CAMBRIDGE LIBRARY COLLECTION

Books of enduring scholarly value

Travel and Exploration

The history of travel writing dates back to the Bible, Caesar, the Vikings and the Crusaders, and its many themes include war, trade, science and recreation. Explorers from Columbus to Cook charted lands not previously visited by Western travellers, and were followed by merchants, missionaries, and colonists, who wrote accounts of their experiences. The development of steam power in the nineteenth century provided opportunities for increasing numbers of 'ordinary' people to travel further, more economically, and more safely, and resulted in great enthusiasm for travel writing among the reading public. Works included in this series range from first-hand descriptions of previously unrecorded places, to literary accounts of the strange habits of foreigners, to examples of the burgeoning numbers of guidebooks produced to satisfy the needs of a new kind of traveller - the tourist.

Discoveries of the World

The publications of the Hakluyt Society (founded in 1846) made available edited (and sometimes translated) early accounts of exploration. The first series, which ran from 1847 to 1899, consists of 100 books containing published or previously unpublished works by authors from Christopher Columbus to Sir Francis Drake, and covering voyages to the New World, to China and Japan, to Russia and to Africa and India. This volume, published in 1862, contains a sixteenth-century Portuguese text first published in translation by Hakluyt himself in 1601; both the original Portuguese and a modified version of Hakluyt's translation are given on each page. The author, António Galvano, (1503–1557), distinguished himself as Governor of the Moluccas, but fell out of favour on his return to Portugal and died in poverty. His book traces the history of exploration from 'the time of the Flood' to 1555.

T0381763

Cambridge University Press has long been a pioneer in the reissuing of out-of-print titles from its own backlist, producing digital reprints of books that are still sought after by scholars and students but could not be reprinted economically using traditional technology. The Cambridge Library Collection extends this activity to a wider range of books which are still of importance to researchers and professionals, either for the source material they contain, or as landmarks in the history of their academic discipline.

Drawing from the world-renowned collections in the Cambridge University Library, and guided by the advice of experts in each subject area, Cambridge University Press is using state-of-the-art scanning machines in its own Printing House to capture the content of each book selected for inclusion. The files are processed to give a consistently clear, crisp image, and the books finished to the high quality standard for which the Press is recognised around the world. The latest print-on-demand technology ensures that the books will remain available indefinitely, and that orders for single or multiple copies can quickly be supplied.

The Cambridge Library Collection will bring back to life books of enduring scholarly value (including out-of-copyright works originally issued by other publishers) across a wide range of disciplines in the humanities and social sciences and in science and technology.

Discoveries of the World

From Their First Original Unto the Year of Our Lord 1555

António Galvano
Edited by C. R. Drinkwater Bethune

CAMBRIDGE
UNIVERSITY PRESS

CAMBRIDGE UNIVERSITY PRESS

Cambridge, New York, Melbourne, Madrid, Cape Town, Singapore,
São Paolo, Delhi, Dubai, Tokyo

Published in the United States of America by Cambridge University Press, New York

www.cambridge.org
Information on this title: www.cambridge.org/9781108010429

This edition first published 1862
This digitally printed version 2010

ISBN 978-1-108-01042-9 Paperback

WORKS ISSUED BY

The Hakluyt Society.

———◆———

GALVANO'S DISCOVERIES OF THE WORLD.

M.DCCC.LXII.

THE

DISCOVERIES OF THE WORLD,

FROM THEIR FIRST ORIGINAL UNTO THE

YEAR OF OUR LORD 1555,

BY

ANTONIO GALVANO,

GOVERNOR OF TERNATE.

CORRECTED, QUOTED, AND PUBLISHED IN ENGLAND,

BY RICHARD HAKLUYT, (1601).

NOW REPRINTED,

𝔚𝔦𝔱𝔥 𝔱𝔥𝔢 Original Portuguese Text:

AND EDITED BY

VICE-ADMIRAL BETHUNE, C.B.

LONDON:

PRINTED FOR THE HAKLUYT SOCIETY.

M.DCCC.LXII.

THE HAKLUYT SOCIETY.

PREFACE.

THE English text was printed from a manuscript copied from Hakluyt's version published in 1601.

We learn from his " Epistle Dedicatorie," that " it was first done into our language by some honest and well affected marchant of our nation."

Hakluyt was not the man to be contented with a translation if better materials could be obtained, and he appears to have made diligent inquiry after the original, but without success.

More fortunate than he, the Hakluyt Society has been able to obtain sight of a copy of the original, published in 1563,[1] and believed to be unique. This valuable work is the property of an American gentleman, Mr. John Carter Brown, of Providence, Rhode Island, who kindly permitted Mr. R. H. Major, of the British Museum, to have it copied ; from this copy

[1] The *Biographie Universelle* speaks of an edition in 12mo. printed in 1555.

the Portuguese text has been printed. The *Nouvelle Biographie Générale* calls this work " rarissime," but speaks of two copies, one in the National Library at Lisbon, the other in the Library of D. Francesco da Mello Manuel.

On comparing Hakluyt's version with the original, some omissions and additions have been noticed. It is not possible at this date to trace the causes of the former, probably they arose from inadvertence in the translator ; they have been supplied within brackets : the latter are due to Hakluyt, who, failing to obtain the original work, supplied what he thought necessary from the " original histories," and to him also are probably due the marginal references.

Antonio Galvano was born at Lisbon in 1503. He embarked for India in 1527, where he soon distinguished himself.

He was selected by the Viceroy Don Nunho da Cunha, to reduce and govern the Moluccas. After a time he succeeded, as much by valour as by judicious conduct, in bringing these islands under Portuguese sway ; and by exercising strict justice and kind dealing towards the natives, both rare in those days, he earned the title of the " father of the country."

But his deeds were not limited to earthly conquest. Galvano, so intrepid at the head of his troops,

might also be seen, with a crucifix in his hand, preaching the Gospel publicly, whereby he became known as the " Apostle" of the Moluccas.

Having spent many years and much treasure in benefiting the people committed to his charge, he was recalled to Europe. But calumny and envy appear to have been at work, and he was coldly received by his sovereign, John III. Finally, he was reduced to such a state of indigence, that he was fain to find refuge in the Royal Hospital at Lisbon, where he died in 1557.

Galvano was a man of rare talent, well versed in religious and secular knowledge, and also well instructed in warlike arts, both military and naval. Faria y Sousa sums up his high qualities in these words :—[1]

" His fame will never perish so long as the world endures ; for neither weak kings, nor wicked ministers, nor blind fortune, nor ages of ignorance, can damage a reputation so justly merited."

He spent the latter part of his life in compiling an account of all known voyages, and thus he may be styled the founder of historical geography. His papers were left at his death to his friend Don F. y Sousa Tavares, who published them.

[1] *Asia Portuguesa.*

This short sketch of an illustrious and hardly used man is taken from the *Biographie Universelle Ancienne et Moderne*, 1816, and *Nouvelle Biographie Générale*, 1857.

The editor's labours have been confined to superintending the press, and he has been careful to retain the quaint language and spelling both in the original and translation.   Perhaps an apology is due for his having undertaken this work, possessing only a slight and superficial knowledge of the Portuguese language.   If excuse be necessary, he has to plead that the work was considered to possess great interest, and that no one else seemed inclined to undertake the labour.   He has been relieved from some responsibility by the kindness of his Excellency the Count de Lavradio and the gentlemen of the Portuguese legation ; but his special thanks are due to M. le Chevalier dos Santos, who kindly undertook to go over the proofs, and who thereby enabled him to supply many deficiencies and avoid many errors.

TRATADO,

QUE COMPŌS O NOBRE & NOTAUEL CAPITĀO
ANTONIO GALUĀO, DOS ᴅIUERSOS & DESUAYRADOS
CAMINHOS, POR ONDE NOS TEMPOS PASSADOS A
PIMENTA & ESPECEARIA VEYO DA INDIA ÁS
NOSSAS PARTES, & ASSI DE TODOS OS
DESCOBRIMENTOS ANTIGOS & MODER-
NOS, QUE SĀO FEITOS ATE A ERA
DE MIL & QUINHENTOS &
CINCOENTA.

COM OS NOMES PARTICULARES DAS PESSOAS QUE OS
FIZERAM : & EM QUE TEMPOS & AS SUAS
ALTURAS, OBRA CERTO MUY NOTA-
UEL & COPIOSA.

FOY VISTA & EXAMINADA PELA SANTA INQUISIÇAO.

*Impressa em casa de JOAM DE BARREIRA impressor del rey nosso
senhor, na Rua de sā Mamede.*

TREATISE

COMPOSED BY THE NOBLE AND REMARKABLE
CAPTAIN ANTONIO GALVANO, OF THE DIFFERENT AND
ASTOUNDING ROUTES BY WHICH IN TIMES GONE BY
PEPPER AND SPICES CAME FROM INDIA TO OUR
PARTS, AND ALSO OF ALL THE DISCOVERIES
ANCIENT AND MODERN WHICH HAVE
BEEN MADE UP TO THE YEAR ONE
THOUSAND FIVE HUNDRED
AND FIFTY.

WITH THE PARTICULAR NAMES OF THE PERSONS WHO
MADE THEM ; AND IN WHAT SEASONS AND IN WHAT
LATITUDES, A WORK CERTAINLY VERY
REMARKABLE AND COPIOUS.

EXAMINED BY THE HOLY INQUISITION.

*Printed in the house of JOAM DE BARREIRA, printer to our lord the
King, in the Street of S. Mamede.*

THE DISCOVERIES

OF THE

WORLD,

FROM THEIR FIRST ORIGINALL VNTO THE YEERE OF
OUR LORD 1555;

Briefly written in the Portugall tongue, by *Antonie
Galuano*, Gouernor of Ternate, the chiefe
Island of the Malucos :

Corrected, quoted, and now publiſhed in English, by RICHARD HAKLUYT,
ſometime ſtudent of Chriſtchurch, in Oxford.

LONDINI :

IMPENSIS *G. BISHOP.*

1601.

To the Right Honorable Sir Robert Cecill,
Knight, principall Secretarie to her Maiestie,
Master of the Court of Wards and Liveries,
the worthy Chancellour of the Universitie
of Cambridge, and one of her Majes-
ties most honorable privie
Counsell.

RIGHT Honorable, while I went about to publish
our English Voyages and Discoveries, I was
advised by master Walter Cope, a gentleman of rare
and excellent parts, to draw them into a short sum,
adding that in his opinion that course woulde proove
most acceptable to the world, especially to men of great
action and employment. Although in that worke then
under the presse I could not conveniently alter my
course, yet holding his advice, as in many things else,
so in this, for sound and very good, I heere present
unto your Honour a briefe Treatie most agreeable to
the same. The authour whereof was one Antonie
Galuano, a Portugall gentleman : of whose pietie towards God, equitie towards men, fidelity to his Prince,
love to his countrey, skill in sea causes, experience in
histories, liberalitie towards his nation, vigilance,

valour, wisedome and diligence in restoring and settling the decaied state of the Isles of Maluco, (where he remained sixe or seven yeeres governour,) if it please your Honour to read Fernando Lopez de Castagneda, or Ioannes Maffeius in their Histories of the East Indies, you shall finde more written in his singular commendation, then a large Epistle can well comprehend.

The worke though small in bulke containeth so much rare and profitable matter, as I know not where to seeke the like, within so narrow and streite a compasse. For heerein is orderly declared, who were the first discoverours of the world since the time of the flood : by what waies from age to age the spicerie, drugs, and riches of the East were conveied into the West : what were the causes of the alterations of those courses, as namely the changes of empires and government : the ceasing of all trafficke for many yeeres by the Gothes invasion of the Romane Empire : the rising up of the Mahumetane sect ; with their overrunning of Africke and Spaine : the renewing againe, after many yeeres disturbance, of the traffic and entercourse of the East Indies ; first by the califas of the aforesaid sect : and eftsoones by the Venetians, Ienowais and Florentines. Then followeth the taking of Ceuta in Barbarie by John the first king of Portugall of that name, in the yeere of our Lord 1415, whose third sonne Don Henry (which he had by the vertuous Ladie Philippa, daughter of John of Gante, and sister to Henry the fourth, King of England) was the first beginner of all the Portugall

discoveries, and continued the same for the space of
fortie and three yeeres even to his dying day. By
whose encouragement the Kings of Portugall found out
with much patience and constancie the last way of the
bringing the Spicerie into Europe by the Cape of
Buona Sperança; and for these hundred yeeres past
have become the chiefe Lords of the riches of the
Orient. By emulation of which their good endevors,
the Antiles and the West Indies began to be discovered by the kings of Spaine. The infancies of both
which most important enterprises, the progresse of the
same from time to time, the discoveries of islands, rivers,
baies and harbours, of many rich provinces, kingdomes,
and countries; the erecting of castles in sundry convenient islands and places, with the drawing of trafficke
unto the same, where, when, by whom, and by whose
authority is heere succinctly and faithfully recorded.
So that if it please your Honour at your convenient
leisure to take a sea card or a mappe of the world, and
carie your eie upon the coast of Africa from Cape de
Non, lying on the mayne in 29 degrees of northerly
latitude, and follow the shore about the Cape of Buona
Sperança till you come to the mouth of the Redde
Sea, and passing thence along by the countrey of Arabia
crosse over to India, and doubling Cape Comory compasse the gulfe of Bengala, and shooting by the citie of
Malacca through the Streite of Cincapura, coast al the
south of Asia to the northeast part of China, and comprehend in this view all the islands from the Açores
and Madera in the West, to the Malucos, the Phillip-

pinas, and Japan in the East : you shall heere finde by
order, who were the first discoverours, conquerours and
planters in every place : as also the natures and commodities of the soyles, togither with the forces, qualities, and conditions of the inhabitants.   And that
which I mention of the Orient, is likewise to be understood of the Occident.

Now touching the translation, it may please you, sir,
to be advertised that it was first done into our language
by some honest and well affected marchant of our
nation, whose name by no meanes I could attaine unto,
and that as it seemeth many yeeres ago.   For it hath
lien by me above these twelve yeeres.   In all which
space though I have made much inquirie, and sent to
Lisbon, where it seemeth it was printed, yet to this
day I could never obtaine the originall copie ; whereby
I might reforme the manifold errours of the translator.

For whereas a good translator ought to be well acquainted with the proprietie of the tongue out of which
and of that into which he translateth, and thirdly with
the subject or matter it selfe : I found this translator
very defective in all three ; especially in the last.   For
the supplying of whose defects I had none other remedie, but to have recourse unto the originall histories,
(which as it appeereth are very many, and many of
them exceeding rare and hard to come by) out of which
the authour himselfe drew the greatest part of this discourse.   And in very deede it cost me more travaile to
search out the grounds thereof, and to annexe the
marginall quotations unto the work, then the translation

of many such bookes would have put me unto. Of
which quotations there is yet a farther use, to wit, that
such as have leasure sufficient, and are desirous to reade
these things more at large, (for brevitie oftentimes
breedeth obscuritie) may fully satisfie their desires by
having recourse by the help thereof to the pure foun-
taines, out of which those waters which are drawne are
for the most part most sweet and holsome. Now if
any man shall marvel, that in these Discoveries of the
World for the space almost of fower thousand yeeres
here set downe, our nation is scarce fower times mentioned : hee is to understand, that when this author
ended this discourse, (which was about the yeere of
Grace 1555) there was little extant of our mens tran-
vailes. And for ought I can see, there had no great
matter yet come to light, if myselfe had not undertaken that heavie burden, being never therein entertained to any purpose, until I had recourse unto your-
selfe, by whose speciall favour and bountiful patronage
I have been often much encouraged, and as it were
revived. Which travailes of our men, because as yet
they be not come to ripenes, and have been made for
the most part to places first discovered by others, when
they shall come to more perfection, and become more
profitable to the adventurers, will then be more fit to
be reduced into briefe epitomes, by my selfe or some
other endued with an honest zeale of the honour of our
countrey. In the meane season nothing doubting of
your favourable acceptation of this my labour, I humbly
beseech the author of all goodnes to replenish and en-

rich you with his best blessings, long to protect and preserve your Honour to the profitable service of her Majestie, and to the common benefit and good of the Realme.

From London this

29. of October

1601.

Your Honors Chaplein, in all dutie

most readie to be commanded,

RICHARD HAKLUYT.

FRANCIS DE SOUSA TAUARES VNTO THE HIGH AND MIGHTIE PRINCE DON JOHN DUKE OF AUEIRO.

ANTONIE GALUANO vpon his death bed left vnto me in his testament among his papers this booke. And because I am certaine he ordained it to bee presented vnto your Grace, I have thought good herein to fulfill his wil and testament, though in other things I have done nothing, the fault remaining not in me. And by all reason this treatie ought to be set foorth by a Portugall, seeing it intreateth of the variable waies from whence the pepper and spices came in

---

PROLOGO.

FRANCISCO DE SOUSA TAUAREZ, AO ILLUSTRISSIMO SENHOR DOM JOHÃO DALEM CASTRO, DUQUE DAUEYRO.

DEXANDO me Antonio Galuão que deos tem por seu testamenteiro, achey antre outros seus papeis este quaderno : & porque sou certo q' elle o ordenou pera o apresentar a vossa illustrissima senhoria, quis ao menos nisto somente comprir sua vontade, pois em seu testamento nam tenho comprido nenhũa cousa, nam por minha culpa. Com razam auia este tractado de ser de pessoa Portuguesa, pois he da materia dos caminhos desuairados, por onde a pimenta & especearia veyo nos tempos passados ás nossa

2

times past into our partes, and also of all the navigations and
discoueries in the old time. In both of which things the
Portugals have most trauailed. In this treatie and in nine
or ten bookes of things touching Maluco and India (which
the Cardinall willed me to give to Damian de Goes, saying
that he should content me, for otherwise I could not deliuer
them) this true Portugall occupied himselfe against the
vnfortunate and sorrowfull times which he had been in
(which were all ended before all our daies and times): for
when he received the captainship and fortresses of Maluco,
all the kings and gouernours of all the ilands about being
agreed to make war against the Portugals, vntill such time
as they might drive them all out of the countrey, he fought
against them all with onely 130 Portugals, when they were
all together, and strong in Tidore; and he gave them the
ouerthrow and killed their king, and one Ternate,[1] the principal author of that war, and he tooke from them their fortresse: so upon this victorie they submitted themselves,

Antonio
Galuano
captaine of
Maluco.

partes: & assi de todas as nauegações & descobrimentos antigos
& modernos: ambas estas duas cousas os Portugueses tem feito
muita auantajem ao passados. Em este tractado com noue ou dez
liuros das cousas de Maluco & da India, que me o Cardeal mandou dar a Damiam de Goes, dizendo que mo[2] satisfaria (que doutra
maneyra eu nam lhos podia dar), se ocupou este verdadeiro Portugues contra os infortunados & tristes tempos em que se via (como
tudo passou āte nossos olhos & tempo), porque entregandolhe a
capitania & fortaleza de Maluco cō todos os Reys & senhores de
todas as ylhas juntos, & conformes a fazer a guerra aos Portugueses
ate os deitar de todo fora da terra, pelejou com todos elles com
soo cento & trinta Portugueses estando todos juntos & fortes em
Tidore, & os desbaratou & matou a el rey, & do Ternate prīcipal
autor da guerra, & lhes tomou a fortaleza: com a qual vitoria logo
se renderam & vieram á obediencia & seruiço del rey nosso señor.

---

[1] And killed the king of Ternate?   [2] Me?

and came under the obeisance and service of our King of
Portugall. Herein two things happened of great admiration. The first, that all the kings and gouernours of Maluco
agreed togither against vs, a thing that never fell out, nor
yet credible to be like to happen : for they are ever at
variance among themselves. The seconde, that the Cap- Variance usually
taine of Maluco with onely his ordinarie soldiers should among the kings of
have the victorie against so many being all together. For Maluco.
sometimes it happeneth that some of the captaines of Maluco
with many extraordinarie soldiers besides their ordinarie,
yea and with the aide of all the kings and lords of Maluco
in their favour and aide, went againste one king onely of
them, and came backe againe with losse. So there may be
reckoned three notable things done in India, I say of qualitie (but of more quantitie and importance there have been
others) ; which were the taking of Muar by Emmanuel
Falcon, and the winning of Bitam by Peter Mascarenas, and
this, whereof we presently treate. For all these three deedes
seemed to be impossible to be atchieved, considering the
small quantitie of soldiers which the captaines had in giving

---

Duas cousas socederam aqui de grande admiraçam : a primeira
serem todos os Reys & senhores de Maluco juntos & conformes
contra nos (cousa q' nunca acōteceo nē se cree q' possa acōtecer
por quā differentes sempre sam antre si). A segunda o capitam
de Maluco com soo a gente ordinaria, auer victoria de todos elles
jūtos, que per vezes aconteceo que algūs capitães de Maluco
com muita gente extraordinaria, alem da sua ordinaria, & com
todos os reis & senhores de Maluco em seu fauor & ajuda, foram
sobre hum soo rey delles, & vieram de là cō muita quebra. Que
se pode dizer, q' tres feitos grandes se fezeram na India, digo em
calidade (q' de mais importancia & de mayor quantidade ouue
outros) os quas sam a tomada de Muar por Manoel falcāo, a de
Bitam por Pedro mascarenhas, & este de que tratamos, porq'
todos estes tres feitos pareciā impossiuel auerē os capitães vic-

the enterprise against so many; with the order and maner by them ordained how and which waies to obtaine their purpose as well by their enimies as by themselves. And they could not be atchieved otherwise but by using a meane and order not thought of at the first by the Portugals, nor yet ever suspected by their enimies. And, besides this, his father and fower of his brethren were all slaine in the king's seruice. And he now being the last of his linage, caried with him into Maluco woorth ten thousand crusadoes [which by share of commercial speculations, and loans, and salaries paid to him, was all gained at Diu[1]], which he spent not in idleness, nor yet in play, but only in bringing of many kings and innumerable townes vnto our holy faith, and in the preserving of Maluco, employing all his power and strength that all the cloues might come vnto the hands of the kings highnes, which with Maluco yielded unto him every yeere five hundred thousand crusadoes; being all

---

torias com a gente com que os cometeram : & com a ordem ou modo que todos cuidauam, por onde a cousa se auia de cometer, assi dos amigos como dos ynmigos : & nam se acabaram por outra nenhũa cousa, se nam porque os capitães os cometeram por lugar & ordem, que nem dos Portugueses, nem dos mesmos immigos foy nunca cuidado nem pensado.   E alem disto sendo seu pay & quatro yrmãos seus todos mortos em seruiço del rey : & sendo elle ja o derradeiro de sua linagem, & leuando cõsigo fazenda a Maluco que valia dez mil cruzados, de contratos q' com partes fez, & emprestemos & ordenados, que lhe pagarão, tudo empregou em Dio : & os gastou, nam em jogos, nẽ em outros maos modos, se nam soo em trazer muitos reys & innumeraueis peuos[2] á nossa sancta fee como em seu tempo fez, & na guerra, & em co'seruar Maluco, & em trabalhar & poer[3] todas suas forças, pera que todo o crauo viesse á mão de S. A. com q' Maluco lhe renderia cada ãno mais

---

[1] A settlement of the Portuguese in the East Indies.   The crusado is now worth about 2*s*.

[2] Pouos ?   [3] Por ?

to his great preiudice, let, and hinderance.   For if he had
gathered cloues for himselfe, as the captaines of Maluco
haue done and doe, then he had come home very rich.   But
when he came home into Portugall in great hope (such is
the simplicite of the best natures) to be rewarded for his   Goodseruice
                                                                                      full ill re-
good service, and to be more fauored and honored, then if   warded.
he had brought home with him an hundred thousand crusadoes, he was greatly deceived.   For he found neither
favour, nor yet honor, but onely among the poor and mise-
rable, to wit, in an hospitall, where he was kept seventeene
yeeres vntill the hower of his death ; and there he had
allowed vnto him his winding sheete to burie him in ; and
the brotherhood of the convent prepared for his buriall as for
a poore courtier cast off by all men, leaving himselfe in-
debted in two thousand crusadoes, whereof part came out of
India, and part thereof many of his friends had lent him to
maintaine him in the hospitall ; for in all these seventeene
yeeres he had not of his highnes for to helpe himselfe with
so much as one riall of plate, nor yet I of the bookes which
I deliuered received any thing to discharge his will with

---

de quinhētos mil cruzados, & sēdo tudo ē grā p' juyzo seu : porq'
fazendo crauo pera si, como fizeram & fazem todos os capitāes de
Maluco viria muito rico.   O gram fraqueza da nossa natureza
humana, q' vindo elle a Portugal com grāo confiança, q' pello q'
tinha feito auia de ser mais fauorecido & honrrado, q' se trouxera
cem mil cruzados, se achou muy enganado, porq' nelle nam achou
outro fauor ou honra, se nam o dos pobres miserauees, quero dizer
o do hospital : onde o teueram dezasete annos, ate que nelle morreo, & delle lhe derāo o lançol pera o amortalhar : & a confraria
da corte como a cortesāo pobre & desamparado lhe fez o enter-
ramento, deixando dous mil cruzados de diuidas, parte que trouxe
da India, & parte q' muitos de seus amigos lhe emprestaram pera
se mant'er no hospital : porq' em todos estes dezasete annos nunca
de S. A. pera se remediar ouue hum soo real, nem eu dos liuros
que dey, nem pera deseucarregar sua alma.   Com tudo assi como

[nor for the good of his soul]. Yet for all this, even
as vpon the prosperitie of his victories he neuer made
any boast, so likewise in his adversities his great stomacke
did nothing abate his hart.[1] As there are good proofes
that with soe many and so continuall disgraces[2] as he
suffered, he neuer vnto the hower of his death left off
A Counto
is 50,000
Crusadoes. to raise and to augment the yeerely rent vnto a counto,[3]
which some made strange[4] and would not give eare
unto. So that euen as he was extreme painfull in the per-
formance of his service, so he was the like in the things
sounding vnto the perfecting of the same,[5] (which was the
cause that he was brought vnto the state that he died in).
For he could not see the qualitie of the time, but onely
those of his great seruice, by reason of the great charges
that it stood him in. And his saying was, that he was
borne, not for to say that his constellation was in the wars
victorious, but in the ouercoming of kings by the arte of

---

cõ as prosperidades das victorias nunca se ensoberueceo, assi nẽ
cõ as aduersidades seu grãde animo se diminuyo nem abaixou :
como heboa proua, que com tamanhos & cõ tam continuos des-
prezos como padeceo, nunca ate ora de sua morte deixou de
requerer & importunar por hum conto de renda cada anno. O q'
algũs estranhauão, nã olhando q' assi como elle foy extreme no
cometer & seruir (de maneira que veyo ao estado em que se vio)
assi o era, no que lhe parecia que seus seruiços mereciam. Porque
nam podia ver a calidade do tempo, se nam a de seus seruiços,
pelo muito que lhe custaram. E dizia q' era nacido por nam dizer
que sua estrella era na guerra vecẽr os reis immigos : com a arte

---

[1] His great soul was never cast down.   [2] Slights.
[3] To require and insist on a yearly income of a conto. A conto is
one million. If a conto of reis is meant, it would be equal to about £200.
[4] Marvelled at, not seeing that...
[5] So he was in what appeared to him that his services merited.

warfare, readines in resolving, prudence in conseruing, and
great loialtie and patience with many seruices vnto his king
and master.   In which of all these he had most contentation
it cannot easily be determined.   Wherefore your noble
Grace may see, that this treatie and the others were made
with sighes and afflictions which his inferiour will might
have raised vp in him against his superiour reason.   Neither
was he willing to take for his remedie that which that great
Turke *Zelim* sonne to the great *Mahumet* did, for he tooke
Constantinople and died in Rome, who vsed to make himselfe drunke, because he would not remember the great
estate which he lost : nor yet woulde he give eare vnto those
things which many of his friends would tell him, wishing
he would settle his mind out of the kingdome (for otherwise
he should neuer be able to live) : whereunto he answered,
that in this point he would rather be compared vnto the
great *Timocles* the Athenian, then to be like the excellent Or rather
Themis-
Romane *Coriolanus*.   Which is a goodly example of a true tocles.
and faithfull Portugall.   Though it were not so as I doe say,

---

de pelejar & presteza de concluir, & a prudencia no conseruar, &
ao seu rey & senhor com muytos seruiços & gram lealdade &
paciencia, & de quael dellas tinha mais contentamento, se nam
sabia determinar.   Pello que vossa illustrissima senhoria pode ver,
q' este tractado & os outros foram feytos de sospiros & afflições
de animo affligido, q' forçadamente contra a parte superior, a in-
ferior lhe auia de dar.   Nam querēdo tomar por remedio o que
tomaua aquelle gram turco Zizimo filho do gram Maamede, q'
tomou Costantinopla, & morreo em Roma, q' se embebedaua por
se nam alembrar do grande estado que perdera.   Nem o que muitos
de seus amigos lhe dauam, dizendo que se possesse fora do Reyno,
que doutra maneira nam teria vida.   Ao qual respondia que nesta
parte mais queria ser comparado ao gram Timocles Atheniense,
que ao excellente Romano Curiolano.   O que he hum gram ex-
emplo de lealde Portuguesa, posto que nam sey como o diga :

yet˙I doe heare, that the hospitals be full of the most faithfull subjects to their prince and country.¹ Wherefore by all
reason this treatie ought to be of your Grace favoured, setting apart all oversights, if there be any, in this worke, of
the author.² I being not able to attaine vnto the vnderstanding of the contrary. God prosper your Grace with long
life and increase of honour.

---

porque també o he, que dos leais estam cheos os hospitaes. Pello
que com razão este tractado deue ser de vossa illustrissima senhoria fauorecido, & leuar em conta algũs descuidos se os na obra
ouuer que por nam ser neste final corregido & emendado, pello
proprio autor pode auer. Cuja vida & estado nosso senhor prospere.

---

¹ What a great example of Portuguese loyalty, supposing even that
it be not as is said : why, moreover, is it that the hospitals are full of
loyal persons ?
² The work not having been finally corrected by its author.

DISCOVERIES IN DIFFERENT TIMES AND
SEASONS, AND ABOUT THOSE WHO
FIRST NAVIGATED.[1]

WHILE I had a desire to gather together some olde and some new discoueries, which haue beene made by sea and by land, with their iust times and situations ; they seemed to be two things of so great difficultie, that being cōfused in the authors of them, I determined once to desist frō any such purpose. For touching the course of time the Hebrewes declare, that from the beginning of the world to the flood were 1656 yeeres. The Seuentie Interpreters make mention of 2242. And S. Augustine reckoneth 2262. In the situations likewise there be many differences. For

Augustine de Ciuit. Dei, lib. xv, cap. 20.

DESCOBRIMENTOS EM DIUERSOS ANNOS & TEMPOS, &
QUẼ FORAM OS PRIMEIROS QUE NAUEGARAM.

QUERENDO ajũtar algũs descobrimentos antiguos & modernos, que por mar & terra sam feytos, cõ suas eras & alturas (como sam duas cousas tã difficultosas) achey me tam confuso como os autores delles, que determiney desistir do tal proposito. Porque os Ebreos dizem que da criaçam do mundo ao diluuio ouue. 1656 annos. E os setenta interpretes. 2242. Sancto Agostinho 2260 & tantos. E assi nas alturas ha muytas differenças : porque nunca se ajunta-

---

[1] This is the rendering of the Portuguese ; it differs from the heading prefixed by the translator, which will appear more properly as the title.

there neuer sailed together in one fleete at sea from ten pilots to the number of 100, but that some of them found themselues by reckoning in one longitude and other some in another.   But[1] considering better with my selfe, that the difficulties are opened and the differences amended by others of more exact judgement and vnderstanding therein, I purposed notwithstanding to proceede in this worke[2] of discoueries.

Some there be that say, that the world hath fully beene discouered ; and they alleage this reason, that as it hath beene peopled and inhabited, so it might be frequented and navigable, and the rather for that the men in that age were of a longer life, and of lawes and languages almost one.

Contrarie opinions touching the discouerie of the world.

There be others of a contrarie opinion to this, holding that all the earth could not be knowne, nor the people conuersant one with another.   For though it had been so once, yet the same would haue beene lost again by the malice of men, and the want of justice among the inhabitants of the earth. But bicause the best and most famous discoueries were made by sea, and that principally in our times, I desire[3] to

---

ram em hũa armada de dez pilotos atè cento, que hũs nam estinessem em hũa altura, & outros em outra.   Mas por ser emmendado de outros que ho melhor entendam, me despus a fazer isto, ainda q' algũs digam que ho mundo foy jaa descuberto & possam allegar pera isso, que assi como foy pouoado, podia ser frequentado, & nauegado.   E mais sendo os homẽs daq'lla idade de vidas mais compridas, leys, linguvagẽs, quasi todas hũas.   Outros tem disto ho contrario, q' dizem que nam podia a terra ser toda sabida, & a gente, cõmunicada hũa com a outra, porque qũado fosse se perderia polla malicia & sem justiça dos habitadores della.

¶ E porque os môres descobrimentos & mais compridos foram por mar feytos principalmẽte em nossos tẽpos, desejey saber quaes

---

[1] But being corrected by others of better judgment.
[2] Although some there be, etc.   [3] Desired ?

knowe who were the first discoverers since the time of the _Who were the first discouerers since the flood._ flood.

Some affirme that they were the Greekes, others say the Phœnicians, others also the Egyptians. The people of India agree not hereunto ; affirming that they were the first that sailed by sea : namely, the *Tabencos, which now we call _* The people of China say they were the first sailors by sea._ the Chinois. And they alleage for the proofe of this, that they be yᵉ lords of the Indiaes, even vnto the Cape of Bona Sperança, and the Island of S. Laurence, which is inhabited by them and al along the sea ; as also the Jauaes, Timores, Celebes, Macafares, Malucos, Borneos, Mindanaos, Luçones, Lequeos, Japones, and other islands, being many in number, and the firme lands of Cauchin-China, Laos [Siamis], Bramas, Pegu, Arracones, till you come vnto Bengala : and _The inhabitants of the West Indies descended from China._ besides this, New Spaine, Peru, Brasil, the Antiles, with the rest adioining vnto them, as appeareth by the fashions and maners of the men and women, and by their proportions, hauing small eies, flat noses, with other proportions to be seene. And to this day many of these ilands and countreies are called by the names of Batochina, Bocho-China,

---

foram os primeiros inuentores disto despois do deluuio. Hūs escreuem que os Gregos, outros dizē que os Fenicios, outros querem q' os Egipcios, os Indios nam consintem nisso, dizendo q' elles foram os primeiros que nauegarão, principalmente os Taybencos, a que agora chamamos Chins, & alegam pera isso serem ja senhores da India, ate ho Cabo de boa esperaça, & a ilha de Sam Lourēço por ser pouoada delles ao lōgo da praya & os Iaos, Timores, Selebres, Macasares, Malucos, Borneos, Mindanaos, Luçoes, Lequios, Japões, & outras Ilhas que ay muytas & as terras firmes dos Cauchenchinas, Laos, Siamis, Bremas, Pegus, Arracões, ate Bengala : & alem disto a noua Espanha, Peru, Brazil, Antilhas, & outras cōjuntas a ellas, como se paresce nas feiçoēs dos homēs, molheres, & seus costumes, olhos peq'nos, narizes rombos, & outras proporcoēs q' lhe vemos. E chamarē

which is as much to say, as the countreies of China. Further it appeareth by histories, that the arke of Noe rested upon the north parts of the mountaines of Armenia, which stands in 40 degrees and upwards : and that immediately thereupon Scythia was first peopled, for that it is an high land and appeared first after the flood. And seeing the prouince and countrey of the Tabencos is one of the chiefest of all Tartarie, as they report, it is to be thought[1] that they were of the most ancient inhabitants, and men of the most ancient nauigations[2] [since in them that country terminates on the east], and the seas being as calme as the riuers be in those parts [by cause of] lying between the Tropicks, where the daies and nights do not much differ, as well in the howers as in ye temperature : where there blow no outragious windes, to cause the waters to rise or be troubled. And by late experience it is found, that the small barks wherein they saile haue onely a great high bough in the

The seas be-
tweene the
Tropicks
very calm.

---

ainda agora a muytas destas ilhas & terras Batochinas, Bocochinas, q' querē dizer terras da China.

¶ Alem disto os nossos escritores deyxarão escrito q' a arca de Noe, se assentara da parte do norte nos mōtes Darmenia, q' está de xl. graos pera cima & que logo daly fora a Scithia pouoada por ser terra alta, & primeyro das agoas descuberta. E como a prouincia de Thaibencos, seja hūa das principaes da Tartaria (se assi he como dizem) bem se mostra ferē elles dos mais antiguos pouoadores & nauegadores, pois nelles se acaba aquella terra da parte do leuante, & os mares sam tam bōs de nauegar como os rios destas partes por jazerē artre os tropicos onde dias & noytes, nam fazem muyta differençia, assi nas oras como na quentura : por onde nam ha ventos tam destemperados que aleuantem as agoas, nem as façam soberbas, & por experiencia o vemos nos pequenos barcos em q' nauegauão com hum ramo por masto & vella, & hū

---

[1] Shewn.   [2] The most ancient peoplers and navigators.

middest of the barke, standing insteed both of mast and An high bough in-stead of mast and saile.
saile, and the master holdeth onely an oare in his hande to
stirre withall : and so they saile swiftly along the coast ; and
the rest of the passengers sit onely upon certaine poles,
which are fastened in the barke, which they call catama-
rones, and so they passe without rowing.[1]

It is further said, that the people of China were sometimes lords of the most part of Scythia, and sailed ordinarily
along that coast, which seemeth to reach vnto 70 degrees
toward the north. Cornelius Nepos is the author of this, Pomponius Mela, lib. 3.
who particularly affirmeth, that in the time that Metellus,
the fellowe consul of Afranius, was proconsul in France, the
king of Sueuia sent vnto him certaine Indians, which came
thither in a ship[2] from this countrey, comming by the north
and by the flats of Germanie. And it is probable that they
were people of China, for that they from 20, 30, and 40
degrees vpwards haue strong ships and clynchers,[3] that can
well brooke the seas, and indure the cold and intemperature
of such northerly regions. As for Cambaia there is ship-

---

remo na mão com q' gouernã, corrē muito mar & costa. E assi
em hūs paos a que chamão Catamarões, em q' se escancham, ou
assentam, & vam com outro remando. E querē ainda q' estes
Chins fossem senhores da mōr parte da Scithia, & q' nauegassem
toda sua costa, que pareçe estar ate setēta graos da parte do norte.

¶ Cornelio Nepote referido, assi nolo aproua, onde diz, que
Metelo colega de Afranio, estando por consul em França, el rey
de Sueuia lhe mandara certos Indios, que vierão em hūa nao cō
mercadorias de sua terra pella parte do norte, aas prayas de Alemanha : & segundo isto deuia ser da China, por estar de vinte,
trinta, corenta graos pera cima, & tē naos fortes & de pregadura
que podiam soffrer mares & terras tam frias & destemperadas como
aquellas : que as nãos de Cambaya, que tambem dizem auer muitos

---

[1] Also logs of wood called "catamarans," on which they either squat
or sit astride, and get along with the others by paddling.
[2] With goods of their country.   [3] Well secured by nails.

ping also in it, and the people by report haue vsed the seas many yeeres : but it seemeth not that they were any of them which came into France ; for that they trafficke onely to Cairo,[1] and are men in deed of little trafficke and lesse clothing.

Joseph. Antiquit. Judaic. lib. i, ca. 5.

As for those which escaped the destruction of the flood, they were therewith so amazed, that they durst not descend into the plaines and lowe countreies, but kept the hils. And we reade of Nimrode, who 130 yeeres after the flood built the Tower of Babell, intending thereby to saue himselfe if there should come any more such floods.

Therefore it seemeth, that they which first came to be sailers were those which dwell in the east in[2] the prouince of China : although others contrariwise hold them which dwell in[3] the west, as in Syria, to haue vsed the trade of the sea soonest after the flood. But this contention about the anti-quitie of nauigation I leaue to the Scythians and Egyptians, who were at great variance and difference in this matter ; for each of them chalenged vnto themselues the honour of the first sea trauaile. But omitting all iars and differences

Justinus, lib. i.

---

annos que no mar andam, não parecem pera isso por ser cozeitas de Cairo, & os homēs de pouco trabalho & vestido.

¶ Tambem os que escaparam do diluuio ficarão tam assombrados q' nam ousaram deçer aos baxos. Mēbroth, depois delle cento & trinta ānos, fez a torre de Babylonia, com entença de se saluar nella vindo outra chea. Pello que parece q' os que mais cedo ao mar chegarão, ora fossem os que hiam ao Leuante & prouincia da China, ora os q' viessem ao Ponente ao fim da Syria aquelles q' primeyro ali pouoassem seriam os q' nauegassem, ho mais deixo aos Scyrios, & Egypcios, q' tiueram grādes debates

---

[1] The translator has misunderstood the expression, " cozeitas de Cairo :" it means "sewn together with coir rope," as the Massoolah boats on the Coast of Coromandel at this day.

[2] Which went to the East and to the, etc.

[3] Which came to the West to the ends of Syria.

thereabouts, I will apply myselfe to my purposed discourse, and speake of that which histories haue left in record.

There be some wel seene in antiquities, which say that in the 143. yeere after the flood, Tubal came by sea into Spaine, whereby it seemeth that in those times nauigations were vsed into our parts out of Ethiopia. Berosus.
The first
nauigation
after the
flood, 143.

And they also say farther, that not long after this, the queene Semyramis went against the Indians in that riuer wherof they tooke their name, and therein gaue battaile vnto the king Stabrobates, wherein he lost a thousand ships. Which being credible by the ancient historie, proueth manifestly that in those parts, in those times were many ships, and the seas frequented in good numbers. Diodorus
Siculus.
lib. ii, cap. 5.

In the 650. yeere after the flood there was a king in Spaine named Hesperus, who in his time, as it is reported, went and discouered as far as Cape Verde and the Island of S. Thomas, whereof he was prince.[1] And Gonsaluo Fernandez, of Ouiedo, the chronicler of antiquities,[2] affirmeth, that in his[3] time the Islands of the West Indies were discouered, and called somewhat after his name Hesperides : Berosus.
Gonsaluo
Fernandez
de Ouiedo,
lib. ii, cap.3.
Generalis
Hist.

---

sobrisso : porq' todos q're adquirir a si esta hōra, & eu vir ao pōto do q' os nossos ātepassados deixarā escripto.

¶ Aquelles que de antiguidades se prezarão, dizem que no anno de 143 depois do diluuio, viera Tubal por mar a Espanha : por onde parece q' ja naquelle tēpo se nauegaua a nossa Ethiopia. E estes mesmos contam, que depois disto não muyto tempo a Raynha Symiramis fora contra os Indios : & naquelle rio de q' elles tomaram ho apellido, dera batalha a el rey Escorobatis, na qual elle perdera mil nauios : por onde parece que naquellas partes auia muytos, & muytos annos que se nauegauam.

¶ No anno de 650 depois do diluuio, ouue hū rey em Espanha que se chamou Hispalo, em cujo tempo diz que foy descuberto ate

---

[1] A mistranslation, " the Island of St. Thomas and Princes' Island," these islands are in the Bight of Biafra.

[2] The Antilles.   [3] This.

Plinius, lib.
vi, cap. 31. and he alleageth many reasons to prove it, reporting particularly that in 40 daies they sailed from Cape Verde vnto
those islands.

There are others that say that the like was done from
this cape vnto the Islands of S. Thomas, and the Isle De
Principe, and that they be the Hesperides, and not the
The ancient
nauigation
was along
the coast,
not far into
the maine
ocean. Antiles. And they doe not differ far from reason : seeing
in those times and many yeeres after they did vse to saile
onely along the coast, not passing through the maine ocean
sea ; for they had neither altitude nor compasse then in vse,
nor any mariners so expert.

[According to the opinion of writers] it cannot be denied
but that there were many countries, islands, capes, isthmos,
Length of
time and
force of
waters haue
much
altered the
situation of
manie
places. and points, which now are grown out of knowledge, because the names of them are found in histories. But the age
of the world and force of waters haue wasted and consumed
them, and separated one countrey from another, both in
Europe, Asia, Africa, New Spaine, Peru, and other places

---

o Cabo verde, & algūs querem dizer que a ylha de Sam Thome,
& Principe. E Gonçalo Fernandez de Ouiedo que fez as coronicas
das Antilhas, que neste tempo fossem ylhas ja descubertas, & do
nome deste rey se chamassem Esperidas : & alega muitas razões
pera ysso, & aquelles quarēta dias q' nauegauam do Cabo verde
a estas ylhas. Mas outros querem dizer que o mesmo se fazia
deste cabo â ilha de sam Thome, & Principe, q' estas sam as
Esperidas : & nam as Antilhas. E nā se apartam da rezam muyto,
poys naq'lle tēpo & despoys muytos annos se navegou mais ao
longo da terra, que pelo mar Oceano, nē auia altura, nem agulha,
nem gēte do mar podia ser tam esperta.

¶ Segundo a openiam dos q' escreueram nam se pode negar que
nam ouue muytas terras, ilhas cabos, ismos, angras, enseadas, que
os tempos & as agoas teram gastadas & apartadas hūas das outras,
assi na Europa, como em Africa, Asia, & Noua Espanha, Peru, &
outras que sam descubertas, & estam occultas pella continua differença que tem a humidade d'agoa, com a sequidam da terra. Diz

that have been discovered, but have been hidden by the continual struggle going on betwixt the water and land.]

Plato saith in his dialogue of Timæus, that there were in ancient times, in the ocean sea Atlanticke, certaine great islands and countries named Atlantides, greater than Afrike and Europe: and that the kings of those parts were lords of a great part of this our countrey : but with certaine great tempests the sea did ouerflow it [with all it contained], and it remained as mud and shingle, so that in a long time after no ships could passe that way. *Plato in Timæa.*

It is also recorded in histories, that fast by the Island of Cadiz, towards the Straights of Gibraltar, there was a certaine[1] island which was called Aphrodisias, well inhabited and planted with many gardens[2] and orchards, and yet at this day we haue no knowledge of this Aphrodisias, but onely a bare mention of it in ancient authors.   The said Island of Cadiz is further said to haue been so large and big, that it did ioine with the firme land of Spaine. *Plinius. lib. iv, cap. 22.*

The Islands of the Açores were sometimes a point[3] of the mountains of Estrella, which ioine vnto the sea ouer the *The Islands of the Açores sometimes ioined to the firme land.*

Platam em os diologos de Thymeo Eclisio, que ouue antigamente no maar oceano Athlantico grandes ilhas & terras chamadas Athlantides, mayores que Africa & Europa, & que os reys daquella terra senhorearam[4] muyta parte desta nossa : & cō grande tormenta se fundio com tudo o que tinha, & ficou tanto lodo & ciscalho, que se nam pode por ali nauegar muyto tempo.   E assi escreueram, que junto da ilha de Calex, contra ho estreyto auia hūas ilhas que se chamauam, Frodisias, bem pouoadas, & frequentadas com muytos jardins, pomares, & ortas, de que ja agora nam temos outra memoria, se nam o que representa a escriptura.

¶ A mesma ilha de Calex se affirma ser tamanha que se ajuntaua aa terra de Espanha, & q' as ilhas dos Açores era hua ponta

---

[1] Were certain islands.
[2] Flower and kitchen.
[3] Or spur.
[4] Governaram.

4

towne of Syntra. And also from Sierra Verde or the greene mountaine, which adioineth vnto the water hard by the citie of Sasin in the land of Cucu (which is the selfe same Island of Mouchin, where Algarbe is) come[1] the Islands of Porto Santo and Madera.

All islands haue their rootes running from the maine land.

For it is held as a true and vndoubted veritie, that all islands have their roots running from the firme land, though they be neuer so farre from the continent: for otherwise they could not stand firme.

Eratoshenes apud Strabonem, lib. i, page 26.

There are other histories which say, that from Spaine vnto Ceuta in Barbarie men sometimes trauailed on foot vpon drie land, and that the Islands of Sardinia and Corsica did ioine the one with the other, as also did Sicilia with Italie, and Negroponto with Greece.

Huls of ships and ankers found on mountaines farre within land.

We read also that there were found hulles of ships, ankers of iron, and other memorials of shipping vpon the mountaines of Suissa farre within the land: where as it seemeth now no salt water or sea euer came.

In India also, and in the land of Malabar, although now

---

das Serras da Estrella, que se mete no mar na villa de Cintra, E que a Serra Verde que se mete nagoa jũto da cidade de Sasim em Teracucu, que he a propria de Mouchim, que do Algarue, & que em estas arrebentam as ilhas do Porto sancto & a Madeira, porque dizem que todas as ilhas tem as rayzes na terra firme, por muyto apartadas q' estẽ della, que doutra maneyra nam se sosteria. Outros querem que Despanha a Ceyta se passase por terra, & q' as ilhas de Cerdenha & Corcega se juntasse hũa cõ outra, Cecilia com Italia, Negroponte com a Grecia. Assi contam q' acharam cascos de naos, ancoras de ferro, nas montanhas de Suissa, muy metidas pella terra, oude parece q' nũca ouue mar, ne agoa salgada.

¶ Tambem dizem que na India & terra do Malabar q' he ta-

---

[1] Have broken off.

there be great store of people, yet many writers affirme that it was once a maine sea vnto the foot of the mountaines; and that the Cape of Comarim, and the Island of Zeilan were all one thing. As also that the Island of Samatra did ioine with the land of Malacca by the flats of Caypassia; and not farre frō thence there stands now a little island, which few yeeres past was part of the firme land that is ouer against it.

Furthermore it is to be seene, how Ptolemey in his tables doth set the land of Malacca to the south of the line in three or fower degrees of latitude, whereas now it is at the point thereof, being called Jentana, in one degree on the north side, as appeereth in the Straight of Cincapura, where daily they doe passe through vnto the coast of Sian and China, where the Island of Aynan standeth, which also they say did ioine hard to the land of China: and Ptolomey placeth it on the north side far from the line, standing now aboue 20. degrees from it towards the north, as Asia and Europe now stand.

Well it may be that in time past the land of Malacca and

---

manha & tam pouoada foy ia tudo mar, ate o pè da Serra: & q' o Cabo de Comorim, & a ilha de Ceilao era tudo hūa cousa, & a ilha de Samatra q' fora pegada cō a terra Malaca, por hūs baixos d' Capasia, & iūto de la està hua ylheta q' não ha muito q' ella & a terra firme tudo era hūa cousa. Ptolomeo em suas taboas põe esta terra de Malaca ao Sul da linha, em tres ou quatro graos daltura, ficando agora a ponta della, que se chama Ojentana em hum grao da banda do Norte (como se vee no estreito de Sincapura), onde cada dia passam pera à costa de Syão, & China, onde està a ilha de Aynão, que tambem dizem q' foy junta cō a terra da China q' Ptolomeo assenta da parte do Norte muyto alem da linha, ficando agora mais de vinte graos della da parte do Norte, de maneira que assi Asia como Europa, ambas agora estam desta banda.

¶ Bem podia ser q' nos tempos passados, a terra de Malaca &

China did end beyond the line on the south side, as Ptolemey doth set them foorth : because it might ioine with the point of the land called Jentana, with the islands of Bintan, Banca, and Salitres being many that waies, and the land might be all[1] slime and oaze ; and so yᵉ point of China might ioine with the Islands of the Luçones, Borneos, Lequeos, Mindanaos, and others which stand in this parallele : they also as yet hauing in opinion that the Island of Samatra did

At this isle of Bali the Hollanders were 1596, and haue largely described it.

ioine with Java by the channel of Sunda, and the Islands of Bali, Anjane, Sambaua, Solor, Hogaleao, Maulua, Vintara, Rosalaguin, and others that be in this parallele and altitude, did all ioine with Jaua [and form one land] ; and so they seeme outwardly to those that descrie them.   For at this day the islands stand so neere the one to the other, that they seeme all but one firme land; and whosoever passeth betweene some of them may touch with the hand the boughs of the trees on the one and on the other side also.   And to come neerer to the matter, it is not long since, that in the east the Islands of

---

China fossem acabar alē da linha de banda do Sul, como Ptolomeo as pinta, porque pegaria aa ponta da terra D'ojentana cō as ylhas de Bintão, Banqua, & Salitres, q' ha por ali muitas, & seria a terra toda mociça : & assi a ponta da China, com as ylhas dos Luções, Borneos, Lequios, Mindanaos, & outras que jazē nesta corda, que tambem tem por opiniao aindagora, q' a ylha de Samatra, foy pegada com a Iaua, pello canal de Sunda, & a ylha de Baly, Anjane, Simbaba, Solor, Hogalcao, Maulua, Vintara, Rosolanguim, & outras q' ha nestacorda & alturas, todas foram pegadas cō a Iaua & a terra hūa, & assi o parece quē as vée defora, porq' ainda- gora ha nestas partes ylhas taõ juntas hūas cō as outras, q' parece tudo hūa cousa, & quē passa per antrellas, vay tocādo cō a mão os ramos do aruoredo dhūa banda & outra.   E nam ha muyto tepō q' ao Leuante das ylhas de Bāda se fundiram muitas : & també

---

[1] Solid land.

Banda were diuers of them overflowen and drowned by the sea. And so likewise in China about nine score miles[1] of firme ground is now become a lake, as it is reported. Which is not to be thought maruellous; considering that which Ptolemey and others haue written in such cases, which here I omit, to return to my purpose.

Nine score miles of firme ground lately drowned in China.

After the flood, 800 yeeres, we reed that the citie of Troy was builded by the Dardans, and that before that time they brought out of the Indies into Europe by the Red Sea, spices, drugs, and many other kindes of marchandises, which were there more abundant than now they be. Whereunto, if credit may be given, we may conceaue that the sea was of old haunted and frequented, seeing that then they of the east had so much and so greate trafficke with them of the west, that they brought their merchandise vnto an hauen which was named Arsinoe, being that which at this day is called Suez, standing in 30 degrees on the north part of the Arabian Gulfe. It is also by authors farther written,

800 yeeres after the flood was trade of spices by the Red Sea.

Arsinoe, now called Suez.

---

dizē agora q' na China se alagarā mais de sesenta legoas de terra: por onde se não deue auer por muito o q' Ptolomeo & outros antigos deixarā escripto, q' tambem eu deixo por tornar a meu proposito.

¶ Depois do diluuio 800 annos, diz q' foy fundada a cidade de Troya pellos Dardanos, & q' antes disto traziā das Indias a Europa pelo mar Roxo, especiarias, drogas, & outras muitas & diuersas mercadorias q' hi auia naquelle tempo mais q' agora. E se assi foy isto bē se pode dar credito q' auia muyto tempo q' os máres se nauegauam, pois naquelle tinham tanto comercio ho Leuante com ho Ponēte q' se traziam estas mercadorias a hū porto q' se chama Arsinoe, q' querē dizer algūs, q' seja aquelle q' agora dizemos Çuez q' està em trinta graos da parte do Norte neste estreyto Arabico.

¶ Declarão mais os escriptores, que deste porto d'Arsinoe, Suez

---

[1] Seventy leagues.

Plinius, lib.
6, cap. 29. that from this hauen of Arsinoe or Suez [or whatever it
may be called], these marchandises were carried by carauans, or great companies of carriers vpon camels, asses,
and mules, vnto the Leuant sea vnto a city called Casson,
standing on the coast in 32 degress of latitude, yeelding vnto euery degree 17 leagues and an halfe, as the maner
is.   And there are by account from the one sea to the
Strabo, lib.
17, pag. 560. other 35 leagues, or 105 miles.   These carriers, by reason of the heate of the countrey, trauailed in the night
onely, directing themselues by stars and by marks of postes
and canes, which they used to sticke in the ground as they
went.   But after that, because this course and iourney had
many inconueniences they changed and altered the same
twise, to find out the most commodious way.

900 yeeres
after the
flood.
Strabo, lib.
17.   900 yeeres or there about after the flood, and before the
destruction of Troy, there was a king in Egypt called
Sesostris, who, perceiuing that[1] the former courses and
passages for the carrying of marchandises by men and
beasts were chargeable to the one and most painfull to the

(ou como lhe quiserdes chamar) traziam estas mercadorias em
carauanas de camelos, asnos, & azemolas, ao mar de leuante, a hūa
cidade q' está nelle em xxxij graos daltura que se chama Cazō,
auerà por aqui de hū mar a outro xxxv legoas : dādo a cada grao
xvii & meyo, como se costumaua : por la terra ser quēte & d'area
nam andauā se nam de noite, gouernādose por estrellas, de q'
tinham conhecimento & por balisas de paos & canas q' na terra
tinhā metidas.   Vēdo q' esta estrada nam era tal como elles dese-
jauam, diz q' duas vezes ho mudaram.

¶ Nouecentos annos pouco mais ou menos despoys do diluuio
antes da destroiçam de Troya ouue hū rey no Egypto q' se chamou
Sesotres, o qual vendo q' estes caminhos & diligencias q' eram
feytas nam escusauā muytos custos, homēs, bestas, carregas &

---

[1] These journeys involved loading and unloading with great labour
to man and beast.

other, prouided to haue a way or streame cut out of the
land from the Red Sea vnto an arm of the riuer Nilus, which
rūneth vnto the citie Heroum, that by the means thereof
ships might passe and repasse with their marchandises from Plinius, lib.
6, cap. 29.
India into Europe, and not be discharged till they came into
Italie.   So that this Sesostris was the first king which built
great caracks to trauaile this way.   But this enterprise for
all that took little effect.   For if it had, Africa had then
been made as an island all compassed with water, being no
more ground between sea and sea, then the space of 20.
leagues or 60 miles.

About this time the Græcians gathered together an army Diodorus
Siculus, lib.
or fleete, which now is called Argonautica, whereof Jason 4, cap. 4.
and Alceus were captains-general.   Some say they went
from the Isle of Creta, others from Græcia.   But whence
soeuer they departed, they sailed through the Proponticke
Sea and Saint George's Sleeue vnto the Euxine Sea, where
some perished, and Jason thereupon returned backe into
Greece.   Alceus reported that he was driuen with a tempest
to the lake Mæotis, where he was forsaken of al his company, The lake
Mæotis.
and they which escaped with great trauaile, passed through

---

descarregas, determinou fazer hūa vala do mar vermelho a hū
braço do rio Nilo, q' vay ter à cidade de Seroum, por onde as
naos podessem ir & vir cō as mercadorias das Indias a Europa,
sem serē tiradas, nē descarregadas ate Italia.   E porisso foy este o
primeiro rey do Egipto q' mādou fazer carracas grandes pera este
caminho, o qual nam teue effeito por que se ho tiuera ficaua Africa
em hūa ilha toda dagoa rodeada por nam ter mais de vinte legoas
este jsmo de terra.

¶ Neste meyo tempo dizem que os Gregos fizeram hūa armada
que chamão dos Argonautas, & hiam por capitães della Jasom &
Alceo, hūs querem que partissem da ilha de Creta, outros da
Grecia, como quer que seja, foram polo mar Pontico & braço de
sam Jorge ao mar Euxino, onde se perderā.   Jasom tornou a
Grecia, Alçeo diz que com tormenta foy ter a lagoa Meotis, onde

Shipping of great anti-quities in the Ger-maine Sea.
by land vnto the ocean sea of Almaine, where they took shipping, passing the coasts of Saxonie, Frisland, Holland, Flanders, France, Spaine, Italie, and so returned vnto Pelo-ponessus and Greece [as far as the province of Thrace], dis-couering the most part of the coast of Europe.

Strabo. lib. 2, pag. 26.
Strabo, alleaging Aristonicus the grammarian, sheweth, that after the destruction of Troy, Menelaus the king came out of the straights of the Levant seas into the sea Atlanticke and coasted Africa and Guinea, and doubled the Cape of Bona Sperança, and so in time arriued in India ; of which voyage of his there may be many more particulars gathered out of the histories. This Mediterrane Sea was also sometimes called the Adriaticke, the Ægæan, and the Herculean sea, with other names, according to the lands, coasts, and islands which it passeth by, running into the great sea Atlanticke, along the coast of Africa.

1 of Kings, 9. 2 Chron., 8.
In the yeere 1300 after the flood, Solomon caused a nauie to be prepared on the Red Sea, at an hauen called Ezeon Geber, to sail to the East India, where by opinion standeth

---

se desfez de todo, & os que escaparam cõ muito trabalho, atraues-saram por terra ao mar Oceano Dalemanha õde se embarcaram, & por la costa de Xaxonia, Frisia, Holanda, Flandres, França, Es-panha, Italia, tornaram a Peloponeso, ou Morea, & Grecia, ate a prouincia da Tracia, deixando descuberto per costa a mór parte da Europa.

¶ Strabon citando Aristonico, diz que despois da destruiçã de Troya, el Rey Menalao sahio do estreyto & mar do leuante ao Athlantico, & costa de Africa, & Guine, & dobrou ho cabo de Boa esperança & em certo tempo foy ter á India. Disto se pode tomar aos autores mais astreyta conta. Este mar Mediterraneo, tambem se chamou Adriatico, Egeo, Herocleo, & outros nomes, segundo as terras, costas & ilhas, que banha ao mar grande Athlantico & costa de Africa.

¶ No anno de 1300, despois do diluuio mãdou Salamão fazer hũa armada no mar do mar roxo que se chamaua Eylam, para ir a leuante da India onde dizem estar aquella jlha & terra a que

the islands called Tharsis and Ophir. This nauie was three yeeres on this voyage, and then returned, and brought with them [much] gold, siluer, cypres, [and pine wood]. Whereby it seemeth that those places and islands were those which now be called the Luçones, Lequeos, and Chinaes. For we know few other parts from whence some of those things are brought, or wherein nauigation was so long since vsed.

It is left vs also in histories, that a king of Egypt called Neco, desiring greatly to ioyne the Red Sea with the riuer Nilus, commanded the Phœnicians to saile from the straight of Mecca to the farther end of the Mediterrane Sea, to see if it did make any turne backe againe vnto Egypt. Which commandement they obeied, sailing towards the south all along the coast and countrey of Melinde, Quiloa, Sofala, till they came to the cape of Bona Esperança, finding the sea[1] continually on the left hand: but when they had doubled the cape, and found the coast[2] continually on the right hand, they maruailed much at it.

Notwithstanding they continued their course forward

Herodotus, lib. 4.

---

chamauam Tarcis & Offir, & q' poseram tres annos neste caminho, de q' trouxerā muito ouro, prata, aciprestes, pinho. Poronde pareçe que aquellas terras & jlhas deuiam ser as q' agora chamāo, Luçoes, Lequios, & Chinas, por que nā sabemos lá em outras partes auer prata, aciprestes, pinhos nē nauegaçā de tātos annos.

¶ Tambē deyxaram escripto os passados q' ouue hū Rey no Egipto q' se chamou Neco, q' desejou muyto ajuntar ho mar roxo cō ho rio Nillo, & mādou aos Fenicios que deste estrèito de Meca nauegassem ate ho fim do mar Mediterraneo pera ver se ternauāo ao Egipto, elles assi ho fizerāo, indo ao sul ao longo da costa & terra de Melinde, Quiloa, Sofala, ate ho cabo de boa esperança ficandolhe sempre ho sol á mão esquerda. Mas dobrando este cabo, & vendo ho sol à mão direita, espantaranse muyto: cō tudo fizeram ao Norte seu caminho pella costa de Guinè, & mar

---

[1] Sun. This means probably that the sun rose on their left.   [2] Sun.

toward the north al along the coast of Guiney and the Mediterrane Sea, till they came backe againe into Egypt, whence they first went out. In which discouerie they remained two yeares. And these are thought to be the first that compassed by sea all the coast of Afrike, and sailed round about it.

In the yeere 590 before the incarnation of Christ, there went out of Spaine a fleete of Carthaginian marchants, vpon their owne proper costs and charges, which sailed toward the west through the high seas to see if they could finde any land : and they sailed so farre, that they found at last the islands which now we call the Antiles and Noua Spagna :

which Gonzalo Fernandes de Ouiedo saith were then discouered, although Christopher Columbus afterwards by his trauaile got more exact knowledge of them, and hath left vs an euident notice where they be. But all these historians, which wrote of these Antiles before, as of doubtfull and vncertaine things, and of places undiscouered, doe now plainly confesse the same to be the countrey of Noua Spagna.

In the yeere 520 before the Incarnation, and after the

Mediterraneo ate tornar ao Egipto dende partirão, & poserão dous annos neste descobrimento, & querem algũs que fossem os primeyros, que o fizerão & andassem a costa Dafrica toda em roda.

¶ No āno de 590 antes da encarnação de Christo partio de Espanha hũa armada de mercadores Cartaginēses feita à sua custa, & foy cõtra ho Ocidente por esse mar grande ver se achauã algũa terra: diz q' forão dar nella, e que he aq'lla que agora chamamos Antilhas & noua Espanha que Gonçalo Fernandez de Ouiedo, quer que neste tempo fosse ja descuberta, ainda que Christouão Colom nos deu della mais vera certeza, & todos os que escrèuerã como falão em cousa duuidosa & terra não descuberta, logo acodem com esta da noua Espanha.

¶ No anno de 520 antes do nacimēto de Christo dizem q'

setting out of the aforesaid army, Cambyses, king of Persia, tooke Egypt; after whom succeeded Darius the sonne of Histaspis, and he determined to make an end of the enterprise which king Sesostris had begun, if they had not told him that the Red Sea was higher then the land of Egypt, and that by meanes of the salt sea comming into the river Nilus, all the prouince would haue been lost and vndone for hunger and thirst. For the fresh water of the riuer Nilus doth overflowe the whole countrey, and the inhabitants [and cattle] haue no other water then that for their drinke : whereupon he left his first purpose of prosecuting that enterprise.

Now by the way I shall not swarue much from my matter, A digression. if I speake a word or two of some things incident to this discourse.[1] The Egyptians say that [in their country the human race was created, and that in it are still pro- Plinius, lib. 9, cap. 58, de miribus Nili. duced] they had in their countrey certaine vermine like vnto[2] rats, wherof many be halfe like earth and the other halfe like a vermine. One kinde of them keepe the water, and another kinde the land.[3] For my part I

Cambisis rey da Persia tomou ho Egypto, ao qual socedeo Dario filho de Histaspis, determinou de dar fim à empresa q' el rey Sesostres começara, selhe nam fizeram certo q' ho mar Erithreo era mais alto q' a terra do Egipto & chegando a agoa salgada ao rio Nillo perderse hia esta provincia á fome & sede, porque delle se rega, & os moradores & gados nã bebẽ outra agoa pelo que deixou de auer fim esta obra.

¶ Ainda que hum pouco me aparte do preposito, nam deixarey dir tocãdo, em algũas cousas em que vou falando, por dar repouso a tam largo caminho. Tinhã, os Egypcios, q' em sua terra se criaua a geraçam humana, & que ainda agora naçem nella hũs bichos tamanhos como ratos, & se vée muytos meyo torrão, & meyo bicho, ate de todo se despedir da terra : cuydo que sam estes

---

[1] To give repose on so long a journey.   [2] As big as.
[3] This translation is wrong : the sense seems to be that several

thinke that these be they which breake the serpents[1] egges, whereof there are many in the riuer Nilus, which also be called crocodiles : which in times past by report were so inchanted, that thereby they could not hurt any persons. But when they were deliuered from their inchantment[2] made by the Egyptians arte, and letters, then they endeauoured to kill people, wilde beasts and cattell, doing very much harme, specially those which liue in the water, which oftentimes come to the land, and liuing altogether on land become very strong poison.[3] The people beyond the citie of Cairo vse to fish for them and eate them, and they take their heads, and set them vpon the walles of their citie.

Joannes Leo Africanus, lib. 9, cap. de Nilo.

Of these crocodiles it is written, that they lay themselues [on the sand] along by the riuer with their mouthes open, and that there come vnto them certaine white birds, little bigger then thrusshes, which flie into the mouth of the crocodile, and picke out the filthines which is betweene his teeth, and in

Plinius, lib. 8, cap. 25.

Joannes Leo Africanus, lib. 9.

---

os que quebram os ouos aos lagartos, que ha muytos no rio Nilo, a que tambē chamão Cocodrilhos. E querem ainda q' em tempos passados fossem encantados, por onde nam fáziam mal a nenhūa pessoa, mas despois de desfazerem sua figura de chumbo, com suas letras Egipcias, tornaram a matar a gente, alimarias, gados, & fazer muyto dāno, principalmente os que saem dagoa, & se vam pela terra dentro, que sam muyto mays peçonhētos que os que ficam no Nilo, que estes pescam da cidade do Cayro pera bayxo, & os comem, & poē as cabeças polo muro.

¶ Tambē se escreue que estes lagartos se deytā na area ao longo de ribeira com a boca aberta, & que vem hūas aues brancas, poueo mayores que mebroas, & se metem dentro, & comem aquella

---

look upon themselves as half beast, half worm, until they take leave of the land altogether.

[1] Lizards.   [2] Literally, but after undoing their figure of lead.

[3] Much more poisonous than those that remain in the Nile.

his iawes, wherewith he is greatly pleased : but for all that the crocodile would close his mouth and deuoure the bird, if nature had not prouided the bird a sharpe pricke as it were, growing out of his head, wherewith he pricketh the crocodile in the mouth ; which causeth him to gape wide, and so the bird flieth away without harme ; yet there come by and by other of those birds, which make an end of cleansing his mouth.

In the same riuer there are also many beastes like vnto horses, and vpon the land certaine fowles like vnto cranes, which warre continually with serpents, that come thither from Arabia, and kill many of them.   Which birds,[1] as also the vermine, which eate the egges of the crocodiles, are greatly esteemed of the Egyptians.

(But now to returne to my matter, and to proceede in the discoueries) : in the yeere 485 before the incarnation of Christ, Xerxes, the king of Persia, commanded Saraspis his nephew to goe and search and discouer India : who according to the precept vndertooke the voyage, and went through the straight of Gibraltar, [which lie in 36 degrees north

çugidade q' tem antre os dentes, & gengiuas, com q' folgam muyto : mas com tudo cerram a boca pera as comerem, o que fariam se a natureza as nam prouera de hũ ossinho agudo que tem na cabeça com q' os picam no ceo da boca, de maneyra que a abrem, & ho passaro se vay embora, mas logo vẽ outros que acabam de alimparlha.   Tambẽ ha nesta ribeira muytos caualos marinhos, & na terra quantidade de cegonhas, q' tem guerra com as serpes que ali vẽ de Arabia, & matam muytas dellas, & assi estas cegonhas, como os bichos que comẽ os ouos dos lagartos, sam dos Egipcios muy venerados.

¶ No anno de 485 antes da encarnaçam de Christo, diz que mandou el Rey Xerxes a Sataspis seu sobrinho descobrir a India, o qual sahio pelo estreito de Gibaltar fora, que estaa em trinta &

---

[1] Storks.

latitude], and passed the promontorie of Africa, which now
we call the Cape of Bona Sperança, standing southward
betwixt 34 and 35 degrees in latitude,[1] and being weary
of so great a nauigation turned from thence backe againe,
as Bartholomew Diaz did in our daies.

Pliuius, lib.
2, cap. 67.   Before the comming of Christ 443[2] yeeres, Himilco, and
Hanno his brother, Carthaginian captaines, gouerning that
part of Spaine which is now called Andaluzia, departed
from thence each one with his nauie.   Himilco, sailing
towards the north, discouered the coasts of Spaine, France,
England, Flanders, and Germanie.   And some write farther,
that he sailed vnto Gotland, and came to the island of
Thule, or Island, standing vnder the circle Arcticke, in 24
degrees from the north pole,[3] and continued in his nauigation two yeeres, till he came vnto this Island, where the day
hath in June 22 houres, and in December the night also
hath 22 houres, whereby it is there wonderfully cold.
[It seems that the inhabitants of this island cry out

---

seys graos da parte do norte, & passou ho promontorio Dafrica, que
he aquelle que agora chamamos Cabo de boa esperança, que esta
da parte do sul em trinta & quatro pera cinco graos daltura.   E
enfadado de tam gram nauegaçam se tornou, como Bertolameu diaz
em nossos tempos fez.

Antes do Saluador do mundo vindo 440 annos Himeleõ, & Annõ
seu hirmão, capitães **Cartagineses**, gouernando a Andaluzia, partiram della cada hum com sua armada Himeleõ contra ho norte
descobrio a costa de Espanha, França, Frandes, & Alemanha : &
algũs querẽ que a Gotica, & q' chegasse á ilha de Thili, em Hislãda,
que está debaixo do circulo artico em sessenta & seys graos do
norte, & poserã nisto dous annos na viagem, ate chegarem a esta
ilha, que tem os dias de Junho de vinte duas horas, & as noytes de
Dezembro doutro tanto, polo que he frigidissima.   Parece que

---

[1] Which is in thirty-four or thirty-five degrees south latitude.
[2] 440 ?   [3] Sixty-six degrees north latitude.

and groan, whereby it is said to be the Purgatory of St. Patrick.

This island has three mountains which throw out fire from the base, while the summit is covered with snow, and in one of these which is called Ecla, the fire is so mild that tow will not burn, while at another part it has such force that it burns up water and consumes every thing.

It is also said that there are in this island two fountains, one like melting wax, the other always boiling, and turning every thing thrown into it to stone, keeping its proper form.

Further, there are in this island bears, foxes, hares, crows, falcons, and other birds, and wild cattle: and there is so much grass that it is mown twice for the cattle; and often they are taken from it that they may not burst.

There are also very large and misshapen fish, and so many as to frighten mariners, and with their bones and ribs a church has been built. There is no bread, wine, oil (olive) nor whereof to make it; they get light from fish oil, for everywhere God provides.]

---

bradam & gemē os homēs nella, por onde dizem que ali he ho pur-gatorio de sam Patricio.

¶ Tem esta ylha tres montes que deitá fogo pe lò pee & encima està neuada, & em hū destes q' se chama Ecla, he o fogo tam brando que nam queima a estopa, & per outra parte tē tanta força q' arde nagoa, & consume a toda. E assi dizem q' ha nesta ylha duas fontes, hua como cera derretida, & outra que sempre ferue, & toda a cousa q' lhe deitam dentro se conuerte em pedra, ficãdo em sua propria figura. Ha mais nesta ilha vssos, raposas, lebres, coruos, falcões, & outras aues, & alimarias brauas: & he tanta a erua, q' asegão duas vezes, pera q' os gados passem[2]: & muitas vezes os tiram della, porque não arrebētem de gordura. Ha hi muy grandes & difformes pescados, & tanto que põe aos nauegantes medo, & de seus ossos & costas fizeram hūa igreja. Na ahi pão, vinho, azeite, nem de que o façõ, alumiam se com o do pescado, porque em toda parte prouee a diuina magestade.[3]

---

[1] Pascem ?   [2] Omitted in the English translation.

Now the other brother Hanno tooke his course towards Africa and Guiney, and[1] he discouered the Fortunate Islands, which we call the Canaries, and besides these he discouered others, as the Dorcades, Hesperides, and the Gorgades, which now be called the Isles of Cape Verde. There he with his company went along the coast till they doubled the Cape of Bona Sperança, and taking their course towards the land, they went along by it vnto another cape, named Aromaticum, which is now called Guardafu, standing south-east[2] from Cape Verde in 14 degrees toward the north; and he came to the coast of Arabia, standing in 16 and 17 degrees, and was five yeeres in this voiage before he returned backe into Spaine. There be others that say that he passed not beyond Sierra Leona, but peopled it,[3] and afterwards discouered as far as the line. But it seemeth he made a full nauigation, because he spent so much time in his travaile. It is reported that the inhabitants of the Cape of Bona Sperança are great witches,[4] and inchanters of certaine

Plinius, lib. 6, cap. 31.

The nauigation of Hanno in Greeke herevnto agreeth.

Enchanted snakes.

¶ Ho capitão Anou tomou na mão a costa Dafrica & Guine, & dizem que descobrio as ylhas bem afortunadas, que agora chamamos Canarias, & alem dellas outras q' dizem Dorcadas, Esperias, & as Gorganas, que se agora chamão do cabo verde: & forão assi ao longo da costa, ate dobrar o cabo de boa esperança, & tomãdo na mão a terra foram ao longo della, à outro cabo q' se chama Aromatico, & agora de Guarda fuy, que esta leste hoeste com ho verde em quatorze graos da parte do norte: & q' chegara à costa Darabia q' está em dezeseys & dez & sete: & posera cinco ānos ate tornar à Espanha. Outros querem q' nam passasse da serra Lioa, & q' Publio[1] despois delle descobrisse ate a linha.

¶ Mas parece q' nam faria tam cõprida nauegaçam pois gastou tanto tempo neste trabalho. Algũs contam agora q' os abitadores desta costa do cabo de boa esperança sam grandes feiticeiros,

[1] It is said.

[2] East, west, or in the same parallel with Cape Verde. Modern observations place Cape Verde in 14° 43', Cape Guardafui, 11° 50'.

[3] And that afterwards he made public the discoveries as far as the line.

snakes,[1] which they bring to such seruice and commande-ment, that they keepe their churches and churchyards,[2] gardens, orchards, barnes, and cattell,[3] as well from wilde beasts as from theeues. For if they see any to doe or to intend hurt, the snake windes her selfe to him[4] or them, holding them as prisoners, and commanding her yoong ones to call their masters vntill they be taken. If the theeues be many, or the wilde beastes of so much strength, that they dare not meddle with them, then they goe vnto the house of him with whom they doe liue ; and if it be in the night time, they giue so many strokes,[5] that at the last they doe awake them, to cause them to prouide for their defence.

A certaine Italian called Aloisius Cadamusta writeth, that he being in the discouerie of Guiney, in the kingdome of Budimol, lay in the house of Bisborol, his sonnes sonne ; and lying in his bed, he heard a great noise and many blowes[6] giuen about the house ; whereupon Bisborol rose, and went out : and when he came againe, Cadamusta demanded of him where he had been : and he answered that

---

encantadores, principalmēte de cobras : & trazem ñas tanto a seu mando, que lhes guardam as semēteiras ortas, pomares & suas grājarias, assi de ladrões, como dalimarias : & se vem algūs fazer dano cinginse com elle, & tem nos presos & mandão aos filhos chamar seus amos & entreganos : & se a gente he muita, ou alimaria poderosa cō que se não atreuem, vamse a casa daquelle com que viuē, & se he de noyte dam tantos Assouios & chirlos, ate q' os acordā pera jr defender, o que lhe entregaram. Aluici Cadamosto Italiano, escreue que se achou no descobrimento de Guine no reyno de Budimol, em casa de Bisborol seu neto : & jazendo na cama ouuio grādes siluos darredor da casa, o q' Bisborol se leuantara da cama & sayra pola porta afora : & quando tornara Cadamosto lhe pergūtara donde vinha, contoulhe como açudira as cobras q' o chamaram. O que se nam deue danar por muyto,

---

[1] Chiefly of snakes.
[2] Not churches, etc.—seed grounds.   [3] Not barns, etc.—farms.
[4] Round him.   [5] Hisses and screams.   [6] Whistlings.

he had been with his cobras or snakes, which called him.
[Which cannot be very hurtful, because] in the Indias there
be many of these kinde of snakes, and some full of poison,
which notwithstanding the Indian people vse to carrie about
their necks, and put them into their bosomes and vnder
their arms: which at some soundes that the people make
will dance, and doe diuers things at commandement.

There was a Portugall that sometime told me, that beyond
the Cape of Bona Sperança, towards Sofala, Quiloa, and
Melinde, where he had been, there were certaine birds,
which would come to[1] the Black Moores at their call, and
according as the Moores did remoue,[2] so the birds would
doe, from one tree to another : and they vsed to follow them
till they did light vpon some tree, from whence they could[3]
not remooue. And as the negros went[4] vp the tree they
should finde waxe and honie thereupon [and knew they were
to take it, and the bird remained there], not knowing whether it grewe there naturally or not.[5] In the same countrey
also vnder ground in ant-holes they did finde much honie

Odericus
writeth the
like of oue
that brought
multitudes
of partridges
to Trape-
zunda.

porq' na India ha muytas & muy peçonhentas, & trazēnas derredor
do pescoço, metēnas pelos peytos & saenlhes polos braços fazēlhe
som q' bailā, & o mais q' lhe mādā.

¶ Assi me disseram algūs Portugueses que por aquella costa do
cabo de boa esperança pera Sofala, Quiloa, Melide andaram, que
auia certos passaros, a que acodiā os negros a seu chamado & como
os viam mudauanse dhūa aruore em outra : & os cafres os seguiam
ate q' se punham em algūa donde se não mudauam : & em olhamdo
os negros pera cima viam mel & cera, sobiā a tomalo, e ho passaro
ficaua ali. Nam me souberam dizer se era isso natural, seho
faziam per ter dali mantēça. Tambē affirmaua q' debaixo da terra
emformigueiros se achaua muyto mel & cera que as formigas

[1] Awaken.
[2] And when they saw them they would change from one tree to another.
[3] Did.   [4] Looked.
[5] Nor could he tell me whether this was their nature, or whether they
did it to find food.

and waxe, which the antes did make, being somewhat bitter.
Vpon the sea coast also they found certaine fishes, which
commonly went vpright in the water, hauing the faces and Mermaides.
natures of women, which the fishermen of those places were
acquainted with[1] [and if they sold them they gave [" the
purchasers?"] an oath that they should sleep with them,
and if they did not do so they bought them [" back?"] for
on no other terms would they give anything for them.][2]

In the yeere 355 before Christ, it is said that the Span- Aristotel. de
yards sailed through the maine sea till they came vnto the natura
flats[3] of India, Arabia, and those coasts adioyning whereunto Strabo, lib.
they caried[4] diuers marchandises, which trade they vsed in de Gadita-
great ships. And, sailing to the northwest, they came vnto longinqua
certaine[5] flats, which, with the flowing of the sea, were bus naui-
couered, and with the ebbe were discouered, finding there bus.
many tunnies of great bignes, where they commonly vsed to
fish them to their great profit, because they were the first vntill
that time that they had seene, and were greatly esteemed.

faziam hū pouco agro. Diziam mais que nesta costa auia grandes
pescados que andauā ho mais do tempo nagoa dereytos, & tinham
rostos & naturas de molheres, com que os pescadores se desen-
fadauā quādo os tomauam : & se os vendiam dauanlhes juramento
se dormiram com ellas, & se ho nam fizeram entamlhas compra-
uam, & doutra maneyra nam lhes dauam por ellas nenhūa cousa.

¶ No anno de 535 antes de Christo, diz que nauegauam os
Espanhões por todo ho maremagno, ate chegarē ás prayas das
Indias, Arabia, & suas costas, donde leuauam & traziam muytas
& diuersas mercadorias : & andauam nestes tratos & outros por
diuersas partes do mundo em grandes nauios : foram ao noroeste
dar em hūs canaes & baixos que com a crecēte do mar se cobriam,
& com ho mingoante apareciā, dōde achauam muytos atuūs de mara-
uilhosa grādeza, fizeram nelles grandes pescarias por serē os pri·
meyros que ate aquelle tempo tinham visto, & por muyto estimados.

[1] With which, when they were taken, the fishermen did amuse themselves. [2] This appears to be something approaching the meaning.
[3] Shores. [4] Whence they brought. [5] Channels and.

The time of Alexander Magnus, as appeereth by the ages of the world, was before the comming of Christ 324 yeeres : we all know that he was borne in Europe; but he trauailed into Asia and Africa, and passed through Armenia, Assyria, Persia, and Bactria, standing northerly in 44 degrees of latitude,[1] which is the farthest countrey in longitude wherein he was in all his iourneyes. From thence he descended into India by the mountaines of Imaus, and the valleyes of Paropanisus, and prepared a nauie in the riuer Indus, and therewith passed into the ocean sea, where he turned by the lands of Gedrosia, Caramania, and Persia, vnto the great citie of Babylon, leauing Onesicritus and Nearcus captaines of his fleete, which afterwards came vnto him by the straight of the Persian sea, and vp the riuer of Euphrates, leauing that countrey and coast discouered.

After this, Ptolemey raigned king of Egypt, who by some is reputed to haue been bastard sonne vnto Philip, father of the foresaid Alexander the Great. This Ptolemey, imitating the forenamed kings Sesostris and Darius, made a trench

---

¶ Alexandre magno segundo polas idades parecem, foy antes da vinda de Christo 324 ānos como todos sabemos, era natural da Europa, passou em Asia, & Africa, & atrauessou a Siria, Armenia, Persia Batuana, q' esta da parte do norte em xliiij graos daltura, q' he amayor, emq' se ele pos nesta jornada, dōde deceo á India polos montes Imãos & valles Paraponistos, e mandou fazer hua armada no rio Indo, e por elle foy sayr ao mar Oceano, donde se tornou por terra de Gedrosia, Carmania, Persya, & Agram, cidade de Babilonia, deixando por capitães darmada Crito & Nearco, q' despois foy ter cō elle polo estreito do mar Persyco, & rio Neufrates acima, deixādo descuberta aq'lla terra & costa.

¶ Despois disso diz que socedeo por rey do Egipto Tholomeu, q' algus querem que fosse filho bastardo de Felipe pay de este grāde Alexādre : ho qual quis imitar a el Rey Secostres & a Dario & pera isso mandou fazer hũ canal de cem pes em largo, & trīta

---

[1] Which is the greatest which he reached in this journey.

or ditch[1] of an hundred foote broad and of thirty foote Plinius, lib. 6, cap. 29. deepe, and ten or twelue leagues in length, till he came to the bitter welles, pretending to haue his worke run into the sea from a mouth of the riuer Nilus, called Pelusium, passing now by the citie Damiata. But this thing tooke none effect; for that the Red Sea was thought to be higher by three cubits then the land of Egypt, which would haue overflowed all the countrey, to the ruine and loss thereof.

In the yeere 277 before the Incarnation, succeeded in the Strabo, lib. 17, pag. 560 & 561. gouernment of the kingdome one Philadelphus, who brought to passe that the marchandises should come out of Europe to the citie of Alexandria, upwards by the riuer Nilus, vnto Coptus. a city named Coptus, and from thence to be conueyed by Myos-Hormos, now Cofir, on the Red Sea. land to a hauen standing vpon the Red Sea, called Myos-Hormos; which way was trauailed in the night, the pilots directing themselues by the stars, which were expert in that practise. And because water was scant that way, they vsed to carrie it with them for all the companie; till, at the last, to auoide that trouble, they digged very deepe wels, and made large cisterns for the receipt of raine water, by which the way furnished with that commoditie, which at the first

---

em alto, & dez ou doze legoas em comprido, ate chegar ás fontes amargas cõ entençam de leuar esta obra ao mar do rio Nillo, q' se chama Peluzio, que entra na cidade Damiata : nam ouue effeito foi desejo, por se achar este mar vermelho ser mais alto tres couodos q' a terra do Egipto, & espalhandose por ella perderse hia tudo.

¶ No anno de 277 antes da encarnaçã de Christo, socedeo neste reyno Philadelphos, & ordenou q' viessem as mercadarias da Europa à cidade de Alexandria pollo rio Nillo acima, ate outra q' se chama o Copto : & della por terra as leuassem a hũ porto que esta em ho mar roxo que se chama Miosormo, andosse este caminho de noite, gouernandose pellas estrellas & pilotos que disso tinham conhecimento, & por esta estrada ser proue dagoa a leuauam pera toda a cõpanhia, ate que fizeram poços muy fundos &

---

[1] Canal.

it wanted, grewe, in continuance of time, to be the more frequented.

But whereas the straight way was dangerous by reason of flats and islands,[1] the aforesaid king, Philadelphus, with his armies, went on the side of Troglodytica, and in an hauen called Berenice caused the ships to arriue[2] which came out of India, being a place of more suretie and lesse perill; from whence they might easily carrie the wares to the citie

The cause of the greatnes of Alexandria. of Coptus, and so to Alexandria. And by this meane Alexandria grew so famous and rich, that in those daies there was no citie of the world comparable to it. And to speake briefly and particularly of the abundance of trafficke there vsed,[3] it is left written for an assured truth, that in the time

Strabo, lib. 17, pag. 549. of king Ptolemey Auletes, father vnto Cleopatra, it yielded in customes vnto him yeerly seuen millions and a halfe of gold, although the trafficke was not then scant twenty yeeres old, by way of that citie.[4]

Strabo, lib. 17, pag. 549. But after that this prouince and countrey became subiect

---

cisternas com q' se sostem, de maneira q' ficou esta estrada mais frequentada.

¶ Dizem q' por este estreito ser perigoso de baixos, Ilhas, Restingas, foy este rey Philadelphos com seus exercitos da parte dos Trogoditas & em hum porto q' se chama Bereniche, mandou q' se descarregassem as naos que vinhā da India por ser lugar mais seguro & podiam chegar sem perigo donde as leuassem a cidade do Copto & dahy a Alexandria: polla qual causa foy esta cidade tam prospera & rica que dizē nam auer naq'lle tempo mais na redō-deza. Veyo este trato em tanto crecimento q' se escreue render em tempo del Rey Tholomeu Aulete pay de Cleopatra sete contos & meyo de ouro: & ainda naq'lla ydade nam auia mais de xx naos neste maneyo.

¶ Mas despois de vir esta prouincia, em poder des Emperadores

---

[1] And sandbanks.   [2] Ordered the ships to discharge.
[3] This traffick increased so much.
[4] Although there were not more than twenty large ships employed.

to the emperours of Rome, as they were greater in power and neerer in couetousnes, so they enhansed the customes; so that within a little time the citie yeelded double[1] the foresaide summe. For the trafficke grew so exceeding great, that they sent euery yeere into India a hundred and twenty ships laden with wares, which began to set saile from Myos-Hormos about the middle of July, and returned backe againe within one yeere.

The marchandise which they did carrie amounted vnto one million two hundred thousand crownes;[2] and there was made in returne of euery crowne an hundred. In so much, that by reason of this increase of wealth the matrones, or noble women, of that time and place, spent infinitely in decking themselues with precious stones, purple, pearles, gum benzoin, frankincense, muske, amber, sandal wood, aloes, and other perfumes, and trinkets, and the like; whereof the writers and historians of that age speake very greatly. ^{Plinius. lib. 12, cap. 18.}

Cornelius Nepos, alleaged by Plinie, maketh report of a king of Egypt that reigned in his time, called Ptolemæus ^{Plinius, lib. 2, cap. 07.}

---

de Roma, como eram mais poderosos, ou cobiçosos, em pouco tempo lhes rendeo o tres dobro: & veo em tanto crecimento, que mandauão em cada hum anno aa India cento & vinte naos de carrega, partiam de Miosormo meado Iulho, & tornauam dētro em hū anno: as mercadorias q' leuauam, dizem q' valeriam hum milhão douro & dozentos mil cruzados, & no retorno faziam cento de hū. Ea fora isto as matronas despendiā em cada hū anno muyto infindo dinheiro em pedraria, pulpura, alsofre, bējoim, encenso, almiscre, ambar, sandalos, aguila, & outros cheiros & brinquinhos, nisto se affirmam os escritores daq'lle tempo.

¶ També escreue Plinio, citando Cornelio Nepote que em su tempo ouue hum rey no Egipto q' se chamou Tholomeu latiro, &

---

[1] Three times the double.

[1] This may mean either one million of gold and two hundred thousand crusadoes,—or, one million two hundred thousand crusadoes.

Lathyrus, from whom one Eudoxus fled vpon occasion, and
the better to auoid and escape his hands, he passed through
the Arabicke gulfe, and the sea all along the coast of Africa
and the cape of Bona Sperança, till he came vnto the island
of Cadiz ; and this nauigation by that course was, in those
daies, as often vsed as now it is, if we may giue credit
to the histories : which appeereth the more manifest by
this, that Caius Cæsar, the sonne of Augustus, going into
Arabia did finde in the Red Sea certaine peeces of those
ships which came thither out of Spaine. It was a vse, also,
long after those daies, to passe to India by land. For so
did the kings of the Soldans and the princes of Bactria,
and other famous captaines, who trauailing thither and into
Scythia by land, had the view of these prouinces and
countreyes so farre till they came that way vnto the
west,[1] and to the seas thereof on the north part, whereunto
many marchants then did trauaile.[2] Marcus Paulus Venetus
writeth much hereof. And although at the first his booke
was taken for a fabulous thing, yet now there is better

Paulus
Venetus
commended.

---

hu Edoxo fogindo delle pello golfam Arabico veyo polo mar ao
lōgo da costa Dafrica & cabo de boa esperança à ilha de Calex, &
querē ainda que se vsasse esta nauegaçam naquelle tēpo como
agora : pelo qual o filho de Cayo Cesar Augusto andando na
Arabia achara neste mar Criteo pedaços de naos da feyçam das
Despanha.

¶ Assi contam q' os reys dos Sudianos & principe dos Batrianos
& outros capitāes famosos forā por terra à India & Sythia, & ounerā
vista daq'llas prouincias & terras todas ate ho leuante & mares
delles da parte do norte, & mercadores & caminhantes que se affirmam andarē por aquellas partes. Marco Paulo largas cousas
escreue dellas ainda que o auiam por fabuloso ja agora lhe dāo
mais credito por acharem nomes de terras, cidades, villas, Angras,
sitios & alturas conformes a suas escrituras.

---

[1] East.

[2] And merchants and travellers declare they have gone in those parts.

credit giuen vnto it; for that by the late experiences of the trauailers and marchants of these daies into those parts, the names of the countreyes, cities, and townes, [anchorages,] with their situations, latitudes,[1] and commodities are now found true, as he and other historiographers of that time haue reported.

In the 200 yeere before the Incarnation it is written, that the Romanes sent an armie into India by sea against the great Can of Cathaia, which, passing through the Straight of Gibraltar, and running to the northwest, found, right ouer against the Cape Finisterre, ten islands, wherein was much tinne.   And they may be those which were called the Cassiterides, and being come to fifty degrees of latitude *Cassiterides.* they found a straight;* and passing through it towards the ** The northwest passage, though the latitude be somewhat mistaken.* west they arriued in the empire of India,[2] and fought with the king of Cathay, and so came backe againe vnto the citie of Rome.   Which thing howsoeuer it may seeme either possible or not possible, true or not true, yet so I finde it *What histories may these be?* left to be recorded in the histories of that time.

In the 100 yeere after the Incarnation of Christ, the emperour Traiane prepared an armie by sea vpon the riuers

---

¶ No anno de 200 antes da encarnaçã de Christo dizem q' os Romãos mandarão hua armada a India cõtra ho gram cão do Cathayo & saindo pello estreito de Gibaltar fora, correram ao Noroeste, & defronte do cabo de Finis terra acharam dez ilhas em q' auia muyto estanho, & deuião ser aq'llas q' chamão Cassiteriacs & posto em cincuenta graos daltura acharam hum estreito por onde forã a loeste a superior India, & pelejando com ho señor de Cathayo se tornaram à cidade de Roma, se he fabula ou certeza pula como a achey escrita.

¶ No anno de cento despois da vinda de Christo ho Emperador Trajano mandou fazer hũa armada nos rios Eufrates, & Tigres foy por elles as ilhas de Zizara, & estreito de Persya, sayram ao Mar

---

[1] And latitudes agreeing with his writings.   [2] Or Upper India.

Xiphilinus in vita Traiani. Euphrates and Tigris, and departed from them and sailed to the islands of Zyzara, and passing the Straight of Persia, entred into the ocean sea, and sailed towards India all along the coast till he came to that place where Alexander had been, and there he tooke certaine ships which came from Bengala, of whom he learned the state of that countrey. But because he was then in yeeres and wearie with his trauaile, but especially because he found there small reliefe for his armie, he returned backe.

After that the Romanes had gotten the most part of the world, there were in that age made many and notable discoueries. But then came the Gothes, Moores, and other Rome taken by the Gothes, 412. barbarous nations, and destroied all. For in the yeere 412 after the Incarnation of Christ, they tooke the citie of Rome : and the Vandales came out of Spaine and conquered Africa.

And in the yeere 450, the king called Atila destroyed many cities in Italie : at which time the citie of Venice The originall of Venice, 450. began. And in this age the Frankes and Vandals entred into France.

In the yeere 474 the empire of Rome was lost, and fell from the Romanes to the Gothes.

Oceano da India, & por aquella costa nauegara alem donde Alexandre chegara, tomara naos que vinham de Bengala, de que se enformara daquella terra & por ser velho & cansado & achar nella pouco mantimento se tornara.

¶ Despois que os Romãos senhorearam a melhor parte do mundo se fizeram muytos & notaveis descobrimentos, mas vieram os Godos, mouros & outros Barbaros & destroirã tudo porq' no anno 412 depois da encarnação de Christo tomarão a cidade de Roma, & os Vandalos sayrã de Espanha a conquistar Africa. E no anno de 450 el rey Atilla destroyo muytas cidades d'Italia & começouse a de Veneza, & neste tempo os Francos, & Vandalos entrarão em França. E no anno de 474 se perdeo o Imperio de Roma & despois disto vieram os Longobardos a Italia no qual tempo andanam os demonios tam soltos pella terra que tomaram à figura de

And after this came the Lombards into Italie, namely in the yeere 560 [in this period devils were let loose on the earth, which took the form of Moses, and many of the deluded Jews were drowned in the sea].

Also about this time the sect of the Arrians preuailed greatly : and at this time one Merline, of England, was famous for his prophecies.

To be short, in the yeere 611 sproong vp the Mahumetane sect and Morisco regiment,[1] which by force inuaded both Africa and Spaine.

The sect of Mahumet began anno 611.

By all this it may appeere, that in that age all the world was in a hurly burly, and all places very tumultuous [and for four hundred years was so defaced and benighted], in so much that trafficke and marchandise ceased : for no nation durst trade one with another, neither by sea nor land : nothing as then remained stedfast, neither in monarchies nor kingdomes, signiories, religions, lawes, artes, sciences, nor nauigations. Nor so much as the records and writings of such things did remaine, but were all burnt and consumed by the barbarous crueltie and vnbrideled power of the Gothes : who became so couetous and ambitious, that they purposed of themselues to begin a new world, and to roote

Trafficke and nauigation cease.

Ramusius, 1 vol., fol. 372, pag. 2.

Moyses, & os Iudeus enganados foram muytos no mar afogados Ea seita Arriana preualecia. E Merlim em Inglaterra foi neste tempo. E no anno de 611 foi Mahamede & os de sua seita, que tomaram por força Africa et Espanha.

¶ Assi que segundo paresce nestas idades todo mundo ardia, por onde dizem q' esteue quatro centos annos tam apagado, & escurecido que nam ousaua nenhum pouo andar dũa parte pera outra, por mar nem terra, tam grande abalo & mudança se fez em tudo q' nhũa cousa ficou em seu ser, & estado ossi monarchias como reynos, & señorios, religões, leis, artes, sciēcias, nauegações escrituras q' disso auia, foy tudo queimado, & consumido segundo contã, porque os Godos eram tam cobiçosos da gloria mundana q' quise-

---

[1] Mahomet and those of his sect.

out the memorie, and blot out the knowledge, of all other nations besides.[1]

But they that succeeded after these times in the government of things, perceiuing the great and huge losse, that the Christian world had by the want of trafficke and ceasing of nauigation,[2] whereby those commodities and marchandises could not be spent, which before went ordinarily from one nation to another by the vse of trade; to the end that this decay and losse might be repaired, and the treasures of the east might be imparted with the west, as it was woont in the times of quietnes and peaceable liuing, they began to deuise a way to passe to India, which was not as the former way was by the Red Sea and the riuer Nilus, but a way of farther sailing and farther length and cost also.[3] For they brought their ware vp the riuer Indus, and there vnladed it, carrying it by land through the countrey of Paropanisus by carauans vnto the prouince of Bactria, and then shipped

Ramusius, 1 vol., fol. 373.

---

ram começar em si outro nouo mundo et q' do passado nã ouuesse nhũa memorias.

¶ Os que despois socederam sentindo tamanha perda e puerto[4] como era ho comercio & trato das gentes hũas com as outras, & q' nã podiam gastar suas mercadorias, nem auer as alheas sem este meo determinaram de buscar maneira como se nam perdesse de todo, & as mercadorias do leuante toruassem ao ponẽte como sohião. Desesperados de as trazeram pollo mar roxo & rio Nilo, abriram outro caminho, ainda q' muito mais comprido & custoso, porque as traziam pello rio Indo acima: & desembarcadas as passaũã por terra & portas Peraponesas à prouincia de Batriana &

---

[1] The foregoing paragraph is very freely translated.

[2] And that neither could they dispose of their own goods nor have others without it, determined to devise means by which all might not be lost, but that the merchandize of the east might flow to the west as before.

[3] Despairing of bringing them by the Red Sea and river Nile they opened another route, though much longer and more costly.

[4] Prejuizo ?

it in barks on the riuer Oxus, which falleth into the Caspian Sea, and so sailed ouer that sea vnto an hauen of the riuer Rha, named Citracan or Astracan, and so vpwards in the said riuer which now is called Volga; and as it appeareth they carried it to the citie of Nouogrode, in the prouince of Resan, which now belongeth to the great duke of Moscouia, standing toward the north in 54[1] degrees of latitude: and therehence they trauailed ouer land vnto the prouince of Sarmatia, vnto the riuer Tanais, which is the diuision of Europe from Asia; where they againe laded it in barks, and caried it downe the riuer, into the lake Mæotis, and to the citie of Caffa, which in ancient time was called Theodosia, which then belonged to the Genowais, who came thither for those wares in their galliasses or great ships.

It is also left written, that the trade this way endured vntill the raigne of Commodita, emperour of Armenia, who[2] prouided for a better course, and commanded this trafficke of the spices to be conueied by the Caspian Sea, and so through the kingdome of Hiberia, which now is called Georgiana, and from thence they entred by the riuer Phasis,

A way by the riuer Oxus, the Caspian Sea, Volga, and ouer land to Caffa.

Strabo, lib. 12.

embarcauanas no rio Oxo, que se mete no mar Caspio & yam a hum porto do rio Ram, q' se chama Sicatrum, et por este rio acima q' se agora diz Volga segundo parece as leuauam aa cidade de Nouogardia, que he agora do gram Duque de Moscouia, & está da parte do norte em 57 graos d'altura & atrauessauam por terra a prouincia de Sarmacia ao rio Tanais, q' a deuide da Europa, onde embarcauā & por elle abaixo as leuauā a alagoa Meotas & cidade de Cafa que antigamente se dezia Theodosia & por ser de Genoeses vinham por ellas as suas galeaças.

¶ E dizem que durou este trato ate ho tēpo do Commodita Emperador Armenio que mādou mudar este caminho ao rio Carius, na fim do qual desembarcauam & atrauessauam ho Reyno de Hiberia q' se agora diz Iorgiana, & tornauam a embarcar no rio

---

[1] 57?

[2] Ordered this route to be changed to the river Cariuscyrus or Kur.

now Phasso, into Pontus Euxinus, and so vnto the city of Trapezunda, standing in 40 and odde degrees of northerly latitude. And to that place came shipping for the marchandises out of Europe and Africa.

The marte of spices at Trapezunda, Ramusius ibidem.

It is further left recorded concerning this way of trafficke, that Nicanor determined or had already begun to open aboue 120 miles of land, which lieth betweene the Caspian Sea and Pontus Euxinus, that they might come and goe by water with their spices, drugs, and other commodities[1] there vsed. But[2] in the meane time this mischiefe happened, that Ptolemey Ceraunvs killed him, and by his death this woorthy and famous enterprise ceased without effect.

Strabo, lib. 11.
Plinus, lib. 6, cap. 11.

But the other way being also at last lost by reason of the wars of the Turks, it pleased God to open[3] another way to these marchandises [and others that were brought] from the isle of Samatra, the citie of Malacca, and the island of Jaua, vnto Bengala, and so carrying them vp the riuer Ganges vnto the citie of Agra, from whence they trauailed ouer

Another way to Boghar, and so by carauans into Persia by the riuer of Ganges.

Facis : & por elle hião ao mar de Latana & cidade de Trapezõda, q' està em quarenta & tãtos graos d'altura, onde vinhā por estas mercadorias as naos da Europa & Africa : & dizē ainda que Nicana determinaua ou tinha ja posto per obra de abrir mais de cento & vinte legoas de terra q' ha deste mar Caspio ao Euxinio pera que podessē yr & vir por agoa as especearias, drogas, & outras mercadorias que por aqui entam caminhauam, se ho nam matara Tholomeu Carauno, por onde nā executou seu generoso pensamento.

¶ Assi que perdido este caminho, pellas guerras do grão Turco, a industria humana abrio logo outro a estas mercadorias & a outras que traziam da ilha de Samatra, cidade de Malaca, ilha da Java : a enseada de Bēgala, et pello rio Gāje acima as leuauam à cidade Dagra, donde atrauessauam por terra a outra que estaa no rio

---

[1] Which travelled this way at that time.

[2] He was killed by Ptolemey Ceraunus, whereby he did not execute his generous intention.

[3] Human industry opened.

land vnto another citie standing neere the riuer Indus, named Boghar,[1] where they discharged, bicause the citie of *Cabor[2] standeth too farre within the land,[3] being the prin- * Or Laor. cipall citie of the Mogores.[4] From thence they went forward to the great citie of Samarcand, standing in the countrey of Samarcande. Bactria: and there the marchants of India, Persia, and Turkie met, bringing thither their seuerall commodities, as cloth of gold, veluets, chamolets, scarlet [carpets, felt] and woollen clothes, which were carried[5] to Cathay and the Woollen cloth good great kingdome of China : wherehence they brought againe marchandise for gold, siluer, precious stones, pearles, silke, muske [camphor, Cathay. aloes, sandal wood] and many other things of great value, and much rubarbe.   After this [it is said] these marchandise, drugs, and spiceries were carried in ships vpon the The way by Ormus and Indian Sea vnto the Streight of Ormus, and to the riuers Balsara, and so to Aleppo Euphrates and Tigris, and were vnladen in the citie of and Barutti. Balsara, standing in 31 degrees towards the north, and from

---

Indio que se chama Bacar, donde hiam pollo sertam dentro a cidade de Cabor, que he a principal dos Mogores : & dahi a gram cidade de Samarcante que estaa na prouincia de Batriana : & juntos os mercadores da India, Persia, Turquia, que traziam borcados, veludos, chamalotes, escarlatas, Alcatifas, fetros,[6] & outros panos de lám que hiam gastando ate ho Cathayo & gram prouincia da China : donde traziam ouro, prata, pedraria, Aljofre, seda, almisere, camfora, aguila, sandalos, & muyto ruybarbo, & outras cousas que ca tinham valia.

¶ Despois disto diz que leuarão estas mercadorias, drogas & especearias, em naos polo mar Indico ao estreyto Dormuz, & rio Eufrates & Tigres & as desembarcauam na cidade de Baçora, que estaa em trinta & hum grao ao norte.   Dahi hiam por terra aa

---

[1] Bokhara or Bukkur.   [2] Cabul ?
[3] Whence they went further inland to the city of Cabor, which is the capital of the Mogores.
[4] Moguls.   [5] Which went to be consumed as far as.   [6] Feltros ?

thence they were caried ouer land vnto the cities of Aleppo, Damascus, and Barutti, standing on the same side, in 35 degrees. And there the Venetian gallies or galliasses, which transported pilgrims into the holy land, came and receiued of those goods.

In the yeere 1153, in the time of Fredericke Barbarossa, it is written that there came to Lubec, a citie of Germanie, one canoa with certaine Indians, like vnto a long barge; which seemed to haue come from the coast of Baccalaos, which standeth in the same latitude that Germanie doth.[1] The Germaines greatly woondered to see such a barge, and such people, not knowing from whence they came, nor vnderstanding their speech, especially because there was then no knowledge of that countrey, as now there is : it may be credible that though the boate was small in respect of those huge seas, yet the winde and water might bring them thither :[2] as we see in these our days that the *Almadie,*

---

cidade Dalepo, Damasco, Baruti, que estaa da mesma banda em trinta & cinco graos : donde as vinham tomar as galees de Veneza, que traziam romeiros a casa sancta.

No anno de 1353,[3] em tempo do Emperador Federico Barba roxa, diz q' foy ter a Lubres cidade Dalemanha hūa nao cō certos Indios em hūa canoa, que sam nauios de remo, parecendo-se aos tones de Cochim : porē esta canoa deuia de ser da costa da Florida bacalhãos & aquella terra, por estar na mesma altura Dalemanha : de que os Tudescos ficaram espantados do tal nauio & gente, por nam saberem donde eram, nem entenderem sua lingoagem, nem terem noticia daquella terra, como agora, porque bem os podia ali leuar ho vento & agoa, como vemos que trazem as almadias de Quiloa,

---

[1] There came to Lubeck a vessel bringing certain Indians in a canoe, which is a vessel propelled by oars, similar to the Cochin boats; but this canoe must have come from Florida, the country of cod fish, which lies in about the same latitude as Germany.

[2] Nevertheless it is quite possible that the winds and currents might bring them there, as we see, etc.   [3] 1153?

which is but a small boate, commeth notwithstanding from Quiloa, Mosambique, and Sofala, to the island of St. Helena, being a small spot of land standing in the maine ocean off the coast of Bona Sperança so farre separated.[1]

In the yeere 1300 after the comming of Christ, the great Soldan of Cayro commanded that the spiceries and drugs, and marchandises of India, should be carried through the Red Sea, as it was vsed before : at which time they vnladed on the Arabian side, at the hauen of Juda, and carried them vnto the house at Mecca, and the carriers of it were the pilgrims.[2] So that each prince vsed a custome to augment the honour and increase the profite of his countrey. And these Soldans had speciall regarde to Cayro, from whence the wares were carried vnto the countreyes of Egypt, Lybia, Africa, the kingdomes of Tunez, Tremessen, Fez, Marocco, Suz : and some of it was carried beyond the mountaines of Atlas vnto the citie of Tombuto, and the kingdome of the Jalophos ; vntill afterwards that the Portu-

JoannesLeo Africanus.

Ramusius, 1 vol., fol. 373.

Tombuto.

Moçambique, Sofala, a ilha de sancta Ilena que he hum ponto de terra, que estaa naquelle gram mar daquella costa & Cabo de boa esperança tam separada.

¶ No anno de 1300 despoys da vinda de Christo ho gram Soldam do Cayro mandou q' tornassem as especiarias, drogas, mercadorias das Indias ao mar Roxo, como em principio acostumauam : somente que desta vez desembarcauam da banda de Arabia, & porto de Juda, as leuauam aa casa de Meca, & as carauanas q' hião a ella em romaria as traziam dõde cada hũ era, por ennobrecer sua terra, principalmente a cidade do Catro, dõde as passauam pola prouincia do Egipto, Libia, Africa, ao reyno de Tunez, Tremecem, Fez, Marrocos, Sus, algũas leuauã alem dos montes Atlanticos á cidade de Tungubutum, & reyno dos Jalopsos, ates que os

---

[1] Far separated from that coast and the Cape of Bona Sperança.

[2] And the caravans that went there in pilgrimage carried them, each to ennoble or enrich their own country ; principally to the city of Cairo, whence the caravans passed by the province of Egypt, Libia, Africa, to the kingdom of Tunez, etc.

8

gals did bring it about the Cape of Bona Sperança vnto the
citie of Lisbone, as in place conuenient we purpose to shew
more at large.[1]

In the yeere 1344, king Peter, the fourth of that name,
reigning in Arragon, the chronicles[2] of his time report, that
one Don Luis of Cerda, sonne vnto the sonne of Don John
of Cerda, craued aide of him to goe and to conquere the
The Canarie Islands. isles of the Canaries, standing in 28 degrees of latitude to
the north, because they were giuen vnto him by Pope Cle-
ment the First, which was a French man.   Whereby in
those daies there grew a knowledge of those islands in all
Europe, and specially in Spaine : for such great princes
would not begin nor enterprise things of such moment without great certaintie.

The Island of Madera discouered by Macham, an English-man. About this time also the island of Madera was discouered
[in 32 degrees] by an English man called Macham : who
sailing out of England into Spaine, with a woman of
his,[3] was driuen out of his direct course by a tempest, and
arrived in that island, and cast his anker in that hauen,

Portugueses as trouxeram Polo cabo de boa esperāça aa nobre
cidade de Lisboa, como se diraa a seu tempo.

¶ No anno de 1344 reynando dom Pedro Daragam ho quarto,
dizem os coronistas de seu tēpo, que lhe pedio ajuda dom Luys
de la cerda neto de dom Joam de lacerda pera ir cōquistar as ilhas
Canarias que estam em vintoyto graos desta mesma banda, por
lhe serē dadas polo Papa Clemente vj natural de França.   E
segundo isto já naquelle tempo auia muyta noticia daquellas ilhas
por toda Europa, quanto mays ē Espanha, porque tamanhos principes nam se auiam de mouer a esta empresa sem muyta certeza.

¶ Tambem querē que neste meyo tempo fosse a ilha da Madeira
descuberta, que esta em trinta & dous graos, por hum Ingres que
se chama Machim, que vindo de Inglaterra pera Espanha com
hūa molher furtada, forā ter á ilha cō tormenta, & fundiaram naq'lle

---

[1] At the proper time.   [2] Chroniclers.
[3] Having run away with a woman.

which now is called Machico, after the name of Macham. And bicause his louer[1] was then seasicke, he there went on land with some of his companie, and in the meane time his ship weyed and put to sea, leauing him there : whereupon his louer for thought died.[2] Macham, which greatly loued her, built in the island a chappell or hermitage to burie her in, calling it by the name of Jesus Chappell : and wrote or graued vpon the stone of her tombe his name and hers, and the occasion whereupon they arriued there. After this he made himselfe a boate all of a tree, the trees being there of a great compasse about, and went to sea in it with those men of his companie that were left with him, and fell with[3] the coast of Africke without saile or oare, and the Moores among whom he came tooke it for a miracle, and presented him vnto the king of that countrey : and that king also admiring the accident, sent him and his companie vnto the king of Castile.

In the yeere 1395,[4] king Henrie the third of that name reigning in Castile, the information which Macham gaue of this island, and also the ship wherein he went thither,

porto que se agora chama Manchico, de seu nome tomado, & pella amiga vir do mar enjoada sayo em terra com algũs da companhia, & a nao cõ tempo se fez á vela, & ella faleceo danojada. Machim q' a muyto amaua pera sua sepultura fez hũa ermida do bõ Jesu, & escreueo em hũa pedra o nome seu & della : & a causa q' os ali trouxera, & poslha por cabeceira : & ordenon hũ barco do tronco de hũa aruore, q' ali auia muyto grossos & embarcouse nelle com os q' tinha, & forã ter à costa Dafrica sem velas, nem remos, Os mouros ouuerá isto porcousa milagrosa, & por tal os apresentaram ao señor da terra, & elle pella mesma causa os mandou a el rey de Castella.

¶ No anno de 1393 reynando em Castela el rey dom Enrique iij pela enformaçam q' Machim desta ilha dera, & a nao d' sua cõpan-

---

[1] Mistress.
[2] And in the meantime the ships made sail and she died of grief.
[3] Reached.   [4] 1393 ?

moued many of France and of Castile to goe and discouer it, and the great Canarie : and they which went were principally the Andaluzes, the Biscaines, and the Guepuscoes, carrying with them many people and horses. But I know not whether the charge of that voiage was theirs or the kings. But by whom soeuer it was set out, they seeme to be the first that discouered the Canaries and landed in them, where also they tooke 150 of the islanders prisoners. Concerning the time of this discouerie, there is some difference among the writers, for some affirme this to be done in the yeere 1405.

The chroniclers of Portugall haue this record, that after the incarnation of Christ 1411-16, [in the month of July], king John the first of that name king of Portugall, departed from the citie of Lisbon with the Prince Don Duarte or Edward, and Don Peter and Don Henry his sonnes, with other lords and nobles of his realme, and sailed into Africa, where he tooke the great citie of Ceuta, standing on the north side thereof, betweene 35 and 36 degrees in latitude : which was one of the principall causes of the enlarging of the dominions of Portugall.[1]

The first discouerie of the Canaries by the Christians, 1405.

The first conquest of the Portugals in Barbarie, 1415. This victorie was gotten by the helpe of the English as Walsingham writeth.

---

hia, moueo a muytos de França & Castela irē a descobrirla & a gram Canaria, principalmente Andalezes Bizcainhos, Lepuzcos : leuādo assaz gente & caualos, mas nā sey se foi isto a sua custa, se d'el rey : como quer que seja, querem q' fossem os primeiros que ouuessem vista das Canarias, & saissem nellas, & captiuassem cento & cincoēta pessoas outros querem q' fosse isto no anno de 1405.

Segundo os nossos cronistas deyxarā escripto, despoys da encarnaçam de Christo 1411 ou 16 annos, no mes de Julho partio el rey dō Joam o primeyro de Portugal da cidade de Lisboa, & o principe dom Duarte, & o ifante dō Pedro, & dom Aurique seus filhos, & outros senhores & nobres do reyno pera Africa, & tomaram a gram

---

[1] Spain. Ceuta was afterwards annexed to Spain, and finally ceded in 1668.

When they were come from thence, Henry, the kings
third sonne, desirous to enlarge the kingdome and to discouer strange and unknowne countryes,[1] being then in
Algarbe [at Cape St. Vincent] gaue direction for the discouery of the coast of Mauritania. For in those daies none
of the Portugals had euer passed the Cape de Non, standing in 29 degrees of latitude. And for the better accom-
plishing of this discouerie, the aforesaid Don Henry prepared a fleete, and gaue commandement to the chiefe captaines to proceede in discouerie from the aforesaide cape
forward :[2] which they did. But when they came to another
cape named Bojador, there was not one of them that durst
goe farther or beyond it :[3] at which fearefull and cowardly
faintnes of theirs the prince was exceedingly displeased.

In the yeere 1417, king John the second reigning in
Castile, and his mother, Ladie Katharine, then vsing the
gouernment, one Monsieur Ruben of Bracamonte, which

*John de
Barros.
Asiæ, decad.
1, lib. 1,
cap. 2.
Cape de
Non.*

*Cape
Bojador.*

cidade de Ceyta, que está da parte do norte em trīta & cinco ate
seys graos d'altura, que foy hūa das principays causas, alargarense
os termos Despanha.

¶ Vindos de lâ, o ifante dom Anrique desejoso de acrecētar este
reyno, & descobrir outro mūdo nouo, se assentou no algarue ao
cabo de sā Vicente, donde começou a mandar descobrira costa de
Mauritania, porque naquelle tēpo ne nhū Portugues passaua do
cabo de Nāo, q' está em xxix graos daltura. E pera isto se por
em effeyto, mandou ho Ifante aparelhar certos nauios : · & deo aos
capitāes por regimento q' deste cabo por diante fosse seu descobrimento : elles assi o faziam, mas como chegauāo a outro q' se
chama Bojador, nenhūa pessoa ousaua auenturar a vida : de q' o
Ifante andaua assaz agastado.

¶ No anno de 1417 reynando em Castela dom Joam ho ij &
gouernando sua māy dona Caterina, hum Mossem Rubem de Bra-

---

[1] Another new world.
[2] And instructed the captains that from this cape forwards should be
his own discovery.
[3] Durst risk his life.

was then admirall of France, craued the conquest of the
islands of the Canaries, with the title to be king of them,
for a kinsman of his called Monsieur John Betancourt:
which being granted him by the queene, and farther also
partly furnished out, he departed from Siuill with a goode
armie: but the chiefe or principall cause that mooued him
to enter into this action, was to discouer and perfectly to
take a view of the island of Madera, whereof Macham before
had giuen so much information.[1] But for all that he went
vnto the Canaries, and carried with him a friar called Mendo
to be as bishop thereof, admitted by Pope Martine the fift.
When they were landed they wonne Lancerota, Forteuen-

The Cana-
rie Islands
conquered. tura, Gomera, and Ferro: from whence they sent into
Spaine many slaues, honie, waxe, camfora or camfire, hides,
orchall, figs, sanguis draconis, and other marchandises,
whereof they made good profit: and this armie also as they
Porte
Santo. report, discouered Porto Santo. The island that they inhabited was Lancerota, where they built in it a castle of
stone for their better defence and securitie.[2]

---

camonte que fora almirante de França, lhe pedira a cõquista das
ilhas Canarias, cõ titolo de rey pera hũ seu parente, q' se chamaua
Mossem Iam Betancor, & que a raynha lhas dera & ho ajudara.
Partio de Seuilha com bõa armada, & querem ainda que a principal causa que a isto ho mouera era descobrir a ilha da Madeyra,
que Machim achara: mas foram ter ás Canarias, leuando consigo
hu Frey Mendo pera Bispo della, concedido pelo Papa Martinho
quinto. Saidos em terra ganharam Lançarote, Forte vētura,
Gomeyra, & ho Ferro, dõde mandaram a Espanha muytos escrauos, mel, cera, cãfora, couros, orchiga, figos, sangue de dragam, &
outras mercadorias, em que fizeram bom dinheyro, por q' esta
armada diz que descobrio a ilha de Porto sancto, assentaram em
Lançarote, onde fizeram hum castelo de pedra & barro, cõ que
sostineram o que tinham ganhado.

---

[1] Which Machan had found out.   [2] To secure what they had gained.

In the yeere 1418 one John Gonzales Zarco, and Tristam Vaz Teixera, householde gentlemen vnto Don Henry the kings third sonne, perceiuing the desire that their master had to discouer new countreyes, and willing in that course to doe him some seruice, craued of him a barke, and licence to vndertake the action : which they obtained, and sailed to the coast of Africa : where they were ouertaken with a terrible tempest ;[1] but they were succoured by falling with the land, and entring into an hauen called Santo, where they landed, and remained two yeeres.

John de Barros, decad. 1, lib. i, cap. 2.

In the yeere 1420 they discouered the Island of Madera [and passed ouer to it], where they founde the chappell and the stone and tombe, whereupon the foresaide Macham had grauen his name.[2] There are others that write that a certaine Castillian, perceiuing the desire and fauour to nauigation which Don Henry had,[3] told him that they had found the Island of Porto Santo ; which being but a small thing

Barros, decad. 1, lib. 1, cap. 3. The chappell built by Macham found in Madera.

Porto Santo

No anno de 1418 Vendo Joam gonçaluez ho zarco, & Tristam vaz teixeyra, caualeyros da casa do Ifante, os desejos que elle tinha de descobrir terra : & elles de ho seruirem na tal impresa, lhe pediram hum nauio & licença em que foram a este descobrimento, & junto da costa de Africa lhes deu tal tormenta que se nã poderãm juntar a ella, & se perderam de todo se os Deos nam socorrera cõ lhes amostrar hũa terra & porto a que poseram nome sancto, onde se saluaram : & estiueram aqui dous annos. No anno de 1420 descobriram as ilhas da madeira, & se passaram a ella, onde ainda acharam a hirmida & pedra que contaua, como Machim ali estiuera. Outros dizem que vendo hum Castelhano os desejos que ho Infante tinha de descobrir nouo mundo, lhe dera conta como elles acharam a ilha do Porto sancto, & por ser

---

[1] And near the African coast they fell in with such a tempest that they could not reach it, and they would have been lost had not God succoured them by showing them a haven, which they named Sancto, where they saved themselves.

[2] Which Machan placed there, as already related.

[3] The desire the Infante had to discover a new world.

they made no reckoning of it. Don Henry sent Bartholomew Perestrello, John Gonzales Zarco, Tristam Vaz Teixera,
and by the signes and likelyhoods that they had receiued,
they went to Porto Santo, and there remained two yeeres :
and after that, namely in the yeere 1420, they sailed also to
the Island of Madera, where they found the memoriall and
monument of the aforesaide Macham the English man.

As for Monsieur Betancourt, who entred into the conquest
of the Canaries as is aboue mentioned, he was slaine in the
middest of the action, and left behind him for his heire a
kinseman of his called Monsieur Menante, who after that
sold the said Islands of the Canaries vnto one Peter Barba
of Siuill.   There are other which speake otherwise, and
say that the Monsieur John Betancourt went into France to
prepare a new army about this conquest, and left there a
nephew of his ; who, because he heard no more of his
vncle, and sawe that he could not maintaine the warres any
longer, he solde the Canaries to Don Henry the king of
Portugals third sonne, for a certaine thing that he gave him
in the Island of Madera.

*The Cana-
rie Islands
sold ouer to
a Spanyard.*

---

cousa pequena nam faziam della estima.   Que foy causa de mandar la ho Ifante Bertolameu perestrelo, Joam gonçaluez ho zarco,
Tristam vaz teyxeira : & polos sinaes & derrotas que ho Castelhano
dera do Porto sancto, foram ter a elle & despoys de ali estar dous
annos, no de 1420 se passaram á ilha da madeyra, onde acharam
como Machim ali estiuera.

¶ Estando assi Mossem Joam Betancort na cõquista das Canarias (como he dito) dizem que ho mataram, & deixara por seu
herdeiro hum parente que se chamaua Mossem Menante, & q' este
as vendera a hum Pero Barba de Seuilha.   Outros querē dizer q'
Mossem Joam Betancort se fosse a França refazer de nouo pera
esta conquista, & deixara aly hũ sobrinho, & como nunca mays
de là viera, vendo ho parente que nam podia sostentar a guerra,
vendera as Canarias ao Ifante dom Anrique por certa cousa que
lhe dera na ilha da Madeira.

In the yeere 1424 they write that the saide Don Henry Barros,
decad. 1, lib.
prepared a nauie and armie to conquer these islands, wherein i, cáp. 12.
there went as captaine generall, one Don Fernando de
Castro ; and by reason of the valiantnes and warlike behauiour of the people they had the repulse : whereupon Don
Ferdinando, considering the great charge, and little or no
good successe, he gaue ouer the action, and returned backe
againe.   After this Don Henry resigned ouer these islandes
to the crowne of Castile, in consideration of the aides which
Betancourt had receiued.   But the Castillians agree not
vnto this report.   For they say, that neither the kings of
Portugall nor Don Henry would render the islands, till
they came in question before Pope Eugenius the fourth [a
Venetian] ; who fully vnderstanding the matter, gaue the
conquest of the islands by order of iudgement vnto the king The Cana-
ries came to
[Don John] of Castile in the yeere 1431, whereupon this the crowne
of Spaine in
contention ceased touching the title of the Canaries be- the yeere
1431.
tweene the kings of Portugall and of Castile.

These islands being in number seuen, were called by the
name of [the Blessed or] Fortunatæ, standing in 28 degrees

No anno de 1424 diz que mandou o Ifante fazer hūa armada para
cōquista destas ilhas, hia por capitam mor della dō Fernando de
castro, & como as gentes dellas eram belicosas, defenderam bem
suas casas.   E vendo dom Fernando ho grande gasto q' fazia, se
tornou, & despois ho Ifante alargou esta terra á coroa de Castella
pellas ajudas q' Abetācor dera.   Mas os Castelhanos contam isto
doutra maneira, que nem os Reys de Portugal nē o Infante dō
Anrique as quiseram alargar, atè chegarem a direito diante do
Papa Eugenio quarto Venezeano, ho qual vīdo isto deu a cōquista
daquelas ilhas por sentença a el Rey dom Joam de Castella, no
anno de trinta & hū, por onde cessou esta contenda das Canarias
ante os Reis de Portugal, & Castella.

¶ Estas ilhas das Canarias diz q' sam sete & q' se chamauā as
Beatas ou bem Afortunadas, estão em vintoito graos da parte do
norte, tē o mayor dia de treze oras, & a noite de outras tātas, estam

to the north : where the longest day is but 13 howers, and the longest night as much, lying distant from Spaine 200 leagues, and from the coast of Africa 18[1] leagues. [In times past] the people were idolaters, and did eate their flesh raw for want of fire : they had no iron, and sowed without any toole : they tilled and raised the ground with (oxe hornes and) goats hornes. Euery island did speake a seuerall language. They tooke many wiues, and knew them not carnally vntill they had deliuered them to the superiours. They had diuers other (Paganish)[2] customes : but now the Christian faith is planted among them.

The commodities of these islands are wheate, barley, sugar, wine, and certaine birdes, called Canarie birdes, much esteemed in Spaine and other places.

In the Island of Ferro they haue none other water, but that which proceedeth in the night from a tree, compassed with a cloud, whence water issueth, seruing the whole island, both men and cattell, a thing notorious and knowne to very many.

In the yeere 1428 it is written that Don Peter, the king

The ancient maners of the Canarians.

The commodities of the Canaries.

A tree yeelding abundance of water in Ferro.

---

de Espanha duzentas legoas, & da costa de Africa dezasete. Em tēpos passados adorauā os ydolos, comiā carne crua, por falta de fogo, nam tinham ferro, semeauā sem nada, laurauā a terra com cornos de bodes, & cabras, cada ilha falaua sua lingoagem, casa-uāse cō muitas molheres, & primeiro que as conhecessem as dauam aos senhores : tinham outros diuersos custumes, agora todos sam da ley de Christo, tem muito trigo, ceuada, açucares, vinho, & hūs passaros q' chamā canarios, que em Espanha sam estimados. Na ilha do Ferro nam ha outra agoa senam a que de noite deita hūa aruore, sobre q' está hūa nuuē, desta bebem as gentes, & gados, cousa a todos muy notorio.

No anno de 1428 diz q' foy o Infante dom Pedro a Inglaterra,

---

[1] 17.   [2] Dele.

of Portugals eldest sonne, was a great traueller.　He went
into England, France, Almaine, and from thence into the
Holy Land, and to other places ; and came home by Italie,
taking Rome and Venice in his way : from whence he
brought a map of the world, which had all the parts of the A most rare and
world and earth described.　The Streight of Magelan was excellent map of the
called in it The Dragons taile : The Cape of Bona Sperança, world.
The forefront of Afrike, (and so foorth of other places :)[1] by A great helpe to
which map Don Henry the kings third sonne was much Don Henry in his dis-
helped and furthered in his discoueries. coueries.

It was tolde me by Francis de Sosa Tauares, that in the
yeere 1528, Don Fernando, the kings sonne and heire, did
shew him a map, which was found in the studie[2] of Alco-
baza, which had beene made 120 yeeres before, which map
did set foorth all the nauigation of the East Indies, with the
Cape of Bona Sperança, according as our later maps haue
described it.　Whereby it appeereth, that in ancient time As much discouered in ancient
there was as much or more discouered, then now there is. times as now is.
Notwithstanding all the trauaile, paines, and expences in Barros, decad. 1,
this action of Don Henry, yet he was neuer wearie of his lib. 1, cap. 4.

França, Alemanha, a casa sancta, & a outras de aquella bãda,
tornou por Italia, esteue em Roma, & Veneza, trouxe de lá hũ
Mapamundo q' tinha todo ambito da terra, & o estreito do Magalhães se chamaua, Cola do dragam, o cabo de Boa esperança, frun-
teira de Africa, & q' deste padram se ajudara ho Infante dom
Anrrique em seu descobrimento.　Francisco de sousa tauarez me
disse q' no anno de 1528 ho Infante dom Fernando lhe amostrara
hũa Mapa que se achara no cartorio Dalcobaça que auia mais de
cento & vinte annos que era feito, o qual tinha toda nauegaçam da
India, com ho cabo de Boa esperança, como as dagora,　se assi he
isto, ja em tempo passado era tanto como agoro, ou mais descuberto.

Com todo do trabalho & gasto que ho Ifante dom Aurique tinha

---

[1] Dele.　　　　　　　　[2] Colloction.

purposed discoueries. At length there was a seruant of his called Gilianes[1] that first passed the Cape Bojador, a place before terrible to all men : and he brought word that it was not so dangerous as it was reported : for on the other side of it he went on land, and in maner of taking possession, set in the ground a crosse of wood, to be as a marke and token afterwards of his discouery so farre.

In the yeere 1433, in the moneth ·of August, Don John died, and his sonne, Don Duarte or Edward, succeeded him in the kingdome.

In the yeere 1434 Don Henry sent out one Alfonso Gonsales Baldaia [a sea captain] and Gilianes aforesaid, and they went to another cape, which was beyond the former, and going on land perceiued the countrey to be inhabited : and because they were desirous to satisfie Don Henry with as much relation and knowledge as they could get, they continued their voyage, and went forward, till they came to a certaine point of land, from whence they turned backe againe.

In the yeere 1438 king Edward, whom the Portugals

---

feyto, nunca desistio de seu preposito & descobrimento, & pera isso mandou a elle Gilianes seu criado, q' foy ho primeiro que passou ho cabo Bojador, tanto por todos arreceado, & trouxe noua nam ser tã perigoso como se dezia, da outra bãda sayo em terra, & como quem tomaua posse, pos hũa Cruz de pao nella por marco : & no anno de 1433 no mes de Agosto faleceo el Rey dom Joam, & aleuantaram por Rey dom Duarte seu filho.

¶ No anno de 1434 mãdou ho Ifante dõ Anrrique Afonso gonçaluez baldaya, capitam de hũ nauio, & Gilianes que descobrio o cabo em outro cabo alem delle, saydos em terra conhecerã ser pouoada, & como sabiam q' ho Infante desejaua auer della lingua forã ter a hũa põta sem ver neuhũa cousa, donde se tornaram, &

---

[1] And to pursue them he sent forth a servant, etc.

call Don Duarte, died, and Don Alphonso the prince being The death of Don Duarte king of Portugall.
yoong, Don Peter his vncle gouerned the kingdome.

In the yeere 1441 Don Henry sent out two ships, and the Barros, decad. 1, lib. 1, cap. 6.
captaines were, in the one Tristan, and Antonie Gonsales in
the other. Being put to sea they tooke a prise vpon the
coast, and sailed on to Cape Blanco, that is the White Cape, Cape Blanco.
standing in 20 degrees, and informed Don Henry of the
state of that coūtrey by the Moores which they brought
from thence. Whereupon he sent one Fernan Lopez de
Sanado to give knowledge thereof to Pope Martine, trusting
to make these things commodious to Holy Church. Vpon
which knowledge the Pope[1] granted indulgences and euer- Indulgences granted to encourage to this enterprise.
lasting pardon, and all other things demanded of him, vnto
those which should die in this enterprise.

After this, in the yeere 1443, Don Henry commanded Barros, decad. 1, lib. 1, cap. 7.
Antonie Gonsales to carrie backe the slaves which he had
brought and to ransome them in their country, (which he
did),[2] and the Moores gaue them in trucke for them againe
blacke Moores with curled haire, and some gold; so that

---

no anno de 1438 faleceo el Rey dom Duarte: & pelo Principe dō
Afonso ficar menino gouernou ho Infante dom Podro suo tio.

¶ No anno de 1441 mandou ho Infante dom Anrriq' dous
nauios, capitães delles Nuno tristam & Antam gonçaluez, sairam
na costa, & fizeram presa, & chegaram ao cabo Branco, que está
em vinte graos, enformado ho Infante das cousas daquella terra
pelos mouros q' estes trouxeram, mandou Fernā lopez dazeuedo
dar cōta ao Papa Martinho do que passaua, & como esperaua re-
sultar gram proueito aa sancta madre igreja, ho Papa lhe concedeo
indulgēcia & doaçam perpetua, & tudo o mais que pedia aos que
nesta empresa falecessem.

¶ Despois disto no anno de 1443 mandou ho Infante Antam
gōçaluez resgatar os escrauos q' trouxera, & os mouros derā por
elles negros de cabelos reuolto, & algum ouro: donde ficou nome

---

[1] And as the Pope hoped that great advantage would result to
Holy Church, etc., etc.   [2] Dele.

Rio de Oro, why so called. now that place is called Rio de Oro, that is, the Golden Riuer, whereby the desire of the discouerie might be[1] the more increased.

Not long after he sent out another, named Nunnez Tris-

The Islands of Arguin. tan, who came vnto the Islands of Arguin, where he tooke more slaves, and brought them to Portugall, in the yeere [following] 1444.

Hereupon, also, one Lansarote, a groome of Don Gilians chamber,[2] with others associated with him, armed out certaine ships, which went coasting til they came to the Islands of

The Islands of Garze. Garze, where they tooke [nearly] two hundred slaves, which were the first that were brought from thence to Portugall.

Barros, decad. 1, lib. 1, cap. 9. In the yeere 1445, there went, as captain of a bark, one Gonsala de Syntra, an esquire belonging to Don Henry, into those parts ; and he went on land, where he was taken with sixe or seuen more of his company, which place was therefore called after his name, Angra de Gonsaluo de

Angra de Gonsaluo de Syntra. Syntra. This was the first losse, which the Portugals received in their discoueries.

In the yeere following, Don Henry sent out three cara-uels, wherein went as captaines, Antonie Gonsales, Diego

---

rio douro, & mais acrecentou ho desejo ao descobrimento : & por isso foy logo lá Nuno tristam, & chegou às ilhas Darguim, donde fez presa, & se tornou cō ella no anno seguinte de 1444.   Lança-rote moço da camara do Infante, Gilianes, & outros armaram certos nauios, foram por costa até as ilhas da Garça, tomarão perto de dozentas almas, que forā as primeiras que até entam de laa vieram.

¶ No anno de 1445 foy por capitam de hum nauio Gonçalo de Sintra escudeiro do Infante, saidos em terra nūa Angra que se agora chama de seu nome, tomaram os mouros com seys ou sete cōpanheiros, foy esta a primeira perda que recebeo Portugal desta ēpresa & no anno seguinte mandou ho Infante tres carauellas, &

---

[1] Was.

[2] Groom of the chamber to the Infant, Don Gilians, etc.

Aloizio, and Gomez Perez, who had their direction not to enter into Rio de Oro, nor to beare themselves disorderly, but to trauaile in peace, and to conuert as many infidels as they could to Christianitie.   But none of these things were performed by them; for they returned without doing any memorable act.

In the same yeere, 1446, another esquire belonging to the king of Portugall, called Denis Fernandes, of the citie of Lisbon, entered into these discoueries, more to win fame, than to reape commoditie by them.   And he being in his voiage, came to the riuer of Sanaga, standing between 15 and 16 degrees of latitude towards the north, [and bordering upon the moors of Jalophos], where he tooke certaine Negroes; and not contented therewith, he went forward and discouered Cape Verde, standing in 14 degrees on the same side; and there he set vp vpon the land a crosse of wood, and then returned with great contentation. *Barros, decad. 1, lib. 1, cap. 9, & cap. 13. The riuer of Sanaga. Cape Verde.*

In the yeere 1447, one Nunnez Tristan, went foorth to discouer in a carauell, and he passed the aforesaid Cape Verde, and Rio Grande, and went past it vnto another *Barros, decad. 1, lib. 1, cap. 14. Rio Grande.*

---

capitães dellas Antā gõçaluez, Diego Afonso, Gomez pirez, a que deu regimento que nam entrasse no rio do Ouro : & asseitassem pazes, & fizessem quantos Christãos podessem : & sem nada d'isto se tornaram.

¶ No anno de 1446 hũ escudeiro del Rey dõ Afonso q' se chamaua Dinis fernandez da cidade de Lixboa, foy a este descobrimento, mais por honra q' por proueito : chegou ao rio á Sanaga, que está em quinze ou dezaseis graos d'altura da parte do norte, & estrema os mouros do Ialophos, onde tomou algũs negros : nã cõtente disto diz q' passou auante, & descobrio o Cabo verde, q' está em catorze da mesma parte, & posta sua Cruz de pao nelle tornou cõtente.

No anno de 1447 tornou Nuno tristã em hũa carauella & passou o Cabo verde, & rio Grāde : & sahio em outro q' está alèm delle em vinte graos, onde o mataram com dezoito Portugueses, & com

standing beyond it in twelve degrees,[1] where he was also taken with eighteen Portugals more; but the ship came home againe in safetie, conducted by fower or fiue (which escaped the hands of the Negroes.)[2]

In this yeere also, 1447, it happened that there came a Portugall ship through the streight of Gibraltar; and being taken with a great tempest, was forced to runne westwards more then willingly the men would, and at last they fell vpon an Island which had seuen cities, and the people spake the Portugall toong, and they demanded if the Moores did yet trouble Spaine, whence they had fled for the losse which they received by the death of the king of Spaine, Don Roderigo.

The island of seven cities.

The boateswaine of the ship brought home a little of the sand, and sold it vnto a goldsmith of Lisbon, out of the which he had a good quantitie of gold.

Don Pedro vnderstanding this, being then gouernour of the realme, caused all the things thus brought home, and made knowne, to be recorded in the house of justice.[3]

There be some that thinke, that those Islands whereunto the Portugals were thus driuen, were the Antiles, or Newe Spaine, alleaging good reasons for their opinion, which here

---

quatro ou cinco se tornou ho nauio em saluamento.   Contam mais que neste meyo tempo vindo hūa nao de Portugueses pelo estreito de Gibraltar fora, lhe dera tal trometa, q' correra a loeste muito mais do q' quisera, & forā ter a hūa ilha em q' auia sete cidades & falauā a nossa lingoa & preguntarā se tinham os mouros ainda occupada Espanha dōde fogirā pola perda del rey dō Rodrigo. O contra mestre da nao diz q' trouxe hūa pouca d'area & q' a vendera a hū ouriues em Lixboa de q' tirara boa cātidade douro: sabēdo isto ho Infante dō Pedro que ainda gouernaua, diz q' ho mādou escreuer na casa do tōbo.   E algūs querem q' estas terras & ilhas q' os Portugueses tocarā, sejam aquelas que se agora chamā as Antilhas & noua Espanha, & alegam muitas razões

---

[1] 20 ?   [2] Dele.   [3] Record.

I omit, because they serue not to my purpose. But all their reasons seeme to agree, that they should be that countrey, which is called Noua Spagna.

In the yeere 1449, the king, Don Alfonso, gave licence vnto his vncle, Don Henry, to inhabit[1] the Islands of the Açores, which were long before discouered.

Don Alfonso king of Portugall come to age. Barros. decad. 1, lib. 2, cap. 1. The Açores first inhabited.

And in the yeere 1458, this king went into Africa, and there he tooke the towne called Alcaçer.

And in the yeere 1461, he commanded Signior[2] Mendez, a gentleman of his house, to build the castle of Arguin, whereof he gave vnto him the gouernment, as to[3] his lieutenant.

Alcaçer taken. The castle of Arguin builded. Ibidem.

In the yeere 1462, there came into the realme of Portugall three Genowais of good parentage, the chiefe of whom was called Antonie de Noli, and of the other two, the one was his brother, the other was his nephew, and each of these had his seuerall ship, crauing libertie of Don Henry to discouer the Islands of Cape Verde, which was granted them. Others say that the places which they discouered, were those which Antiquitie called the Gorgades, Hespe-

Barros, decad. 1, lib. 2, cap. 1.

The isles of Cape Verde discouered by three Genowais.

---

pera isso, em que nam falo por nã tornar isto à minha conta, mas com tudo toda a cousa de que nam sabiam dar rezam era dizer, he a noua Espanha.

¶ No anno de 1449 el Rey dõ Alonso deu licença ao Infante dõ Anrriq' seu tio p'ra mandar pouoar as ilhas dos Açores q' auia dias q' erã descubertas : & no anno de 1458 passou este Rey a Africa, & tomou a villa Dalcacere, & no de 61 mandou Soeiro mendez fidalgo de sua casa fazer o castello Darguim aque deu alcaydaria.

No anno de 1462 vieram a este reyno de Portugal tres Ianoeses pessoas nobres, o primeiro delles era Antã de Noly & hũ seu jrmão & sobrinho, cada hũ em seu nauio, pedirã licẽça ao Infante p'ra descobrir as ilhas do Cabo verde & elle lhe aprouue : algũs querem dizer que fossem aquellas que os antigos chamaram Gorga-

---

[1] People.   [1] Soeiro.   [3] Dele.

rides, and Dorcades ; but they named them Mayo, Sainct Jago, and Sainct Philip, because they discouered them on those Saints daies : but they are also called by some, the Islands of Antonio.

The death of Don Henry, 1463.

[In this same year or] in the yeere following (1463, this good noble man)[1] Don Henry died, leauing from Cape De

Sierra Leona.

Non discouered vnto the mountaine called Sierra Leona, standing on this side the line in eight degrees of latitude (where no man had beene before that time.)[2]

In the yeere 1469, the king [Don John] of Portugall did

Barros, decad. 1, lib. 2, cap. 2. The countrey of Guiney let out to farme.

let out for yeerely rent the trade of Guiney vnto one called Fernan Gomez, which countrey afterwards was called The Mine. He let it out for fiue yeeres, for two hundred thousand Reyes by the yeere (which is of our English money £138 17s. 9d. ob.)[3] and added vnto his lease this condition, that euery yeere he should discouer an hundred leagues.

Ibidem.

In the yeere following, which was 1470, this king went

Arzila taken. Tanger taken.

into Africa with his sonne, Prince John, where they tooke the towne of Arzila, and the people of the citie of Tanger

---

nas, Esperidas, Orcadas, mas elles lhes poseram nome a Maya, Sanctiago, Sam Felipe, polas verem em seu dia, outros lhe chamão as ilhas Dantao ou Dantonio. Neste mesmo āno, ou no outro seguinte faleceo este Infante dom Anrique, deixando descuberto do cabo do Não ate a Serra lioa que estaa desta nossa banda, em oyto graos daltura.

¶ No anno de 1469 arrendou el rey dom Ioão, o trato de Guine a Fernam Gomez, que se despois chamou da Mina, por cinco annos, a rezā de dozentos mil reis cada hum anno, & q' mandasse em cada hum delles descobrir cem legoas alem das descubertas. No anno seguinte de 1470 passou este Rey & o principe dom João seu filho em Africa, & tomarão a villa Darzilla & a cidade de Tangere se despejou com medo, tēdo muyto custado, paresce que per-

---

[1] Dele.   [2] Dele.   [3] Present value about £40 or £50.

fled out for fear, and that he tooke also.   It seemeth that
good fortune followeth a couragious attempt.[1]

In the yeere 1471, Fernan Gomes gave commandment Ibidem.
that the coast should be discouered as it lay.[2]   Which was
vndertaken by John de Santeram, and John de-Scouar; and
they went and found the Mine in 5 degrees of latitude.   La Mina.

And the next yeere, which was 1472, one Fernando da Ibidem.
Poo discouered the Island, now called after his name.   Also The isle de Fernan de Poo.
about this time the Islands of Sainct Thomas and Del Sainct Thome.
Principe were discouered, standing vnder the line, with the Rha del Principe.
firme land also, wherein is the kingdome of Benin, reaching Benin.
to the Cape de Santa Catarina, standing on the south side Cape de Santa Catarina.
of the line in 3 degrees.   The man that made this dis-
couerie was a seruant of the king, and his name was
Sequeira.

Many suppose, that then also there were those places,
countreys and Islands discouered, which before were neuer
knowne to vs since the flood.

In the yeere 1480, the magnanimous and valiant king

---

mitio Deos isto por amostrar q' os ousados sam delle fauores-
cidos.

¶ No āno de 1471 mandou Fernam Gomez descobrir a costa
como se obrigara, & foram a isso, João de Santarem & João
Descouar, & em cinco graos daltura acharam a Mina.   E no āno
seguinte de 1472 descobrio Fernão do poo a ilha q' se chama como
elle, & neste mesmo tempo foram descubertas as ilhas de Sam
Thome & prīcipe que estam na linha, & na terra firme o reyno de
Benij ate ho cabo de Caterina que estaa da parte do Sul em tres
graos, & o q' fez este descobrimento era criado de S. A. chamauase
Siqueira.   Muitos querē dizer que neste tempo fossem terras & ilhas
descubertas, de que ja nā ha memoria q' sera de Noe ate agora.

¶ No anno de 1480 faleceo este magnanimo & esforçado Rey

---

[1] It appears that God permitted this to show that He favours the
brave.

[2] As he had bound himself.

Don John
the Second.
Barros,
decad. 1,
lib. 3, cap. 2.
Castell de
Mina built.
Don Alphonso died, and left many things woorthy of memorie behinde him; and his sonne Don John the second succeeded him. Who in the yeere 1481, gaue direction for the building of the castle De Mina to one Diego d'Azambuxa, who did so, and was made captaine of it.

Barros,
decad. 1,
lib. 3, cap. 3.

Rio de
Congo.
In the yeere 1484, the foresaid king John sent out one Diego Caon, a knight of his court, to discouer; and he went to the river of Congo, standing on the south side, in 7 or 8 degrees of latitude; where he erected a pillar of stone, with the royall armes and letters of Portugall, wherein he wrote[1] the commandement that he had receiued from the king, with the time and day [in which were placed the wooden crosses] (of his being there).[2] From thence he went

Discouerie
neere vnto
the Tropick
of Capri-
corne.
vnto (a riuer neere)[3] the Tropicke of Capricorne, setting still vp pillars of stone where he thought it conuenient, and so came backe againe vnto Congo, and to the king of that

An ambas-
sadour from
the king
of Congo.
country: who thereupon sent an ambassadour and men of credite into Portugall.

In the next yeere or the second following, one John Alonso d'Aueiro came from the kingdome of Benin, and

---

dom Afonso deixando muytas cousas feytas dignas de memoria, & começou logo a Reynar dō João seu filho, q' no anno de oytenta & hum mandou por Diogo Dazambuja fazer a fortaleza da Mina, & ficou por capitam della.

No anno de 1484 foy mādado por este Rey dom João a este descobrimēto Diogo Cão caualeiro de sua casa: chegado ao rio de Manicōgo, que estaa da parte do Sul, em sete ou oyto graos daltura, pos nelle Padram de pedra com armas. & letras reaes q' denunciauam que o mādaua, & o anno & era em q' se poseram as Cruzes de pao, daqui foram ter ao rio Pico de Pico[3] de Capricornio, pondo padrões, oude lhe pareceo ser necessario, tornando a Manicōgo viose cō el rey delle, q' mandou embaixador & homēs de credito a este reyno, & no anno sequinte ou no outro despois

---

[1] Were set forth.   [2] Dele.   [3] Ao Tropico?

brought home pepper with a taile: which was the first of Pepper of Benin.
that kinde seene in Portugall.

[In the year 1486 the king Don John sent on this discovery Bartholomew Diaz, a gentleman of the court, with
three sail: coasting along he placed pillars of stone, and
discovered the Cape of Good Hope, and beyond as far as
the river Infante,[1] and it may be said that he saw the land
of India, but, like Moses and the promised land, did not
enter in.]

In the yeere 1487 king John sent to discouer India ouer Barros, decad. 1,
land. In which iourney went one Pedro de Couillan, a lib. 3, cap. 5
Pedro de
servant of the kings, and Alfonso de Payna, because they Couillan
and Alfonso
could speake the Arabian toong. They went out in the de Payna
sent to dis-
moneth of May of the same yeere, and they tooke shipping couer India.
at Naples, and arriued in the isle of Rhodes, and lodged in
the house that was prouided for the Portugall knights of

---

delle chegou João alonso Daueiro do Reyno de Benij com pimenta
de rabo, que foy a primeira que se vio nesta terra.

¶ No anno de 486 mandou el rey dõ Joaõ a este descobrimento
Bertholameu diaz cavaleiro de sua casa cõ tres vellas, yndo assi ao
longo da terra poseram padrões de pedra, & descobrio o cabo de
boa esperança & alem delle ate ho rio do Infante, q' se pode dizer
q' via terra da India, mas nã entrou nella, como Mouses na terra
de promissam.

No ãno de 487 madou el Rey dom João descobrir a India por
terra, foy a isso hũ Pero de couilhã seu criado, & Afõso de Paiua
por saberẽ a lingoa Arabia, partiram no mes de Mayo do mesmo
ãno, & na cidade de Napoles embarcarã. Chegaram à ilha de
rodes, pousaram em casa dos comendadores Portugueses, passaram

---

[1] Probably a little beyond Cape Agathere: this seems but a meagre
account of the remarkable voyage of Bartholomew Diaz, who pushed
discovery a thousand miles further than his predecessors. The cape he
reached was named by him Cabo Tormentoso; but on his return to
Portugal the king, with what seems a presentiment that it lay on the
road to the Indies, gave it the name Good Hope.

Alexandria. that order : from thence they went to Alexandria, and so
Cayro. to Cayro, and thence to the hauen of Toro,[1] in the companie
Toro.
of the carauans or carriers which were Moores. There they
tooke shipping, and being on the Red Sea they arriued at
Aden. the citie of Aden, and there they separated themselues : for
Alfonso de Payna went towards Æthiopia, and Pedro de
Cananor. Couillan into India. Who came vnto the cities of Cananor
Calicut. and Calicut, and came backe vnto Goa: where he tooke
Goa.
shipping vnto Sofala, being on the coast of Africa, in the
southerne latitude of 20 degrees, to see the mines that were
Sofala. of so great name. From Sofala he turned backe to Mosam-
Mozam-
bique. bique, and vnto the cities of Quiloa, Mombaza, and Melinde,
Quiloa.
Monbaza. till he came backe againe vnto the citie of Aden : where he
Melinde.
and Alfonso de Payna diuided themselues : and thence he
sailed againe through the Red Sea vnto the citie of Cayro,
where he thought to haue met with his companions : but
there he heard that he was dead[2] by the letters that he receiued from king John his master ; in which letters he was
farther commanded to trauaile into the countrey and dominions of Presbyter John.

Vpon this commandement he[3] prouided for his farther

à cidade Dalexandria, dahi foram ao Cayro, & ao porto do toro em
Carauanas, & em Recouas de mouros, onde embarcarā no mar roxo,
chegaram à cidade Dadem, onde se apartaram João de paiua pera
Thiopia, & Pero de Couilhaā á India, & foy ter aa cidade de Cana-
nor, Calecut, & tornou a Goa, onde embarcou pera Sofalla, costa
Dafrica, a ver aquellas Minas cousas tam nomcadas.

¶ De Sofala tornou a Moçambique, & aa cidade de Quiloa,
Bombaça, Melinde, ate a cidade Dadem donde Afonso de paiua se
apartara delle, & foy pelo mar roxo à cidade do Cairo, ōde ficaram
de se ajuntarem, mas achou noua como ahy falecera, & cartas del
Rey dom Joam em q' mandaua q' se visse cō o preste Joā da India.

¶ Vendo Pero de couilham este recado, partio do Cairo ao porto

---

[1] Cosseir ?   [2] And at the same time received letters from, etc.
[3] Set out from, etc.

iourney, and from Cairo went backe againe to the hauen
of Toro, and from thence to Adens, where he had been
twise before: and there hearing of the fame of the citie
of Ormuz, he determined to goe thither; and therefore
went along the coast of Arabia vnto the Cape Razal-
gate, standing vnder the Tropicke of Cancer, and from
thence he went to Ormuz, standing in twenty-seuen degrees
on that side.   There he learned and vnderstood of the
streight of Persia, and of that countrey : and entred there
into the Red Sea, and passed ouer to the realme of the
Abassini, which commonly is called Presbyter Johns countrey or Æthiopia : and there he was detained till the yeere
1520, when there came thither the ambassadour Don Roderigo de Lima.   This Pedro de Couillan was the first Portugall that euer knew and saw the Indias and those sea, and
other places[1] adioyning thereunto.

   In the yeere 1490 the king sent vnto Congo one Gonzalo
de Sousa, a gentleman, with three ships, and in them sent
home the ambassadour of Congo, which was sent into Portugall, whom Diego Caon had brought from thence : who
at his being in Portugall was baptised, both himselfe and
others of his companie.

The voiage of Pedro de Couillan vnto the countrey of Prete Ianui.

Abassini. Pedro de Couillan the first Portugal that came into the East India and Æthiopia by the Red Sea.

Barros, decad. 1, lib. 3, cap. 9.

---

do Toro, & dahi á cidade Dadem onde ja duas vezes estiuera, &
tendo noticia de camanha cousa era & quam prospera a cidade
Dormuz, determinou d'ir a ella, & foy ao longo da costa Darabia
ao cabo de Resalgate que estaa no Tropico de Cancro, & dahi a
Ormuz, que estaa situada em vinte sete graos da mesma banda.
Enformado do estreito da Persia, & daquella terra, se tornou ao
mar roxo & passouse ao Reyno do Abexim, que vulgarmēte se
chama Preste João da india, onde esteue ate ho anno de 520 que
ho achou lá o embaixador dõ Rodrigo de Lima.   Este Pero de
couilhaã foy o primeiro Portugues que eu sayba q' vio as Indias &
seus mares, & outras cousas a nos muy remotas.

---

[1] Far removed from us.

The aforesaid Gonzalo de Sousa died in that iourney by the way, and in his roome they chose his nephew, Ruy de Sousa, for their capitaine ; and so being come vnto Cogo, the king was very glad of their comming, and yeelded himselfe and the greater part of his realme to be baptized :[1] whereof the Portugals had good cause to reioice, seeing by them so many Infidels were conuerted from gentilitie and paganisme to Christianitie.

A great parte of the kingdome of Congo baptized.

¶ No anno de 1490 mandou el Rey a Manicongo com tres nauios Gonçalo de Sousa homē fidalgo, tornou em sua companhia o embayxador de Manicongo, que Diogo cam trouxera, tendo ja tomado agoa de baptismo & outros que com elle vieram, Gonçalo de Sousa faleceo no caminho & enlegeram por capitā mor a seu sobrinho Ruy de Sousa, chegado a Manicongo, fez lhe el Rey muyto gasalhado & baptizouse logo com a mòr parte de sua terra, que foy grande louuor, & honra ao reyno de Portugal & sua coroa.

---

[1] Which was cause of great praise and honour to the kingdom of Portugal and its crown.

[DISCOVERIES OF THE ANTILLES AND INDIES MADE BY THE SPANIARDS.]

THE FIRST BEGINNING OF THE DISCOUERIES OF THE SPANYARDS, WITH THE CONTINUATION OF THE DISCOUERIES OF THE PORTUGALS.

In the yeere 1492, in the time of Don Ferdinando, king of Castile, he being at the siege[1] of Granada, dispatched one Christopher Columbus, a Genoway,[2] with three ships to goe and discouer Noua Spagna: who first had[3] offered his seruice for a westerne discouerie vnto king John of Portugal; but he would not entertaine him.

He *being sufficiently furnished for this enterprise*,[4] departed from the towne of Palos the third day of August, hauing with him as captaines and pilots, Martin Alfonso Pinzon, Francis Martinez Pinzon, Vincent Yannes Pinzon,

---

DESCOBRIMENTOS DAS ANTILHAS & INDIAS POLLOS ESPANHŌES FEYTOS.

No anno de 1492 estando el Rey dom Fernando de Castella sobre a cidade de Grada, despachou Christouam Colom Italiano, cõ tres Nauios ao descobrimento da noua Espanha o q'l primeiro viera a Portugal a el rey dom João & o nam quis aceitar. Partio da villa de Pallos aos tres dias do mes Dagosto leuando consigo por capitāes & pilotos Martim Alonso pição, Francisco martīz pição, Vicēte

---

[1] Near the city.   [2] An Italian.

[3] Come to Portugal to the king Don John, who did not desire to accept him.

[4] Not in Portuguese.

The first
that in sail-
ing are
thought to
haue ob-
serued
latitudes.
and Bartholomew Columbus his brother, with 120 persons
more in his companie : and some affirme that they were the
first that sailed by latitudes.   They tooke the Canaries in
their way, and there refreshed themselues ; taking their
course thence [through the Sargassum Sea] *towards Ci-
pango :*[1] but finding the sea by the way full of weeds they
were amazed, and with great feare arriued at the Antiles
the tenth day of October, and the first island that they
The Isle of
Guanahany
first dis-
couered.
descried was called Guanahany : where they went on land,
and tooke possession of it, and named it San Saluador. *This
island standeth in 25 of degrees northerly latitude.*[2] And after
that they found many islands, which they called the Princes,[3]
because they were the first that they had discouered.

The sauages of these parts call these islands by the name
Lucaios
Islands.
of Lucaios, hauing in deede seuerall[4] names for them.   And
they doe stand on the north side almost vnder the Tropicke
of Cancer.   As for the Island of S. James or Jamaica, it
standeth betweene 16 and 17 degrees.

Thence they went to the islands which the naturals of the

---

anez piçāo, & Bartholameu Colō seu hirmao, & cēto & vinte
pessoas.   E querem dizer algūs q' fossem os primeiros q' nauegassem por alturas.   Nas ilhas Canarias tomarā refresco, dahi foram
na volta do Sagarço : & vendo o mar delle coalhado ficaram espantados, & com grande arreceo chegaram às Antilhas a dez dias do
mes de Ouctubro.   E a primeira ilha que viram se chamaua
Greinani,[5] sayram em terra, tomaram posse della, poseram lhe
nome sam Saluador : despois viram muytas a q' chamaram as
princesas, per serē as primeiras por elles vistas : mas os da terra
lhes chamā os Lucayos, ainda q' todas tē nomes separados, &
estam da parte do Norte, quasi debaixo do Tropico de Cancro, de
parte do Norte de dezeseys graos ate dezesete, que he a ilha de
Santiago.

¶ Daqui foram á ilha a que os da terra chamā a Cuba, & os

---

[1] Not in Portuguese.   [2] Not in the Portuguese.
[3] The Princesses.   [4] Distinct.   [5] Guanani ?

countrey call Cuba, and the Spanyards call it Ferdinandina, ^{Cuba.}
bicause their kings name was Ferdinando, standing in 22
degrees : from whence the Indians conducted them vnto
another island, which they call Hayti, and the Spanyards
called it Isabella, in the memorie of the Queene of Castile,
which was so called, and they named it also Hispaniola. ^{Hispaniola.}
In that island the admirall ship of Columbus was cast
away : of the timber and planks whereof they made a forte,[1]
wherein they left 38 men, and a captaine called Roderigo de
Arana, to learne the language and customes of the countrey.
They brought from thence musters and shewes of gold,
pearles,[2] and other things which that countrey yielded ; and
ten Indians also, whereof six died,[3] the rest were brought
home and baptized.

Hereupon there grewe such a common desire of trauaile[4]
among the Spanyards, that they were ready to leape into
the sea to swim, if it had been possible, into those new
found parts. The aforesaid company of Columbus at their
comming home tooke in their way the isles of the Açores,
and the 4 day of March, in the yeere 1493, they entred into

Castelhanos poserā nome Fernandina por el rey dō Fernando, a qual
estaa em vīte dous graos, donde os Indios os leuarā á outra que elles
chamāo Ahyti, & os Castelhanos Isabela, em memoria da Rainha
de Castella : & tābem a Espanhola. Aqui se perdeo a nao capitania, & da madeira della fizeram hūa tranqueira, onde deixarā
trinta & oyto homēs, & capitam delles Rodrigo darena, pera
aprenderem a lingoa & costumes da terra, donde trouxeram
mostras douro, papagayos, & outras cousas q' la auia, & dez
Indios de que escaparam seys que se ca baptizaram. E pos isto
tam grande aluoroço & desejo aos Espanhões q' a nado queriā hir
aq'lla terra. E na volta vierā pellas ilhas dos Açores, & a quatro
dias de Março do anno de 1493 entraram pella barra de Lisboa : de

---

[1] Or blockhouse.   [2] Parrots.
[3] Whereof six did not die, and were brought home and baptized.
[4] And this raised such transport and desire.

the bar of Lisbon : which discouerie pleased not the king of Portugall. Whereupon rose a contention betweene those two kings.

Christopher Columbus being arriued went presently into Castile with the newes of all things, and acquainted the king Fernando with the discontentednes of the king of Portugal : whereupon he and the Queene Isabella his wife sent streight word thereof vnto Pope Alexander the 6., whereat he and the Italians were in great admiration, marvailing that there was any more land besides that which was vnder[1] the Romanes. But the end of this matter was this : Alexander the Pope gaue these countreies by his judgement vnto the kingdomes of Leon and Castile ; with this condition, that they should labour to extirpate idolatrie, and plant the holy faith in those countreyes.

Fernando the king hauing receiued this answere, was glad of it, and sent Christopher Columbus againe on the former voiage, hauing made him admirall, and giuen him other honors, with particular armes,[2] and a posie written about his armes to this effect :

---

q' el rey dom Joam lhe pesou tanto q' teue differença sobre estas terras com ho de Castella.

¶ Tanto q' Christouã colõ chegou a Castella cõ esta noua, & de como el rey dõ Joã lhe pessaua della, el Rey dõ Fernãdo & dona Isabel, mãdarã logo ao Papa Alexandre sexto, da qual noua elle & todo o pouo ficaram marauilhados, auer terra q' os Romãos nam tiuerã noticia, auẽdose por señores da redondeza & fez logo doa-çam dellas aos reynos de Lyam & Castella, cõ tal cõdiçam q' trabalhassẽ com q' a jdolatria desarreigasse, & a nossa sãcta fee multiplicasse. Chegada esta reposta tornou logo el rey dõ Fernãdo mãdar Christouam colõ ao descobrimẽto, ja Almirante cõ outras honras, merces & insignias, & derredor das suas armas hũa letra q' dezia, por Castella & Leõ nouo mũdo achou Colõ.

---

[1] Known to. [2] Favours and decorations.

For Castile and for Leon
A new world found out Colon.

In the yeere 1493, the 25 of the moneth of October, Christopher Columbus went backe vnto the Antiles, and frō Cadiz he tooke his course, hauing in his companie 17 ships, and 1500 men in them, with his brethren Bartholomew Columbus and Diego Columbus, with other knights, gentlemen, men of law, and religious men, with chalices, crosses, rich ornaments, and with great power[1] *and dignitie*[2] from Pope Alexander; & the 10 day after their setting foorth, they arriued at the Canaries; & from thence, in 25 or 30 daies, they sailed vnto the Antiles; & the first island that they saw standeth in 14 degrees towards the north, due west from Cape Verde, on the coast of Africa. They say that the distance from thence to the Canaries is 800 leagues. The name they gaue it was Deseada, that is, the desired or wished Island, for the great desire which the company had to come to sight of land. After that they discouered many more, which they named the Virgines, which the naturals of the countrey call the Caribas, for that the men of that countrey are good warriers, and shoote well in bowes.

Columbus second voyage.

Deseada discouered.

Caribas.

No anno de 1493 aos 25 do mes Doctubro, tornou Christouã colõ ás Antilhas, & da barra de Calez tornou sua derrota, leuãdo dezasette vellas, & mil & quinhentos homẽs nellas, & seus hirmãos, Bertholameu colom, & Diogo colom, & outros fidalgos, caualeiros, & letrados, & religiosos com calezes, Cruzes, & ricos ornamentos, & grandes poderes do Papa Alexandre. E aos dez dias chegaram aas Canarias: & dellas a vinte cinco ou trinte dias ás Antilhas. A primeira ilha que viram estaa em quatorze graos da parte do Norte leste hoeste com ho cabo Verde, diz que auera della ás Canarias oito centas legoas, poseran lhe nome a Desejada, pelos desejos que leuauã de ver terra, logo viram outras muitas, a que poseram nome as Virgens: ainda que os da terra lhe chamã as

---

[1] Powers.   [2] Not in Portuguese.

They poison their arrowes with an herbe, whereof he that is hurt dieth, biting himselfe like as a mad dog doth.

From these islands and others they went vnto the principall island there, which they of the countrey doe call Boriquen, and the Spanyards call it S. John, and thence to Hispaniola or Isabella, where they found all the men dead which they had left [from injuries (or diseases) incident to the countrey]. Here the admirall left the most part of the people to plant it,[1] and appointed his brethren to be gouernours there : and so tooke two ships, and went to discouer the other side of the Island of Cuba, and from thence to Jamaica [which is now called Santiago]. All these islands stand from 16 vnto 20 degrees of northerly latitude. In the meane time that the admirall sailed about, his brethren and they that were left with them were much troubled, because the sauages did rise against them. So that Christopher Colon went backe againe into Spaine, to tell the king and queene of his aduentures.

Boriquen, or S. John de porto ricco.

Jamaica.

Quiribas, por ser de hómes guerreiros & bōs frecheiros, tiram com erua tā peçonhenta que quem morre della morde a si mesmo como cāo danado.

¶ Destas ilhas em outras foram ter à principal dellas, a que os da terra chamā Boriquem, & os Castelhanos sa Joāo, dōde chegarā a Espanhola ou ilha Bela[2] & acharāo todos os homēs mortos que nella deixaram, por offensas que aos da terra fizeram aqui, deixou ho Almirante a mayor parte da gēte pera pouoala, & seus jrmāos gouernadores della, & embarcando em dous nauios foy descobrir a costada da ilha da Cuba, & dahi a Jamaica, q' se agora chama Santiago, todas estas ilhas estam de dezasete ate vinte graos daltura da parte do norte. E em quanto laa andou ho Almirante, seus jrmāos com os q' aly ficaram passaram assaz trabalho & desauētura por se aleuantar a terra, tornou Christouā colō outra vez a Castella a da conta a el Rey & à Rainha do que là passara.

---

[1] Or people it.　　　　[2] Isabella?

In the yeere 1494, and in the moneth of Januarie, there was an agreement made of the differences which were betweene the two kings of Spaine and Portugall. For the which agreement there were sent out of Portugall Ruy de Sosa, and Don John his sonne, and the Doctor Ayres de Almada : and for the king of Spaine there were Don Henry Henriques, Don John de Cardenas, and the Doctor Maldonado. All these met in the towne of Tordesillas, and they deuided the world frō the north to the south by a *The first line of partition.* meridian which standeth west from the Islands of Cape Verde 300[1] leagues : so that the one halfe which lay vnto the east should belong vnto Portugall, and that which lay to the west to the king of Spaine, whereby notwithstanding libertie to trauell [by sea and land] was left equall vnto both.

In the yeere following, 1495, John king of Portugall *The death of Don John the second.* died, and Emmanuel his cosen began to reigne.

In the yeere 1496 there was a Venetian in England called *The great discouerie of John Cabota and the English.* John Cabota, who hauing knowledge of such a new discouerie as this was, and perceiuing by the globe that the

No anno de 1494 & mes de Janeiro se aueriguaraõ as differenças que antre estes dous Reys auia : & foy a isso Ruy de sousa & dõ João seu filho, & o doctor Ayres Dalmada : & da parte de Castela dom Anrique Anriquez, dom Jorge de Cardines, & o doctor Maldonado, ajuntaramse todos em Torresilhas, & partiram ha redondeza de Norte Sul por hum meridiano q' está ao ponente das jlhas do Cabo verde 370 legoas, & que ametade que ficasse ao Leuante fosse de Portugal, & Ocidente de Castella, & o mar & terra pera caminhar fosse a todos iqual. No anno seguinte de nouenta & cinco faleceo el Rey dom João, & começou a reynar dõ Manoel seu primo.

No anno de 1496 achandose hum Venezeano por nome Sebastião Gaboto em Inglaterra, & ouuindo noua de tam nouo descobri-

---

[1] 370 ?

islands before spoken of stood almost in the same latitude
with his countrey, and much neerer to England than to
Portugall, or to Castile, he acquainted king Henrie the
seuenth, then king of England, with the same, wherewith
the saide king was greatly pleased, and furnished him
out with two ships and three hundred men : which departed and set saile in the spring of the yeere, and they
sailed westward til they came in sight of land in 45 degrees
of latitude towards the north, and then went straight northwards till they came into 60 degrees of latitude, where the
day is 18 howers long, and the night is very cleere and
bright. There they found the aire cold, and great islands
of ice, but no ground in [seventy, eighty] an hundred
fathomes sounding [but found much ice, which alarmed
them] : and so from thence [putting about] finding the
land to turne eastwards they trended along by it [on
the other tack] discouering all the bay and riuer named
Deseado,[1] to see if it passed on the other side : then they
sailed backe againe [diminishing the latitude] till they came

---

mento como este era : & vendo em hūa poma como estas jlhas
acima ditas estão quasi em hū paralelo & altura, & muyto mais
perto de sua terra hūa a outra, que de Portugal nē Castella, o
amostrou a el Rey dō Anrrique o septimo de que elle ficou tam
satisfeito, que mandou logo armar dous nauios, partio na prima-
vera cō trezētos companheiros, fez seu caminho a Loeste a vista da
terra, & quarēta & cinco graos daltura da parte do norte, forão por
ella ate sessenta onde os dias sam de dezoyto horas, & as noytes
muy claras & serenas. Auia aqui muyta frialdade & ylhas de
neue que não achauam fundo em setenta, oitenta, cem braças, mas
achauā grandes regelos, do que tambem se arreceauā. E como
daqui por dianta tornasse a costa ao leuante, fizerāose na outra
volta ao lōgo della descobrindo toda a baya, rio, enseada, p'ra ver se
passaua da outra banda, & foram assi diminuindo naltura ate trinta

---

[1] Or inlet.

to 38 degrees toward the equinoctiall line, and from thence This is to the south of the Chesepian Bay. returned into England. There be others which say that he went as far as the Cape of Florida, which standeth in 25 degrees.

In the yeere 1497 the king of Spaine, Don Fernando, Columbus third voiage Gomara, historiæ general, lib. 1, cap. 21. sent out Christopher Columbus with sixe ships, and he him-selfe prouided two ships at his owne cost, and sending his brother before, he made saile from the Bay of Cadiz, carry-ing with him his sonne, Don Diego Colon. It was then reported that he went to take the Island of Madera, because he mistrusted the French men, and therefore sent thither three ships: others say it was to the Canaries. But how-soeuer it was, this is true, that he and three more went vnto the Islands of Cape Verde, and ran along by the line, find-ing great calmes and raine, and the first land which they came vnto of the Antiles was an island standing in 9 degrees of latitude towards the north, ioining fast vnto the maine land, which they called La Trinidada; and so he entred Trinidada. into the Gulfe of Paria, and came out of the mouth which they named Bocca de Dragone, or the Dragons mouth: and

---

& oyto graos, donde se tornaram a Inglaterra. Outros querem dizer que chegasse á ponta da Florida que estaa em vinte cinco graos.

No anno de 1497 tornou el rey dõ Fernando a mandar ás Antil-has Christouão Colõ com seys nauios, elle armou dous aa sua custa, mandou seu yrmão diante: partio elle da baya de Calez, leuando consigo dõ Diogo Colon seu filho. Diz que foy tomar a ylha da Madeira, cõ receyo de Franceses, dõde mãdou tres nauios, outros querem dizer das Canarias, como quer que seja, elle & tres foy aa ylha do cabo Verde, & correo ao longo da linha, em que achou grã calmaria & chuueiros. Ea primeira terra que viram das An-tilhas, foy hũa ylha que estaa em noue graos daltura da parte do norte, pegada com a terra firme, poserãlhe nome a Trindade: entraram ne golfam de Parea, & sayrã por hũa boca, a q' chamam do Dragõ, tomaram na mão a costa, & acharam tres pontas, a que

12

they tooke their course hard by the coast, where they found three[1] small islands, which they named Los Testigos, that is to say, the Witnesses, beyond which standeth the Island of Cubagua, where is great fishing of muscle pearles : where also, as they say, there springeth a well of oile : and beyond that island they came to the Isles of Frailes, Roques, Aruba, and Curaçoa, with other small ones all along the bay.:[2] and they came to the point of Cabo de Vela, and discouered along the coast almost 200 leagues,[3] from whence they crossed ouer to Hispaniola, hauing had also sight of the island called Beata.

[There are in these parts certain insects or birds, called Cocoyos ; they are furnished with four stars ; two in the eyes, and the others under the wings, which shine like candles. They write, spin, sew, and weave with them, and carry them to give light, and when these stars are stuck on their hands and faces they seem to be on fire.

There is another insect called Nigu ; it skips like a flea,

---

poseram nome Testigos, & diante a ylha Cubaga, que he gram pescaria D'aljofre. Tambem dizem q' tem fonte d'azeyte, & mais adiante viram as ylhas de Paragry, Roques, & Heruma : & o Coraceo, & outras pequenas ao longo da praya. Chegaram aa ponta que se chama da Vela, descobriram por costa cento & cincoenta ou dozentas legoas, onde atrauessaram a ylha Espanhola & ouueram vista da que se chama Beata.

Ha nestas ylhas & terras hũs bichos ou passaros a que chamam Cocoyos, tem quatro estrelas, duas nos olhos, & as outras debaixo das asas, dam claridade como candeas : podem escreuer, fiar, cozer, & tecer com ellas, & as leuam pera alumiarem, & se untam as mãos & rostros com estas estrelas, parece que ardem em fogo.

Ha outro Bicho que chamam Nigu, salta como pulga, he muyto

---

[1] Peaks.   [2] Shore.
[3] One hundred and fifty or two hundred leagues.

but is smaller : it fixes itself in the flesh under the nail, and there produces so many grubs, that if not presently removed they multiply in such a way that people lose their fingers, and some become maimed for life.

There is also in these parts another vermin as large as a cat, it lives among trees, hanging from the branches by the tail, and after its young ones are born they take to a pouch, with which nature has furnished them ; in this entresol of the belly there is a teat which suckles them, whence it appears that it goes big with its young until of such age that nature delivers them, and then the young ones go to seek their own living.

There are in these islands many different fishes, and one which no one knows whether it be beast or fish : it has hands and feet like a lizard, snout and tail like a greyhound, feeds in the water, and on land among the trees, lays eggs like a fowl, from which they are produced : these have a soft shell, and if fried with oil or butter they do not thicken ; with water I do not know. When these creatures are small they pass on the surface of the water so rapidly that

---

mais pequeno, mete se entre a unha & carne, & poem aly emprouiso tanta lendea, que se lhe nam acodē logo multiplicam : de maneira que perdem os dedos & ficam aleijados algūs a vida.   Ha tambem nestas partes outro bicho de tamanho de hum gato, anda pellas aruores, dependura se dos ramos pello rabo, & depois que pare, hos filhos tornam se a meter por hum buraco que tem junto da natura : neste antresolho da barriga tem hūa mama cō que ho cria, por onde parece que anda prenhe ate ser de ydade que ha natureza o despede, & vay buscar sua vida.

¶ Ha nestas jlhas muitos & diuersos pescados, & hum que se não entende se he alimaria se pexe, tem pes & mãos como lagarto, focinho & rabo como galgo, cria se nagoa & na terra pelas aruores, poē ouos como de galinhas, de que se geram, tem a casca delgada, se os frigem nam se coalham com azeite nem manteiga, senão com agoa ; em quanto estes bichos sam pequenos, passam per cima

they do not sink; it further appears that at a certain season
they run upon land, then turning about they go under the
water along the sand, for they know not how to swim, nor
have they that fashion. They are eaten during carnival
and Lent.

There is also a fish called Monatim: it is large and in-
durated; it has the head and countenance of a cow, and also
resembles it much in its meat; it has arms joined to its
shoulders with which it swims; its principal food is the
grass that grows along the edge of the water; it is very
savoury; it has some stones in its head which are profitable
for the grief of stone, and the female has teats on her
breast, with which she suckles her young, which are born
living.

There is another fish called Reverso, a little greater than
a span; it has spikes like a hedgehog. They feed them
in the sea in a basket tied to a long line, and take by
their means monatis and other large fish, and use them
as ferrets for rabbits. Here are many sardines; these
small fish are seen in Maluco and among those islands,

---

d'agoa com tāta presteza, que se nam vão ao fundo, mas parece que
corrē por terra ate certo tempo, dahi por diante andam por baxo
dagoa ao longo d'area por nam saberē nadar, nem tem pera isso
maneira, comem nos no carnal & quaresma.

Ha la hum pexe que se chama Monatim, he grande & de coiro,
tem a cabeça & rostro de vaca, & tābē na carne parece muito a
ella, tē hūs braços junto dos hombros com que nadā, o mais de seu
comer heeru a q' nace ao longo d'agoa, he muy saboroso, tem hū
as pedras na cabeça q' sam proueitosas pera a dor de pedra, & a
femea tem tetas nos peitos çom q' criam os filhos que nacem viuos.
Ha outro pescado a q' chamā Reuerso pouco mayor de hum palmo,
tē espinhos como ouriço cacheiro, crião nos no mar em hū couão,
atam nos em hū cordel comprido, tomā com elles monatīs, & outros
grandes pescados & trazenos como forais aos cohelhos. Aqui ha
muitas sardinhas, estes bichos pescados se vem em Maluco, &

and the inhabitants resemble those of New Spain, and also some eat human flesh.]

In this same yeere 1497, on the 20 day of the moneth of June, one Vasques de Gama sailed from Lisbon by the king Emmanuels commandement to India with three ships, wherein there went for captaines, Vasquez de Gama, Paulus de Gama his brother, and Nicolas Coello, with 120 men; with whom also there went one ship laden only with vittailes, and in 14[1] daies they came vnto Cape Verde, vnto the Island of Saint Jago, where they refreshed themselues, and from thence they went along the coast beyond the Cape of Bona Sperança, whereupon they erected certaine pillers of stone, and so came vnto Mosambique, standing in 15[2] degrees to the south of the line, where they staied not long, but went from thence to Mozamba, and vnto Melinde: where the king of that place gaue them pilots, which conducted them into India, in which discouerie they found out Los Baxos do Padua, that is to say, the flats of Padua.

In the yeere 1498, in the moneth of May, they came to

Barros, decad. 1, lib. 4, cap. 2, and to the end of the 11 chapter.

The Cape of Bona Sperança.

Mosambique.

Mombaza. Melinde.

Los Baxos de Padua.

---

naq'llas ylhas, & a gente se parece cõ a da noua Espanha, & assi comem algũs a carne humana.

No mesmo anno de 1497 a vinte dias do mes de Julho, partio Vasco da Gama por mandado del Rey dom Manoel, de Lisboa pera aa India com tres vellas, hiam por capitães Vasco da Gama, & Paulo da Gama seu hirmão, & Nicolao Coelho, & cēto & vinte homēs nellas, hia mais hum nauio cõ mantimento, & em treze dias foram ao Cabo verde á ilha de Santiago a tomar refresco, & dahi foram ao longo da terra: & alem do cabo de Boa esperança poserã padrões nella. Chegados a Moçambique, que está em treze graos da parte de meyo dia, fizeram ahi pouca detença: foram a Mombaça & a Melinde, el Rey delle lhe deu pilotos, que os poseram na India, na qual trauessa descobrirão os baixos de Padua.

No anno de 1498 no mes de Mayo, surgirã na cidade de Calecu

---

[1] 13?   [2] 13?

an anker before the citie of Calicut and Panana, where they remained all the winter: and the first day of September they set saile towards the north, discouering the coast all along till they came to the Island of Angediua, which standeth on that side in 15 degrees of latitude, where they came to an anker in the beginning of October, and so they departed from Angediua in Februarie in the yeere 1499, and came in sight of the coast of Africa about Melinde, towards the north 3 or 4 degrees, and from thence they sailed vnto the said citie, and so vnto Mozambique againe, and to the Cape of Bona Sperança, sailing along by the coast, and then they came to the Islands of Cape Verde, and last of al to the citie

of Lisbon in the moneth of September, hauing beene in the voiage 26 monethes.

In the yeere 1499, on the 13 day of the moneth of Nouember, there departed frō Palos one Vincent Yannez Pinson and his nephew Aries Pinson with fower ships well appointed at their owne cost and charges, to discouer the new world vnder the licence of the king of Castile, and with commandement not to touch there, where the admirall Columbus had beene. And so they went to the Islands of

---

& Panane, & estiuerā todo ho inuerno, & o primeiro de Setembro se fizeram a vella, & foram contra ho Norte descobrindo aquela costa atee a ylha D'angediua que està daquella parte em quinze graos d'altura, onde surgiram na entrada do mes Doctubro, partiram de Angediua, & no de Feuereiro do anno de 1499 ouueram vista da terra de Africa, acima de Melinde cōtra ho norte tres ou quatro graos: d'ahi foram àquella cidade, & della a Moçambique, & ao cabo de boa Esperança, & tomaram na mão a costa, & vieram as ylhas. do Cabo verde, & a cidade de Lisboa na entrada do mes de Setembro, & poseram vinte & seis meses neste caminho.

No anno de 1499 a treze dias do mes de Nouembro, partiram de Pallos, Vicente Anez piçā & seu sobrinho Aires piçam cō quatro nauios que armaram á sua custa, pera descobrimēto do nouo mūdo, cō licença del rey de Castella, & regimēto q' nam tocasse no q' o

Cape Verde, and passed the line to the southward, and discouered the Cape of Saint Augustine standing on that side The Cape of
in 8 degrees of latitude, and there they wrote on the rindes S. Augustine.
of pine trees the names of the king and of the queene [with
some of their own], also the yeere and day when they
arriued there. They fought with the people of Brasil, but
got nothing; they tooke their course all along the coast
towards the west vnto the riuer Maria Tambal, and at that Rio de Maria
Tambal.
time they had taken thirtie and odde prisoners.[1] The chiefe
places where they touched were the Cape of S. Augustine, Angla de
San Lucas.
and the angle or point of S. Luke, and Tierra de los Humos, The riuers
of Maran-
the riuers of Marannon and of the Amazons, and Rio dolce, non, Amazons, and
or the Sweete riuer, and other places along the coast: and Rio Dolce.
they came to [Para in] ten degrees of latitude on the north
side, where they lost two ships and their companie, and remained in that voiage of discouery ten moneths and 15
daies.

In the yeere 1500 and in the moneth of March, one Pedro Barros,
decad. 1, lib.
Aluarez Cabral sailed out of Lisbon with 13 ships, with com- 5, cap. 2.

---

almirante Colō tinha descuberto, pelo q' foram as ilhas do Cabo
verde & passarā a linha da outra parte do sul, & descrobrirā o cabo
de sancto Agostinhō q' estaa daquella banda en oyto graos daltura,
& escreueram em troncos de aruores & penedos ho nome del Rey
& Raynha com algūs delles, & ho anno & dia q' ali chegaram,
pelejaram cō hos Brasis, & nam guardaram nada. Tomaram na
mão ha costa contra ho Ponente, & no Rio Maria, Tambal, capti-
uaram neste tempo trinta & tantos Indios, tomaram ho cabo
primeiro, Angra de sam Lucas a terra dos Fumos, o rio Maranhō
& o das Mazonas, & rio Doçe & outras partes ao longo da costa,
chegarā aa Paria em dez graos daltura da parte do norte, perderāo
dous nauios & gente. Poserā na viagem & descobrimento dez meses
& meyo.

No anno de 1500 & entrada de Março, partio Pedraluarez Cabral

---

[1] Indians.

mandement not to come neere the coast of Africa to shorten
his way; and he losing the sight of one of his ships went to
seeke her, and in seeking of her lost his course, and sailed
till he came within sight of the land.   The generall was so
long in seeking his ship, that the companie were wearie of
it, and entreated him to leaue his enterprise.   The next
day they fell in sight of the coast of Brasil : whereupon the
generall commanded a barke to goe to land and seeke an
hauen : which they did, and found a good and safe hauen,
and they named it Puerto Seguro, that is to say, the Safe
Hauen, standing on the south side in 17 degrees of latitude.
From thence they sailed towardes the Cape of Bona Sperança and Melinde, and crossed ouer to the riuer of Cochin,
which before was not knowne, where they laded themselues
with pepper, and at their returne Sancho de Thouar discouered the citie of Sofala vpon the coast of Africa.

    In this same yeere 1500 it is reported that Gaspar Corte-
real craued a generall licence of the king Emmanuel[1] to
discouer the New found land.   He went from the Island

*Puerto
Seguro in
Brazil.*

Sofala.

---

com treze velas, com regimento que se afastasse da costa D'Africa,
para encurtar a via. E tendo hūa nao perdida em sua busca perdeo
a derrota, & indo fora della, toparā finaes da terra, por onde o
capitão môr foy em sua busca tantos dias, q' os d'armada lhe re-
quererão que deixasse aquella profia : mas ao outro dia virão aa
costa do Brasil. E mandou o capitam môr hum nauio apalpar se
achaua porto, tornou, dizendo, que achaua bem & seguro, & assi
lhe poserão o nome, & dizem que está da parte do sul em dezasete
graos daltura. Daqui se fizerā à vela na volta do cabo de Boa
Esperança & de Melinde, & atrauessarão á outra banda, & no rio
de Cochim que se ainda nā sabia, & carregarão de pimēta. E à
tornada Sācho de Thouar descobrio a cidade de çofala.

    Neste mesmo anno de 1500 diz q' pedio Gaspar corte real licença
a el Rey dom Manoel pera yr descobrir a terra Noua. Partio da

---

    Don Manuel.

Terçera with two ships well appointed at his owne cost, and he sailed vnto that climate which standeth vnder the north in 50 degrees of latitude, which is a land nowe called after his name; and he came home in safetie vnto the citie of Lisbon : and making another time this voiage the ship was lost wherein he went, and the other came backe into Portugall. Wherefore his brother, Michael Cortereal, went to seeke him with three ships well appointed at his owne cost; and when they came vnto that coast, and found so many entrances of riuers and hauens, euery ship went into her seuerall riuer, with this rule and order, that they all three should meete againe the 20 day of August. The two other ships did so, and they seeing that Michael Cortereal was not come at the day appointed, nor yet afterwards in a certaine time, returned backe into the realme of Portugall, and neuer heard any more newes of him nor yet any other memorie. But that countrey is called the land of Cortereall vnto this day.

Terra Corterealis.

Many entrances of riuers in the northwest.

In the yeere 1501, in the moneth of March, John de Noua departed from the citie of Lisbon with fower ships,

Barros, decad. 1, lib. 5, cap. 10.

---

ilha terceira com dous nauios armados á sua custa, foy áquelle clima que está debaixo do norte em cincoēta graos daltura. He terra que se agora chama de seu nome, tornou a saluamento á cidade de Lixboa. Fazendo outra vez este caminho, se perdeo o nauio em que elle hia, & o outro tornou a Portugal. Pola qual causa seu yrmāo Miguel corte real foy em sua busca cō tres nauios armados á sua custa. Chegados àquella costa, como virão muytas bocas de rios & abras, entrou cada hum pela sua com regimento que se ajūtassē todos ate vinte dias do mes Dagosto: os dous nauios assi o fizerāo. E vendo que nāo vinha Miguel corte real ao prazo, nem despois algum tempo, se tornaɪá a este Reyno, sem nūca mais delle se saber noua, nem ficar outra memoria, se nāo chamarse esta terra dos Corte reaes ainda agora.

No anno de 1501 & mes de Março, partio Joāo de noua com quatro velas da cidade de Lixboa, & alem da linha da parte do sul

and passed the line on the south side into 8 degrees of lati-

tude, and he discouered an island, which he called the Isle
de Ascension : and he went vnto Mosambique, and to
Melinde, and from thence he crossed ouer vnto the other
side, where they tooke lading, and so came back and

doubled the Cape, and found an island called Santa Helena,
being but a small thing, but yet of great importance in
respect of the situation thereof.

In this same yeere 1501 and in the moneth of May there
departed out of Lisbon three ships, upon the commandement
of Emmanuel[1] the king, to discouer the coast of Brasil ;
and they sailed in the sight of the Canaries, and from thence
to Cape Verde, where they refreshed themselues in the towne

of Bezequiche, and passed from thence beyond the line
southward, and fell with the land of Brasill in five degrees

of latitude, and so went forward till they came in 32 degrees,
little more or lesse, according as they accounted it, and
from thence they came backe in the moneth of Aprill, because it was there at that time cold and tempestuous.   They

---

em oyto graos daltura descubrirā a ilha a que poserao nome da
Concepção[2] & forāo a Mozambique, & de Melinde atrauessaram a
outra banda, tomādo carregase tornaram, & dobrādo o cabo em
dezasete graos daltura, acharam a ilha aque poseram nome de
santa Elena cousa pequena, mas muito nomeada.

Neste mesmo anno de 501 & mes de Mayo partirā tres nauios
da cidade de Lixboa por mandado del Rey dom Manoel, a descobrir
ha costa do Brazil, & foram a ver vista das Canarias, & da hi a
cabo Verde, tomarā refresco em Beziquiche, passada a linha da
parte do sul, foram tomar terra no Brazil em cinco graos daltura,
& forā por ella ate trinta & dous pouco mais ou menos, segundo
sua cōta, donde se tornaram no mes de Abril por auer já la frio,

---

[1] Don Manuel.

[2] There is here some confusion betwixt the names Conceicāo and
Ascensāo.   The discovery of Ascension is attributed to Tristran da
Cunha in 1508.

were in that voiage fifteene monethes, and came to Lisbon againe in the beginning of September, 1502.

In the yeere 1502, one Alfonso Hoieda went to discouer Terra firma, and followed his course till he came to the prouince of Vraba.

Gomara, historiæ general, lib. 2.

Vraba.

The next year following, also, one Roderigo Bastidas of Siuill went out with two carauels at his owne cost, and the first land of the Antiles that he saw was an island, which he named Isla Verde, that is, the Greene Island, standing fast by the Island of Guadalupe, towards the land ; and from thence they took their course towards the west to Santa Martha, and Cape De la Vela, and to Rio Grande or the great riuer, and they discouered the hauen of Zamba, the Coradas, Carthagena, and the islands of S. Barnard of Baru, and Islas de Arenas, and went forward vnto Isla fuerte, and to the point of Caribana standing at the end of the Gulfe of Vraba, where they had sight of the Farallones standing on the other side hard by the riuer of Darien, and from Cape De la Vela vnto this place are two hundred leagues[1] ; and

& tormenta, poseram neste descobrimento & viagẽ quinze mezes, por tornarem a Lixboa na entrada de Setembro.

¶ Neste anno ou no seguinte, forã ao descobrimento da noua Espanha Alonso de hijada, & trouxe sua derrota até reconhecer a prouincia de Sinta. E no anno seguinte partio Rodrigo de bastidas de Seuilha, com duas carauellas armadas à sua custa & ha primeira terra que das Antilhas tomaram, foy hũa ylha a que poseram nome Verde, que está junto Daguadalupe contra a terra, & tomado na mão ha volta contra ho Ponente a sancta Martha, & a cabo dauella & ao Rio grande, & descobriram ho porto do Zamba, hos Coroados, Cartagena, & has ylhas de sam Bernardo de Baru, & has areas, foram diante à ylha forte, & a ponta da Caribana, que estaa no cabo do golfam de Vraba, vieram hos Farelones, que estam da outra banda junto Dariem, & do cabo da villa atee esta

[1] The distance from Cape de la Vela to the Point of Caribona is about one hundred and fifteen leagues.

it standeth in 9 degrees and two parts of latitude. From
thence they crossed over vnto the island of Jamaica, where
they refreshed themselues. In Hispaniola they graued their
ships because of the[1] holes which certaine wormes of the
water had eaten in the planks. In that country they got
fower hundred markes of golde, although the people there
be more warlike than in Noua Spania, for they poison their
arrowes which they shoote.

The fourth
voiage of
Columbus.
In this same yeere, 1502, Christopher Columbus entered[2]
the fourth time into his discouerie with fower ships at the

Gomara,
historiæ
general,
lib. 1, cap.
24.
commandement of Don Fernando, to seeke the Streight,
which, as they said, did diuide the land from the other side,
and he carried with him Ferdinando, his sonne. They went
first to the Island of Hispaniola, to Jamaica, to the riuer

Cabo de
Higueras.
Azua, to the Cape of Higueras, and vnto the Islands Ga-

Cabo de
Hunduras.
mares, and to the Cape of Honduras, that is to say, the Cape
of the Depthes; from thence they sailed towards the east

Cabo de
Gracias a
Dios.
Veragua.
vnto the Cape Gracias a Dios, and discouered the prouince
and riuer of Veragua, and Rio Grande, and others, which

---

enseada a [cem ?] trinta legoas, estaa em noue graos & meyo daltura. Daqui atrauessaram ha ylha de Zamayca, onde tomaram
refresco, & na Espanhola deram com hos nauios aa costa pelo
gusano que ha muyto, leuarem quarenta marcos douro que por
essa terra resgataram, ainda que ha gente da terra he mays guer-
reira que ha na Noua Espanha, & tiram com erua.

No anno de quinhētos & dous, tornou Christouam Colom ha
quarta vez a este descobrimento com quatro nauios per mandado
del Rey dom Fernando a buscar ho estreyto, que deziam cortar a
terra a outra banda leuaua cōsigo dom Fernando seu filho : foram
ter a ilha Espanhola, & de Jamaica, & ao Rhio Nheser, & ao cabo
de Figueira, & ao ylhas dos Gamares, & ao porto das fonduras ;
& dahi contra o Leuante ao cabo de Graças a Deos, & descobrio a
prouincia & Rio Veraga, & o Rio grande, & outros que os da terra

---

[1] Worms, which are numerous.   [2] Returned.

the Indians call Hieura. And from thence he went to the riuer of Crocodiles, which now is called Rio de Chagres, Rio de Chagres. which hath his springs neere the South Sea, within fower leagues of Panama, and runneth into the North Sea ; and so he went vnto the island which he called Isla de Bastimentos, Isla de Bastimentos. that is, the Isle of Victuailes, and then to Puerto Bello, that Puerto Bello. is the faire hauen, and so unto Nombre de Dios, and to Rio Nombre de Dios. Francisco, and so to the hauen of Retrete, and then to the Gulfe of Cabesa Cattiua, and to the Islands of Caperosa, and lastly to the Cape of Marble, which is two hundred The Cape of Marble. leagues vpon the coast ; from whence they began to turne again unto the Island of Cuba, and from thence to Jamaica, where he grounded his ships, being much spoiled and eaten with wormes.

In this yeere also, 1052, Don Vasques de Gama, being now admirall, went again into India with 19 or 20 carauels. Barros, decad. i, lib. 6, cap. 2. He departed from Lisbon the tenth day of Februarie, and by the last day of that moneth he came to an anker at Cape Verd, and from thence he went vnto Mosambique, The Island of Mosambique. and was the first that crost from that island into India ; and

chamam Hieura. E dahi foy ter ao Rio dos Lagartos, que se agora chama Chegres, que tem seu nascimento ao mar do Sul, & sae ao do Norte, passa de Panamaa quarenta[1] legoas, & foy aa ylha que pos nome dos Bastimentos, & ao porto Bello, & a nombre de Dios, & ao Rio Francisco, & ao porto do Retrete, & ao golfam de Secatiua, & aas ylhas de Caparrosa, & ao cabo de Marmol, que sam dozentas legoas de costa, donde começaram, tornou a ylha de Cuba, & dahi a Jamaica, onde acabou de dar com os quatro nauios a costa por serem ja muy gastados do gusano.

No anno de 502 tornou dom Vasco da Gama ja Almirante aa India, leuou xix ou vinte carauelas : partio de Lisboa a x de feuereiro, no fim delle surgio no Cabo verde, donde foy a Moçambique, & o primeiro q' desta ilha atrauesou pr'a India, & descobrio outra em quatro graos daltura, a que pos nome a do Almirante,

---

[1] Quatro ?

he discouered another in 4 degrees of latitude, which he called the Island of the Admirall, and there he took his lading of pepper and drugs, and left there one Vincent Sodre to keep the coast of India, with fiue ships.

These were the first Portugals that with an army did run along the coast of Arabia Felix. It is there so barren, that their cattell and camels are onely maintained with drie fish brought from the sea, whereof there is such plenty and abundance that the cats of the countrey doe vse to take them.

Cattell and camels fed with dried fish.

In the yeere following, as it is reported, one Antonie de Saldania discouered the island, which in old time was called Caradis, and now Socotora, and the Cape of Guardafu, which adioineth vnto that countrey.

Socotora. Cape de Guardafu.

In the yeere 1504,[1] Roderigo de Bastidas obtained licence of king Ferdinando, and by the means of John de Ledesma and others of Seuill named and furnished out two ships, hauing for his pilot one John de Cosa of St. Mary Port, and he went to discouer that part of Terra firma where now standeth Carthagena, being in ten degrees and a halfe of

Cartha-gena.

---

tomou carrega de pimenta & drogas, & deyxou la por guarda da costa da India cō cinco vellas, Vicente sodrè, estes forā os prime-iros Portugueses q' d'armada correram a costa de Arabia, a q' chamāo Felix, ella he tam esteril que se nā mantem os gados & camelos senam em peixe seco que lhe do mar leuam, & seram elles tātos q' os gatos os tomā. E no anno seguinte segundo dizem descobrio Antonio de Saldanha a ilha que se chama Dioscorodis, & agora Socotora, & o cabo de Guarda foy com aquela terra.

No anno de 1504 armaram Joam de cosa, vezinho de Sancta Maria del Puerto, & o piloto Rodrigo de bastidas, cō ajuda de Joam de Ledesma, & outros de Seuilha, com licença del Rey dom Fernando quatro carauelas, & forā a descobrir a terra noua onde se chama Cartagena, q' está em dez graos & meyo da parte do

---

[1] John de Cosa, of Santa Maria del Puerto, and the pilot, Rodrigo de Bastidos, with the aid of John de Ledesma and others of Seuille, by license from the king Ferdinand, fitted out four caravels.

northerly latitude. And it is said that they found the captaine, Luis de la Guerra, and they together tooke land in[1]
the Isle of Codego, where they tooke six hundred persons   Codego.
of the sauages. And going farther along the coast they entred into the Gulfe of Vraba, where they found sand mingled with gold, being the first that was brought to the king,
Don Ferdinando ; from thence they returned to the citie of
Santo Domingo, laden with slaues, without victuailes, because they of the countrey would not bargaine with them,
which grew to their great trouble and griefe.

In the later end of this yeere died Ladie Isabella, Queene   The death
of Castile, which queen, while she liued, would not suffer   Isabella,
                                  1504.
any man of Arragon, Catalunia, Valencia, nor any borne in
the countrey of Don Fernando her husband, to enter into
these discoueries, saue those which were their seruants, or
by speciall commandement ; but only the Castilians, Biscaines, and those which were of her owne Signiories, by
whom all the lands aforesaid were discouered.

In the yeere 1505, vpon our Lady day in March, Fran-

---

norte, & diz que acharam aly o capitã Luis da guerra, & juntos
todos saltarã na ilha do Codego, tomaram nella seis centas pessoas,
foram por aquela costa, & entraram no Golfam de Vrába : & na
area acharam ouro mesturado cõ ella, & foy o primeiro que se daly
trouxe a el Rey dom Fernãdo oude foram á cidade de sam Domingos carregados de escrauos sem resgate nem mãtimento; porque
os da terra nã quiseram contratar com elle lhe fizera muito dano.
E no fim deste anno de 1504 falaceo a Raynha dona Isabel de Castella, & em quanto foy viua nã consentio que fossem do descobrimento da noua España, Aragões, Cathelões, Valencianos, nem
nenhũs do patrimonio del Rey dom Fernando seu marido, saluo se
fosse seu criado, ou por especial mandado, somente Castelhanos,
Galegos, Biscaynhos, & os de·seu senhorio que esta terra descobriram.

No anno de 1505 dia de Nossa Senhora de Março, partio dom

---

[1] Fell upon.

Barros,
decad. 1, lib.
8, cap. 3.

cisco de Almeida, Viceroy of India, tooke his course with 22
sailes towards India [by way of Brazil] as now is accustomed.

A fort built
in Quiloa.

He came vnto the city of Quiloa, where he built a fort, ap-
pointing one Peter Fereira to be captaine thereof; and

Augediua
possessed.

beyond Melinde he trauersed to the Island of Augediua,
where he placed as captaine one Emmanuell Passania.   In

Forts
builded in
Cananor
and in
Cochin.

Cananor also he built another fort, giuing the captainship
of it to Laurence de Brito.   In Cochin he did the like,
where Don Alfonso de Neronia was made captaine.   This

A fort
builded in
Sofala.

yeere one Peter de Anhaya did build the fortress of Sofala,
whereof also himselfe was made captaine.

In the later end of this yeere [or at the beginning of the
next] the viceroy commanded his sonne, whose name was
Don Laurenço, to make some entrie upon the Islands of
Maldiua, and with contrairie weather he arriued at the
islands, which of ancient time were called Tragana, but the

Ceilan.

Moores called them Ytterubenero, and we call them Ceilan,
where he went on land, and made peace with the people
there, and afterwards came back vnto Cochin, sailing along
the coast and fully discouering it.   In the middest of this

Francisco Dalmeyda, Viso Rey da Indio com vinte & duas vellas,
fez seu caminho na volta do Brasil, como se ja costumaua. Chegado
á cidade de Quiloa, assētou fortaleza, capitam della Pero ferreira,
& alem de Melinde atraueouss a ilha Daugediua, onde fez capitā
Manoel Paçanha. Em Cananor edificou outra, deu a capitania a
Lourenço de Brito.   Em Cochim o mesmo, & capitam dō Affonso
de Noronho.   Neste anno fez Pero danhaya a fortaleza de Sofala,
de que teue a capitania.

Na fim deste anno, ou na entrada do outro, mandou ho Viso rey
a dom Lourenço seu filho ás ilhas de Maldiua, & com tempo contraria, arribou às ylhas, a que os antiguos chamaram Tragana &
os mouros Itterubenero, & nos agora Ceilam, onde sahio em terra,
& assentou paz com os della, tornou a Cochim ao longo da costa,
deixandoa toda sabida.

No meo desta ylha estaa hum pico de pedra muy alto, & hūa

island there stands a rocke of stone, very high, hauing the
signe of the foote of a man vpon the top of it, which they
say to be the footestep of Adam, when he went up into the
heauens, and the Indians haue it in great reuerence.

In the yeere 1506, after the death of the Queene of Spain,
King Philip and Queene Joan his wife came into Spaine to
take possession thereof, and King Don Fernando went into
Arragon, being his owne patrimonie. In this same yeere
the said King Philip died, and then Fernando came againe The death of
Philip the
fyrst of
Spaine,1505.
to gouerne Spain, and he gaue licence vnto all Span-
yards to goe vnto the New land, and to the Antiles, but not
to the Portugals. In this yeere, and in the moneth of May,
Christopher Columbus died, and his son Don Diego Colum- The death of
Christopher
Columbus.
bus succeeded in his roome.

In the year 1506, and entring into the moneth of March, Barros,
decad. 2, lib.
1, cap. 1.
Tristan de Acunna and Alfonso de Albuquerque went into
India with 14 ships in their companie, and sailed till they
came to an anker at the towne of Bezequiche, where they Bezequiche
is by Cape
Verde.
refreshed themselves ; and before they came to the Cape of
Bona Sperança, in 37 degrees, they found certaine islands,

---

pegada de homem, & na sumida delle que dizē ser do nosso padre
Adam, quando sobio aos ceos, tem no os Indios em grande vene-
raçam.

No āno de 1506 depois da Raynha dona Isabel falecer, veyo el
Rey Felipe, & a Raynha dona Ioana sua molher a Espanha tomar
posse, el rey dom Fernando se foy Aragam por ser seu patrimonio :
& neste mesmo anno faleceo el rey Felipe, & tornou gouernar Castella el rey dō Fernando, & deu licença aos Espanhoes que podessem
hir aa terra noua & Antilhas, saluo os Portugueses. E neste
mesmo anno & mes de Mayo faleceo Christouam columbo, & socedeo
em seu lugar seu filho dom Diogo columbo.

Neste mesmo anno de 1506 & entrada do mes de Março, partio
Tristam da cunha & Afōso Dalbuquerq' pera India, & xiiij. vellas
ē sua cōpanhia, foy surgir em Bezequichi, pera refrescarem, &
antes q' chegassem ao cabo de boa esperança ē trinta & sete graos

The Isles of Tristan de Acunna in 37 degrees. which now are named the Isles of Tristan de Acunna, where they had such a tempest that therewithal the fleete was dispersed. Tristan de Acuna and Alfonso de Albuquerque went vnto Mossambique, and Aluaro Telez ran so far that Samatra discouered. he came to the Island of Samatra, and so backe againe vnto the Cape of Guardafu ; hauing discouered many islands, sea, and land neuer seene before that time of any Portugall. Emmanuel Telez de Meneses was also driuen without the great island of S. Lawrence, and he ran along the coast thereof, and arriued at last at Mosambique, and there met with Tristan de Acuña, who was the first captaine that wintred there ; and by them it was told that in this island was much ginger, cloues, and siluer ; whereupon he went The inland of S. Laurence discouered. and discouered much of it within the land ;[1] but, finding nothing, he came backe againe into Mozambique ; from whence he sailed vnto Melinde, and ran along that coast, Braua. and entred into Braua, and from thence they crost ouer to A fortress builded in Socotora. Barros, decad. 2, lib. 2, cap. 1. the island of Socotora, where they built a fortresse, and made one Don Antonio de Noronia captaine thereof.

---

d'altura acharam hũas ylhas, q' se agora chamam de Tristam da cunha, onde lhe deu tam grande tormenta, q' se espalhou toda a frota. Tristam da cunha & Alfonso Dalbuquerque foram ter a Moçambiq', Aluaro telez, correo tā largo, q' foy a terra de Samatra, dōde se tornou ao cabo de Guardafui deixando descuberto muitas ylhas, mar, & terra, nũca ate aq'lle tēpo por Portugueses vista.

Manoel telez de Meneses tambem varou por fora daquella gram ylha de sam Lourenço, & correo todas na costa, foy ter a Moçambique cō Tristam da cunha, q' foy o primeiro capitam q' ali inuernara, & por lhe dizerem q' nesta ylha auia muito gengibre, crauo, & prata, tornou a descobrir muita della pella parte de dentro, & nam achando nada se tornou a Moçambique, donde partiram pera Melinde, correram aq'lla costa, sahiram em Braua, & dahi passaram aa ylha de Sacatoraa, onde fizeram fortaleza, capitam della dom Antonio de Noronha.

---

[1] The interior.

In the yeere 1507, in the moneth of August, Tristan de Acuña tooke shipping for India, and Alfonso de Albuquerque remained there with fiue or sixe ships to keepe the coast and entrie of the streight : but being not therewith satisfied, he tooke his course ouer vnto Arabia, and, running along that coast, he doubled the Cape of Rosalgate, standing vnder the tropicke of Cancer. ^{The Cape of Rosalgate.}

In the year 1509, one Diego Lopez de Sequeira went out of Lisbon with fower sailes vnto the Island of Saint Laurence, and continued in his voiage almost a yeere, and in the moneth of May the same yeere he arriued in Cochin, where the viceroy gave him one ship more : and, in the beginning of the moneth of September, he tooke his course vnto Malacca, passing betweene the islands of Nicubar, and many others. He went also to the land of Samatra, to the cities of Pedir and Pacem, and all along by all that coast vnto the Island of Poluoreira, and the flats of Capacia : and from thence he went ouer vnto Malacca, standing in 2 degrees of latitude towards the north; but in that citie the people killed and tooke as prisoners some of his men : and thereupon he turned backe againe into India, hauing dis-

[margin: Barros, decad. 2, lib. 4, cap. 3. The Isle of S Laurence. The Islands of Nicobar. Samatra. The Isle of Poluoreira. The flats of Capacia.]

No ano de 1507 no mes Dagosto partio Tristã da cunha p'a India : & Afõso dalbuq'rq' q' ali ficaua cõ v. ou vj. nauios p'a guarda da costa & boca daq'le estreito, não se contētando disto se passou Arabia, & correndo a toda, dobrou o cabo de Rosalgata, q' está no tropico de cancro.

No anno de quinhentos & noue partio Diogo lopez de Seq'yra de Lisboa cõ quatro velas pera ylha de Sam Lourēço, andou derredor della q'si hũ anno, & no de noue & mes de Mayo chegou a Cochim, ho Visorey lhe deu mais hum nauio. E na entrada do mes de Setembro, partio pera Malaca, passou per entre as ylhas de Nicobar, & outras muytas : & foy a terra de Sumatra ás cidades de Pedir, & Pacem : & per toda essa costa ate a ylha da Poluoreira, & baixos de Capacea : & dahi se passaram a Malaca, que está em dous graos daltura da parte do norte, & por lhe matarem & capti-

couered in this voiage fiue hundred leagues.   This Island of
Samatra is the first land wherein we know man's flesh to be
eaten by certaine people which liue in the mountaines called
Bacas, who vse to gilde their teeth.   They hold opinion
that the flesh of the blacke people is sweeter then the flesh
of the white.   The buffes, kine, and hennes which are in
that countrey are in their flesh as blacke as any inke.   They
say that there are certaine people there called Daraquc
Dara, which haue tailes like vnto sheepe ; and some of their
welles yield oile.

The king of Pedir is reported to haue a riuer in his land
running with oile ; which is a thing not to be maruelled at,
seeing it is found written, that in Bactria there is also a well
of oile : it is farther said that there groweth here a tree, the
iuice whereof is strong poison ; and, if it touch the blood of
a man, he dieth immediately ; but if a man doe drinke of it,
it is a soueraigne remedie against poison, so seruing both for
life and death.   Here also they doe coine peeces of gold,
which they call drachmas, brought into the land, as they
say, by the Romanes ; which seemeth to haue some resem-

Rarities in Sumatra.

In Sumatra the buffes, kine, and hennes haue flesh as blacke as inke.

Peoples hauing tailes like sheepe.

Gold coined in Samatra.

---

uarem nesta cidade gente, se tornou pera à India deixãdo quinhentas legoas descubertas.

Esta ylha de Sāmatra he a primeira terra q' la sabemos, em q' se
come carne humana, hūas gentes que viuem nas serras que se chamam Bacas, douram hos dentes, dizem que a carne dos homēs
pretos he mais saborosa que a dos brancos : & assi as bufaras,
vacas, galinhas que ha naquellas partes, sam de carnes tam pretas
como esta tinta,   Diziã auer ahi homēs a que chamão Dara que
dara, que tem rabos como carneiros, aqui ha azeite que tiram de
poços : El Rey de Pedir me disse q' por sua terra corria hū rio
delle, nam se deue dauer por muito, pois se acha escripto, que na
Batriana ha hūa fonte doleo : & assi contam auer aqui hūa aruore
que o çumo della he forte peçonha, & se toca em sangue logo a
pessoa morre, & bebendoo he cousa muy provada contra ella, assi
que dà morte & vida : batese aqui moeda douro a que chamam

blance of truth, because that from that place forward there is no coined gold ; but that which is thus coined doth run currant in the buying of marchandise and other things.

In the year 1508, one Alfonso de Hoieda, and Diego de recusa, with the fauour of Don Fernando, purposed to goe vnto tierra firma to conquer the prouince of Darien. He went foorth at his owne charges, and discouered the firme land, where it is called Vraba, which he named Castilia del Oro, that is, Golden Castilia, bicause of the gold which they found among the sand along the coast. And they were the first Spanyards that did this. For this, one governed Vraba, the other Beraga. Alfonso de Hoieda went first from the Island of Hispaniola and the citie of San Domingo with fower ships and three hundred soldiers, leauing behinde him the bachiler[1] Anciso, who afterwards compiled a booke of these discoueries. And after him there went also one ship with victuals, munition, and 150 Spanyards. He went on land at Carthagena, but there the people of the countrey tooke, slew, and eate 80 of his soldiers, whereupon he grew uery weake.[2]

Gomara, historiæ general, lib. 3, cap. 7.

Castilia del Oro.

The booke of the Bachiler Anciso of these discoueries.

---

dragmas, dizem q' os Romãos a trouxeram a esta terra, parece algũa cousa, porque daqui por diãte nam se bate moeda douro, mas corre se ele por mercadoria.

No anno de 1508 armaram a sua custa com licença del Rey dom Fernando, Alonso de hijada, & Diogo de recusa, pera hir pouuar & conquistar a prouincia Doriem, & descobrir a terra firme, onde se chama Vraba q' poserão nome Castella do ouro, pello q' acharam na area ao longo da praya, & foram os primeiros Castelhanos q' isto fizeram : porq' hum tinha a gouernança de Vraba, & outro de Beraga. Partio primeiro Alonso de hijada da ylha Espanhola, & cidade de Sanctiago cõ quatro nauios & trezẽtos soldados, deixando o Bacharel Ansiso, q' depois fez hũ liuro deste descobrimẽto, p'a yr tras elle hũ nauio cõ mantimẽtos & monições, & cẽto & cincoẽta Espanhoes. Chegou Alõso de hijada a Cartagena, onde tomou

---

[1] Bachelor of Arts. [2] Angry.

In this year 1508, one Diego de Niquesa prepared seuen
ships in the port of Beata to goe vnto Veragua, and carried in
them almost 800 men.   When he came to Carthagena, he
found there Alfonso de Hoieda forespoiled with his former
losse ;[1] but then they both ioined together, and went on
land, and auenged themselves of the people [and went each
to his government].   And in this voiage Diego de Niquesa
went and discouered the coast called Nombre de Dios, and
went vnto the sound of Darien, and called it Puerto de
Misas, which is vpon the riuer of Pito.   When they were
come vnto Veragua, he went on shore with his armie,[2] his
soldiers being out of hope to returne to Hispaniola.   [And
though this stratagem of war was put in practice afterwards
by Fernan Cortez, he was not the first in that land, as some
hold and believe].   Alfonso de Hoieda began a fortress in
Caribana against the Caribes ;[3] which was the first towne
that the Spanyards builded in the Firme land ; and in Nom-

Beata is a
prouince in
the west
part of His-
paniola.

Gomara,
gen. hist.,
lib. 3, cap. 6.

---

terra, & os dela lhe matarão & comeram oytenta soldados, de que
ficou muyto agastado.

Neste mesmo āno de 1508 armou Diogo de Nequisa no porto
de Beata sete vellas pera hir a Beraga, & leuou nellas perto de
oytocentos homēs.   Chegado a Cartagena, achou ahi Alonso de
hijada assaz agastado pello q' lhe socedera, sahiram ambos em
terra, tomaram vingança, & se foram cada hum a sua gouernança,
Diogo de recusa foy descobrindo a costa que he de nombre de
Dios aos Roquedos de Dariē, chamou porto de Misas ao rio Pito :
chegado a Beraga deu com a armada á costa, por os soldados perderem esperança de tornarē a Espanhola : & ainda q' este ardil de
guerra tiuesse despois Fernam cortez, nā foy elle primeyro naquella
terra (como algus tem, & cuidam) Alonso de hijada começou hua
fortaleza em Caribana Solar dos Caribas, & foy a primeira villa q'

---

[1] Very angry at what had happened to him.

[2] He ran his ships on shore that his soldiers might lose the hope of
returning to Hispaniola.

[3] Country of the Caribs ?

bre de Dios they built another, and called it Nuestra Sen- ^{Nuestra}
nora de la Antigua. They builded also the towne of Vraba. ^{la Antigua}
And there they left for their captaine and lieutenant one
Francis Pisarro, who was there much troubled [and afterwards discovered Peru]. They builded other towns also,
whose names I here omit. But these captaines had not that
good successe which they hoped for [and this is enough for
my purpose].

In the yeere 1509, the second Admirall, Don Diego
Columbus went into the Island of Hispaniola with his wife
and houshold And she being a gentlewoman carried with
her many other women of good families, which were there ^{Many}
married, and so the Spanyards and Castillians began to ^{women went}
people the countrey :[1] for Don Fernando, the king, had ^{Hispaniola.}
giuen them licence to discouer and people the townes of
Hispaniola; so that the same place grew to be famous and
much frequented. The foresaid Admirall also gaue order to
people the Island of Cuba, which is very great and large, ^{Cuba}

os castelhanos em terra firme fizerā, & assi em Nombre de Dios,
cidade de nossa senhora del antiga, & a villa de Vraba, donde
deixaram por capitam & teniente Francisco piçarro, q' leuou ahi
assaz trabalho, (& descobrirā despois a de Peru) E assi fizeram
outras q' nam nomeo, por que estes capitāes nam tiueram tā bom
socesso como cuydauā, & isto abasta a meu proposito.

No anno de 1509 chegou ho segundo Almirante dom Diogo
colom a ylha Espanhola com sua molher & casa, & como era nobre
& fidalga, leuou muitas molheres & de boa casta q' la casaram, &
começaram de Castelhanos de encher a terra, porque el Rey dom
Fernando tinha dado licença que podessē la yr descobrir, pouuar,
todo los pouos de Espanha, por onde aq'lla terra foy mais enno-
brecida & frequētada & tambē este Almirante deu ordē como se
pouoasse a ilha da Cuba, q' he cousa grande & pos nella pera isso

---

[1] And began to fill the land with Castilians.

and placed there as his lieutenant one Diego Velasques, who went with his father in the second voiage.

Barros, decad. 2, lib. 5, cap. 10, & lib. 6, cap. 2. In the yeere 1511, in the moneth of Aprill, Alfonso de Albuquerque went from the citie of Cochin vnto Malacca. Barros, decad. 2, lib. 6, cap. 5. In which yeere and moneth[1] the Chineans went from Malaeca into their owne countrey, and Alfonso sent with them [to Siam] (for master[2]) a Portugall called Duarte Fernandes, with letters [and greeting] (also, and order[3]) vnto the king of the Mantias, which now is called Sian, standing in the south. The Streight of Cincapura. [Coasting along], they passed through the streight of Cincapura, and sailed towards the north, went along the coast Odia the chiefe citie of Siam. of Patane, vnto the citie of Cuy, and from thence to Odia, which is the chiefe citie of the kingdome, standing in 14 degrees of northerly latitude. The king greatly honoured and welcomed Duarte Fernandes, being the first Portugall that he had seene, and with him he sent backe ambassadours to Albuquerque. They passed ouer land towards Tanaçerim. the west vnto the citie of Tanaçerim, standing upon the sea on the other side in 12 degrees, where they imbarked them-

---

por seu adiātado a Diogo valhasquez que fora com seu pay na armada segūda.

No anno de 1511, & mes de Abril partio Afonso dalboquerque da cidade de Cochim pera Malaca & neste mesmo anno, & mes de Julho forā os Chins de Malaca pera sua terra, & mandou Afonso dalbuquerque cõ elles a Syāo hum Portugues q' se chamaua Duarte fernandez com cartas & recado a el rey dos Muātais que agora chamamos siāo ao Sul, ao lōgo da terra passaram pelo estreito de Sincapura & tomaram a norte correndo aquella costa de Pāpatane, ate a cidade de Cuy, & della ao Dia, q' he cabeça, deste reyno, que estara ate quatorze graos daltura. El Rey fez a Duarte fernandez por ser o primeiro Portugues q' vira muita merce & honra, & madou cõ elle embaixadores a Afonso dalbuquerq', atrauessarā pola terra a loeste a cidade de Tanasarim q' esta no mar da outra banda em doze

---

[1] And in the same year and month of July.   [2] Dele.
[3] Dele. And greeting.

selues in two ships, and sailed along the coast unto the citie of Malacca, leauing it all discouered [so much as it can be by sailing along a coast].

The people of this countrey of Sian are people that eate of all kinde of beastes, or vermine [or fish which land and water produce]. They haue a delight[1] to carrie round bels within the skin of their priuie members, which is forbidden to the king and the religious people. It is said that of all[2] other people of those parts, they be most vertuous and honest. They commend themselues much for their chastitie and pouertie. They bring no hennes nor doues vp in their houses [nor other female thing]. This kingdom hath in length 250 leagues, and in bredth 80 [besides those who are subject to it]. Of this only kingdom the king may bring foorth into the field thirtie thousand elephants, when he goeth to warre, besides those which remaine in the cities for the garde of them. The king much esteemeth a white elephant, and (a red)[3] one also, [with red] (that hath)[3] eies like vnto flaming fire.

There is in this countrey a certaine small vermine, which

M. Ralph Fitch which had beene in this country brought diuers of these bels into England.

---

graos, embarcados em dous nauios se vieram ao longo da costa ate a cidade de Malaca, deixando a toda vista, segundo alcança os que vam per mar ao longo de terra.

A gente deste reyno de Syão he gentia, come toda alimaria, bicho, pescado q' a terra & agoa produzem, prezā fe de trazer cascaneis em suas naturas, a el Rey & religiosos he vedado : & dizem que sam dos mais virtuosos & honestos q' ha na redondeza, prezam se muito de castidade & pobreza : em sua casa nam criam galinha pomba, nem outra cousa femea. Terá este Reino dozentas & cincoēta legoas em comprido, & oitenta de largo, afora os q' lhe obedecē. Deste soo reyno poē el rey em cāpo trinta mil alifantes de guerra, afora os q' lhe ficam nas cidades por guarda, tē hū branco em grande estima, & outro ruyuo de olhos q' escamecham, como fogo. Ha nestas terras hū bicho peq'no, q' se lhes pega na

---

[1] To wear rings, etc.   [2] The world they be, etc.   [3] Dele.

vseth to cleaue fast to the trunke of the elephant, and
draweth the blood of the elephant, and so he dieth thereof.
The skull of this vermine is so hard, that the shot of a hand-
gun cannot enter it : they haue in their liuers the figures of
men and women, which they call Toketa, and are much like
vnto a mandrake.   And they affirme that he which hath one
of them about him cannot die with the stroke of any iron.
They haue also wilde kine in this countrey, in the heads of
whome they finde stones, which are of vertue to bring good
hap and fortune to marchants.

After that Duarte Fernandes had been with the Mantales
or people of Siam, Alfonso de Albuquerque sent thither a
knight called Ruy Nunnez de Acunna, with letters and ambassage vnto the king of the Seguies, which we call Pegu.
He went in a Iunco of the countrey in sight of the Cape
Rachado, and from thence went vnto the citie of Pera which
standeth fast by the riuer Salano,[1] and [to] many other
villages standing all along this riuer, where Duarte Fernandes had beene before, vnto the cities of Tanaçerim and
of Martauan, standing in 15 degrees toward the north, and

The liuer of
a little beast
good against
any wound
of iron.

Pegu.

Pera.

---

tróba, & os ensanguenta ate q' os matã, tem a concha tã dura, q'
hũ arcabuz o nã passa, & cria nos figados hũa figura de homẽs ou
molheres ã q' chamã toy'ta, q' he coma mẽdracola, & quẽ as traz
consigo, dizẽ q' nam podẽ morrer a ferro, & nas cabeças de vacas
brauas achãse pedras muy ditosas pera mercadores.

Depois de Duarte fernandez hir aos Mantuis, mandou Affonso
Dalbuquerque hũ caualeiro q' se chamaua Ruy nunez da cunha
cõ cartas & embaixada ao Rey dos Sequĩs, q' nós chamamos Pegus,
foy em hũ junco dos da terra ao lõgo della, & vista do cabo
rachado, & dahi à cidade de Perá, & aquẽ da Iunsalão, & outras
muytas pouoações q' jazem ao longo desta ribeira, por onde ja
Duarte fernandez viera, ate a cidade de Tanasarim, & de Bartabão,
que está en quinze graos da parte do Norte, & á cidade de

---

[1] And on this side of the river Solano ?

the citie of Pegu standeth in 17. This was the first Portugall which trauailed in that kingdome, and he gaue good
information of that countrey and of the people, which vse to Master
Ralph Fitch
wear bels[1] in their priuities, euen as the Mantales doe.   saw this in
Pegu also.
   In the end of this yeere 1511, Alfonso de Albuquerque Barros,
decad. 2, lib.
sent three ships to the Islands of Banda and Maluco. And 6, cap. 7.
The Iles of
there went as generall of them one Antonio de Breu, and Banda and
Maluco.
with him also went one Francis Serrano; and in these ships
there were 120 persons. [Not more vessels nor men went
to discouer New Spain with C. Columbus, nor with Vasco
de Gama to India ; nor in comparison with these is Maluco
less wealthy, nor ought it to be held in less esteem.] They
passed through the Streight of Saban, and along the Island
of Samatra, and [in sight of] many others, leauing them on
the left hand, towards the east ; and they called them the
Salites. They went also to the Islands of Palimbam and The Salites.
Lusuparam, from whence they sailed by the noble Island of
Iaua, and they ran their course east, sailing betweene it and Iaua.
the island of Madura. The people of this island are very Madura.

Pegu em xvij. Este foy o primeiro Portugues q' trilhou aq'le
reyno, & deu enformação da terra & de como traziã cascaueis
como os Muãtais.

   No fim deste anno de 1511 mandou Affonso Dalbuquerque tres
nauios ás ilhas de Banda & Maluco : & por capitão mór delles
Antonio Dabreu, & hum Francisco serrão : hiam nelles cento &
vinte pessoas, porq' nam foram mais velas nē homēs ao descobrimento da noua Espanha com Christouam columbo, nem com Vasco
da Gama á India, porq' Maluco depois destes nam he menos em
riqueza, nē se deue de ter em menos estima, foram pello estreito
de Sabam ao lōgo da ylha de Samatra, & à vista doutras que ficam
da mão esquerda contra o Leuante q' chamam dos Salites, ate as
ylhas de Palimbão, Lusuparam, donde atrauessaram pella nobre
ylha da Jaua, foram a Leste correndo sua costa, per antre ella & a
ylha da madeira. A gente desta ylha he mais belicosa, & que

---

[1] Rings.

warlike and strong, and doe[1] little regard their liues [as any known in the world].   The women also are there hired for the warres : and they fall out often together, and kill one another, as the Mocos doe, [and they contrive that cocks should fight with spurs, as their principal diversion is bloodshedding], delighting onely in shedding of blood.

Beyond the Island of Iaua they sailed along by another called Bali ; and then came also vnto others called Aujaue, çambaba, Solor, *Galav, Mallua, Vitara, Rosalanquin, and †Arus, from whence are brought delicate[2] birds, which are of great estimation because of their feathers : they came also to other islands lying in the same parallele on the south side in 7 or 8 degrees of latitude.   And they be so nere the one to the other, that they seeme at the first to be one entire and maine land.   The course by these islands is aboue fiue hundred leagues.   The ancient cosmographers call all these islands by the name Iauos ; but late experience hath found their names to be very diuers, as you see.   Beyonde these [it is said] there are other islands (towards the north,)[3]

Bali.

---

menos tem em cōta a vida que se sabe na redondeza, & dizem q' as molheres ganham soldo polas armas, & por qualquer cousa se desafiam & matam hūs a outros, como se fazē a Mocos, & inuentam pelejarem galos cō naualhas, porq' ho principal seu desenfadamento he sanguinolento.

Alem desta ylha da Jaua, vam ao longo doutra q' se chama Balle, & outra logo (q' se diz) Anjano, Simbaba, Solor, o Galao, Mauluca, Vitara, Rosolanguim, Arus, donde vē os passaros myrrados, q' sam mui estimados pera penachos, & outras q' jazem nesta corda da parte do Sul, em sete ou oito graos daltura, & tam juntas hūas com as outras, q' parece toda hūa terra.   Auera nesta derrota mais de quinhentas legoas hos Cosmographos lhes chamaram as Jaoas, ainda que agora tem nome differentes como aqui vedes.   Auante destas ylhas dizem que ha outras de gentes mais aluas,

---

which are inhabited with whiter people going arraied in
shirts, doublets and slops, like vnto the Portugals, hauing
also money of siluer. The gouernours among them doe
carrie in their hands red staues, whereby they seem to haue
some affinitie with the people of China, [and not only these
but] there are other islands and people about this place,
which are redde ;[1] and it is reported that they are of the
people of China.

The people
of the Iles
of Maluco
weare such
apparell.

  Antonie de Breu and those that went with him tooke their
course toward the north, where is a smal island called Gumnape (or Ternate),[2] from the highest place whereof there fall
continually into the sea flakes or streams like vnto fire ;
which is a wonderfull thing to behold. From thence they
went to the Islands of Burro and Amboino,[3] and came to an
anker in an hauen of it called Guliguli, where they went on
land and tooke a village standing by the riuer, where they
found dead men hanging in the houses ; for the people there
are eaters of man's flesh. Here the Portugals burnt the
ship wherein Francis Serrano was, for she was old and

Ternate.

Burro.
Amboino.
Guliguli.

que andam vestidas de camisas, gibões, & ceroulas como portugueses, & tem moeda de prata, os q' gouernam a republica, trazè
nas mãos varas vermelhas, por onde parece que deuem de ser da
China, & nam tam somente estas, mas ha por aqui outras de
gentes pintadas, que dizem ser dos Chins pouoadas.

  Antonio Dabreu & os que com elle hiam, tomaram sua derrota
contra o norte dhũa ylheta que se chama o Gumuapè : porque do
mais alto della corre sempre, & de contino ate o mar ribeiras de
fogo, cousa muito pera ver. Daqui foram aa ylha de Burro, &
Damboino, & costearam a costa daq'lla q' se chama de Muar
Damboino, surgiram em hũ porto, q' se diz Guli Guli, saltaram
em terra, tomaram hũa pouoaçam que ali estaua, & acharam nas
casas homẽs mortos dependurados : porque comem carne humana,
onde queimaram a nao em que hia Francisco serrão por ser ja

_____

[1] Painted.   [2] Not in Portuguese.
[3] And coasted along what is called Muar d'Amboina.

Cloues, nut-
megs, and
mace are in
8 degrees
toward the
south.rotten. They went to a place on the other side standing in
8 degrees toward the south, where they laded cloues, nut-
megs, and mace, in a Junco or barke, which Francis Serrano
bought here.

They say that not farre from the Islands of Banda there
is an island where there breedeth nothing else but snakes,
and the most are in one caue in the middest of the land
[some great and others small go always rolled together].
This is a thing not much to be woondred at ; for as much as
in the Levant Sea, hard by the Isles of Maiorca and Minorca,
there is another island of old named Ophiusa, and now
Formentera, wherein there is great abundance of these vermine : and in the rest of the islands lying by it there are
none.

In the yeere 1512 they departed from Banda toward
Malacca, and on the baxos or flats of Luçapinho Francis
Serrano perished[1] in his Junke or barke, from whence escaped[2] vnto the Isle of Mindanao [with] nine or ten Portugals which were[3] with him, and the kings of Maluco sent

Mindanao.
Maluco.

---

velha, & foram ter a banda q' estaa em oito graos da parte do Sul,
dõde carregaram de crauo, noz, e maça, e hũ junco q' Francisco
Serram aqui comprara. Dize q' nam muito lõge destas ylhas de
Banda ha hũa em q' senã cria senã cobras, & as mais nũa coua q'
tem no meo, hũas grandes & outras peq'nas, andão sẽpre enrola-
das, mas nã se deue dauer por muyto, tanto como os da terra,
fazẽdo disto espãto pois os nossos deixarã escrito q' junto das
ilhas de Mayorca & Menorca auia hũa q' se chamaua Eufuria, ẽ
q' auia muita cãtidade destas bichas, ñã as auẽdo ẽ todalas outras
ilhas jũto cõellas.

No ãno de 1512 partiram de Banda pera Malaca, & nos baixos de
Lusupino, se perdeo Francisco Serram cõ o seu junco, donde se
tornou ailha de Mĩdanao cõ ix ou x portugueses q' cõ ele hia, &
os reis d' Maluco mãdarã por eles estes foram hos primeyros

---

[1] Was wrecked with his junk.   [2] Had returned.   [3] Went.

for them. These were the first Portugals that came to the
Islands of Cloues, which stand from the equinoctiall line
towardes the north in one degree, where they liued seuen
or eight yeeres. [A. Dabreu made his way to Malacca
having discovered all the sea and land above named.]

The island of Gumnape, now called Ternate, is much to
be admired, for that it casteth out fire.[1] There were some
princes of the Moores and couragious Portugals which determined to goe neere to the firie place to see what it was,
but they could neuer come neere it [so as to give any
account.] But Antonie Galuano hearing of it, vndertooke
to goe vp to it, and did so [with the help of God and our
Lady, and the thing that most astonished him in this journey
was] (and found)[2] a riuer so extreme cold, that he could not
suffer his hand in it, nor yet put any of the water in his
mouth : [it appears that nature has provided there this cold,
as in other waters immense heat]. And yet this place

Espanhoes que viram as ylhas do crauo, que jazem da linha
contra ho Norte em hum grao, onde esteueram sete ou oyto annos.
Antonio Dabreu fez seu caminho pera Malaca, deixando descuberto
todo aquelle mar & terra nomeadas.

A ylha de Guape em que está nossa fortaleza, q' se agora chama
Ternate, he das mais altas cousas que no mundo se sabe, deita
fogo pello mais alto, cousa tam espantosa q' se nam sabe la falar
em outra. Algũs principes mouros, & nobres portugueses de altos
pensamẽtos, cometeram per vezes ver ysto, mas nunca la chegaram : pello que se fazia ainda mõr conta, o q' Antonio Galuão
ouuindo, determinou cometelo, quis deos & nossa senhora q' lhe
deu cima & da cousa q' se mais espantou desta jornada, foy por
hũa ribeira tam frigidissima, q' nam auia pesoa q' podesse ter a
mão nella, nẽ metela na boca : parece q' proueo a natureza ali esta

---

[1] The Island of Guape, where our fort is situated, is one of the most
sublime objects which is known in the world; it throws out fire from its
summit, a thing so frightful that its equal cannot be spoken of.

[2] Dele.

standeth vnder the line, where the sunne continually
burneth. In these Islands of Maluco there is a kinde of
Monstrous men that have spurres on their ankles like vnto cocks. And
meu.
it was told me by the king of Tydore, that in the Islands of
Batochina. Batochina there were people that had tailes, and [in Amboine
a he goat that gaue milk from some teats he has between
his testicles] (had a thing like vnto a dug between their
cods, out of the which there came milke.[1] There are smal
hennes also which lay their egges vnder the ground aboue a
fathome and an halfe, and the egges are bigger than duck's
egges, and many of these hennes are blacke in their flesh.
There are hogs also with hornes, and parats which prattle
much, which they call noris. There is also a riuer of water
so hot, that whatsoeuer liuing creature cometh into it, their
skins will come off, and yet fish breede in it. There are
crabs which be very sweete, and so strong in their clawes,
that they will break the iron of a pikeaxe. There be others

frialdade, como em outras agoas à immensa quẽtura : sendo isto
debaxio da linha, onde continuadamente o sol reuerbera.

Há nestas ylhas de Maluco homẽs com esporões nos artelhos
como galos, disse me el rey de Tidore q' na ilha da Batachina os
auia cõ rabos & nas Dāboino hũ bode q' deitaua leite por hũs
peitos q' antre os cõpanhões tinha : ha lá galinhas peq'nas q' debaixo da terra mais de braça & mẽa, põe ouos mayores q' patas :
ha muitas de carne pretas & porcos com cornos, & papagayos muy
chorarreiros a que chamã Noris : ha hũa ribeira dagoa tam quẽte
que se pela tudo nella, & cria peixes : ha cranguejos dos matos
muy saborosos & tam forçosos das bocas q' quebram o ferro de
hũa azagaya : ha outras no mar velosos & pequenos, que quẽ os
come emprouiso morre : ha hũas ostras a q' chamã Bras, que tem
tamanhas conchas, que baptizam nellas : ha no mar pedra vina q'
nasce & cria como peixe : & faz cal muy boa, & se a tiram fora &
está ate que morre nũca mais arde. Ha hũa arvore que como

---

[1] Dele.

also in the sea little and hairie, but whosoeuer eateth of them dieth immediately. There be likewise certaine oisters, which they doe call Bras, the shels whereof haue so large a compasse, that they doe christen in them. In the sea also there are liuely stones, which doe grow and increase like vnto fish, whereof very good lime is made : and if they let it lie when it is taken out of the water, it looseth the strength, and it neuer burneth after. There is also a certaine tree, which beareth flowers at the sunne set, which fall down as soon as they be growne. There is a fruit also, as they say, whereof if a woman that is conceaued of child eateth, the child by and by mooueth. There is further a kinde of herbe there growing, which followeth the sunne, and re-mooueth after it, which is a uery strange and maruailous thing. *The flowers of Xistus and Arbor-tristus are such.*

In the year 1512, in the moneth of Januarie, Alfonsus de Albuquerque went back from Malaca vnto Goa, and the ship wherein he went was lost, and the rest went from his companie. Simon de Andrada and a few Portugals were driuen into the Islands of Maldiua, being many and full of palme trees, and they stand lowe by the water : which staied there till they knew what was become of their gouernour. These were the first Portugals that had seen those islands, *Barros, decad. 2, lib. 7, cap. 1.* *The Isles Maldiua.*

---

ho sol se poē enflorece : & caelhe como nace : a hi fruta que dizem que como hūa prenhe a come logo moue, ha hūa erua que segue o sol de maneira que sempre anda cō elle, & he causa de admiraçam vella.

No anno de 1512 no mes de Janeiro tornou Afonso dalboquer-que de Malaca pera Goa & se perdeo a nao em q' elle hia, & outras se partiram de sua companhia, & Simão dandrade & algūs Portugueses foram ter ás ilhas de Maldiua, que sam muitas & cheas de palmeiras, & rasas cō a agoa, aqui o retiueram ate saberem q' ho Gouernador era vindo. Estes forā os primeiros portugueses q' aq'llas ilhas viram, nas quaes dizem q' se criam cocos debaxo dagoa, que sam muy proueitosas contra toda peçonha.

wherein [it is said] there grow cocos [beneath the water] which are very good against all kinde of poison.

John de
Solis.
In this yeere 1512, there went out of Castile one John de Solis, borne in Lisbon, and chief pilot vnto Don Fernando [the king]. And he hauing licence went to discouer the coast of Brassill. He tooke the like course that the Pinsons had done : he went also to¹ the Cape of S. Augustine, and went forwards to the south, coasting the shore and land [league by league] (and he came vnto the port De Lagoa) ;² and in 35 degrees of southerly latitude he found a riuer which they of Brassill call Parana-guaçu, that is, the great water. He sawe there signes of siluer, and therefore called
Rio de
Plata.
it Rio de Plata, that is, the riuer of siluer. And it is said that at that time he went farther because he liked the countrey well ; but he returned backe againe into Spaine, and made account of all things to Don Fernando, demaunding of the king the gouernment thereof, which the king granted
Pet. Martyr,
decad. 3,
cap. 10.
him. Whereupon he prouided three ships, and with them in the yeere 1515 [in the month of September] he went

---

Neste anno de 1512 partio de Castella Ioam de Soliz, natural de Lebrixa,³ piloto mòr Del rey dom Fernando, com sua licença foy descobrir a costa do Brasil, leuou a derrota dos Piçōes. Tornou o cabò de Sancto Agostinho, seguio sua via contra o meio dia, costeando a ribeira & terra legoa por legoa, & em xxxv graos daltura achou hū rio, a q' os Brasis chamã Paranagaco, q' quer dizer grāde agoa, vio nellas mostras de prata, & assi lhe pos nome Rio da prata : & dizē ainda q' foy mais adiante por lhe parecer bē a terra. Tornando a Espanha, deu de tudo a el rey dō Fernando conta, & pediolhe aq'lla gouernança, el rey lhe fez merce della, Armou em Lepe⁴ tres nauios, & no āno de 1515 & mes de Setēbro tornou a este reino, onde o matarā, estes Solizes piçōes forā grādes descobridores naq'las partes, ate gastarem nisso vida & fazenda.

---

¹ He doubled.   ² Not in Portuguese.   ³ Lisboa ?   ⁴ (?)

againe into that kingdome; but he was there slaine. These [gallant] Solisses were great discouerers in those partes, and spent therein their liues and goods.

In the same yeere, 1512, John Ponce of Leon, which had beene gouernour of the Isle of S. John, armed two ships and went to seeke the Isle of Boyuca, where the naturals of the countrey reported to be a wel, which maketh old men young. Whereupon he laboured to finde it out, and was in searching of it the space of six monethes, but could finde no such thing. He entred into the Isle of Bimini, and dis- couered a point of the firme land standing in 25 degrees towards the north, vpon Easter day, and therefore he named it Florida. And because the land seemed to yeeld gold and siluer and great riches, he begged it of the king, Don Fernando, but he died in the discouerie of it, as many more haue done.

Pet. Martyr, decad. 2, cap. 10. Gomara historiæ general, lib. 2, cap. 10. Bimini Islands.

Florida.

Martyr. decad. 3, cap. 10.

In the yeere 1513 Vasco Nunnes de Valboa hearing speech and newes of the South Sea, determined to goe thither, although his company dissuaded him from that action.[1] But being a man of good valure, with those soldiers

Pet. Martyr, decad. 3, cap. 1.

Neste mesmo āno de 1512 Ioam ponso de Liā q' foy gouernador da ylha de S. Ioā, armou dous nauios, & foy buscar a ilha Boihuca, onde diziā os da terra q' estaua hūa fonte q' sua agoa tornaua os velhas moços, & andou em sua busca seis meses cō assaz trabalho sem achar de la noua, nē q' visse tal cousa, entrou ē Bemini, & descobrio aqlla ponta de terra firme q' está em xxv graos da parte do norte dia de pascoa florida, & por ysso lhe pos o tal nome, & por lhe parecer q' acharia nella ouro, prata, & grāde riq'za, a pedio a el rey dō Fernādo, q' foy causa de sua morte & dano, como muitos na tal empresa tē recibido.

No anno de 1513 tendo Vasco nunez de Valboa, noua do mar do sul, determinou passar a elle, cō quanto lhe punham medo da gente da terra, por onde auia de fazer este caminho, mas elle como

---

[1] Although his company tried to inspire him with fear of the people of that country.

that he had, being 290, he resolued to put himself into that
ieopardie.   He went therefore from Dariene the first day of
September, carrying some Indians of the countrey with him
to be his guides, and he marched ouerthwart the land, sometimes quietly, sometimes in war ; and in a certaine place called
Careca he found Negroes captiues with curled haire [and
never up to that time were others seen or known until now,
in all these parts of New Spain, Golden Castile and Peru.]

The South
Sea dis-
couered.

This Valboa came to the sight of the South Sea on the 25
day of the said moneth, and on Saint Michael's day came
vnto it, where he imbarked himselfe against the will of
Chiapes, who was the Lord of that coast, who wished him
not to doe so, because it was very dangerous for him.   But
he[1] desirous to haue it knowne that he had beene vpon those
seas, went forwards, and came backe againe to land in
safetie, (and)[2] [He returned] with great contentment, bringing with him good store of gold, siluer, and pearles, which
there they tooke.   For which good seruice of his, Don

---

era esforçado & belicoso, cõ esses soldados q' tinha q' eram
dozentos & nouenta, determinou de se põer neste perigo : & partio
do Doriem dõde estaua.   O primeiro de Setẽbro leuando algũs
Indios da terra por guia, atrauessou toda a terra, ora por paz, ora
por guerra, & em hũ certo senhorio q' se chama Careca, acharam
negros captiuos de cabeça reuolta, q' nũca ate entam se viram,
nem se sabe outros ategora em todas aq'llas partes da noua
Espanha, Castella do ouro, & Peru.   Ouue vista Valboa do mar
do Sul a vinte cinco dias do mes, chegou a elle dia de sam Miguel,
& por isso pos aq'lle golfam tal nome, embarcouse em certas
barcas cõtra võtade de Chipe, q' era senhor daq'la costa, que lhe
rogaua que o nã fizesse por ser perigosa, mas elle quis saber o que
era & dizer que ho nauegara : tornouse assas contente, com
muito ouro, prata, aljofre que se lá pescaua, por onde el Rey dom
Fernando lhe fez merçe & hõra.

---

[1] Wished to know what it was like, and to say that he had sailed on it.
[2] Dele.

Ferdinando the king greatly fauoured and honoured him.

This year, 1513, in the moneth of Februarie, Alfonsus de Albuquerque went fro the city of Goa [by Aden] towards the Streight of Mecha with twenty ships. They arriued at the citie of Aden and battered it, and passed forward and entred into the streight. They say that they saw a crosse in the element[1] and worshipped it. They wintered in the Island of Camaran. This was the first Portugall captaine that gaue information of those seas, and of that of Persia, being things in the world of great account.

Barros,
decad. 2, lib.
7, cap. 7.

The streight
of Mecha or
of the Red
Sea disco-
uered.

The Isle of
Camaram.

In the yeere 1514, and in the moneth of May, there went out of Saint Lucar one Pedro Arias de Auila, at the commandement of Don Ferdinando. He was the fourth gouernour of Castillia del Oro or Golden Castile, for so they named the countreyes of Dariene, Carthagena, and Vraba, and that countrey which was newly conquered [and brought under government]. He carried with him his wife the Lady Elizabeth[2] and 1500 men in seuen ships; and the king appointed Vasco Nunnez de Valboa gouernour of the South Sea and of that coast.

Pet. Martyr,
decad. 3,
cap. 5.

Neste anno & mes de Feuereiro partio Afonso dalbuquerq' da cidade de Goa pera Adē & estreito de Meca, com vinte vellas, chegados áquella cidade, deram lhe cōbate : & passados a diante entraram o estreito, & dizem q' viram no ceo hũa Cruz, a que todos adoraram : & na ylha de Camaram inuernaram, este foy o primeiro capitam Portugues que deu enformação daquelle mar & da Persia, cousas pelo mundo tam celebradas.

No anno de 1514 & mes de Mayo, partió de sam Lucas de Barramedo Pedraires dauilla, por mandado del Rey dom Fernādo quarto, gouernador de Castella douro, que assi poseram nome a esta prouincia do Dariem, Cartagena, Suraba, & aquella terra que nouamēte se conquistaua, descobria, & senhoreaua, leuou sua molher dona Isabel sete naos mil & quinhētos homēs nellas, assi

---

[1] Heavens.   [2] Isabel ?

In the beginning of the yeere 1515 the gouernour, Pedro
Arias de Auila, sent one Gaspar Morales with 150 men vnto
the Gulfe of S. Michael to discouer the Islands of Tararequi,
Chiapes, and Tumaccus.   There was a casique, Valboa's
friend, which[1] gaue him many canoas or boates made of one
tree to row in, wherein they passed vnto the Island of

pearles ; the lord whereof resisted them at their comming
on land.   But Chiapes and Tumaccus did pacifie him in
such order, that the captaine of the isle had them home vnto
his house, and made much of them, and receiued baptisme
at their hands, naming him Pedro Arias after the gouernour's
name, and he gaue vnto them for this a basket full of pearls
waying 110 pounds,[2] whereof some were as big as hasell
nuts of 20, 25, 26, or 31 carats ; (and euery carat is fower
graines.)[3] There was giuen for one of them 1200 ducats.
This Island of Tararequi standeth in 5 degrees of latitude
towards the north.

---

fez el Rey a Vasco nunoz de valboa adiantado do mar do sul & de
toda aquella banda.

Na entrada do anno de 1515 mandou o Gouernador Pedraires
dauila a Gaspar de morales cõ cento & cinquenta homẽs ao golfão
de sam Miguel buscar a ylha de Tararequi, Chiapi, & Tumugoa,
Casiquas amigos de Valboa, lhe derã muitas conoas q' sam barcos
de remo, com q' passaram a ylha das perolas, o senhor de la lhe
defendeo a desembarcaçam, mas Chiapi & Tumaco os concertaram
de maneira, que ho capitáo da ylha hos leuou a sua casa, & lhe
fez bom gasalhado, & tomou agoa de baptismo, pos se nome
Pedraires como o Gouernador, & lhe deu pera elle hum cesto de
perolas q' pesara cem marcos, em que entraua algũas dellas como
auelãas, & tinham vinte & cinco, & vinte & seis, & trinta quilates,
& deuse por esta mil & dozentos castelhanos : esta ylha de Tara-
querj está em cinco graos daltura da parte do norte.

---

[1] Chiapi and Tumagoa, caciques and friends of Valboa.
[2] 100 marcs. The marc was eight ounces.   [3] Not in Portuguese.

In this yeere 1515, in the moneth of March, the gouernour sent one Gonsaluo de Badaios with 80 soldiers to discouer new lands, and they went from Dariene to Nombre de Dios, where came vnto them one Lewis de Mercado with fiftie men more, which the gouernour sent to aide him. They determined to discouer toward the south, saying that that countrey was the richest. They tooke with them Indians to be their guides, and going along the coasts they found slaues marked with irons as the Portugals doe vse; and hauing marched a good way through the countreyes with great trauaile they gathered together much golde and fortie slaues to do them seruice : but one Casique, named Periza, did set vpon them and[1] slue and tooke the most part of them.

Pet. Martyr,
decad. 3,
cap. 10.

The gouernour hearing of these newes, the same yeere 1515, sent foorth his sonne, John Arias de Auila, to be reuenged and to discouer also by sea and by land. They went westward to Cape de Guerra, standing in little more than

Cape de
Guerra.

Neste mesmo anno de 1515 & mes de Março mandou o gouernador descobrir terra a Gonçalo de Badajoz, & deulhe oitenta soldados, partiram de Dariem, & foram a Nombre de Dios, onde chegou a elles Luis de mercado cõ cinquẽta homes mais q' o Gouernador mandaua.   Em sua ajuda assentarã descobrir da parte do Sul, por dizerem q' era terra mais rica, tomaram Indios por guias, foram ao longo daquella costa, onde viram escrauos ferrados, como nós acostumamos, depois de passarem assaz terras, & trabalhos, ajuntarã muito ouro & quarenta escrauos pera seu seruiço, o Casique palisa deu sobre elles, & tomou lhes tudo.

Sabẽdo ho gouernador esta noua no mesmo anno de 1515 mandou a vingar por seu filho Ioã ayres Dauila, & descobrir por mar & costa, (ho alcayde Gaspar despinosa, q' era passagem muy freq'ntada do Peru & Nicaraga,)[2] daqui forã ao Ponẽte ao cabo da guerra, q' está em pouco mais de seis graos da parte do norte, &

---

[1] Took them all.   [2] This line appears to be interpolated by mistake.

sixe degrees towards the north, and from thence vnto Punta
de Borica, and to Cape Blanco or the White Cape, standing
in 8 degrees and an halfe ; they discouered 250 leagues as
they affirme, and peopled the citie of Panama.

In this very yeere 1515, in the moneth of May, Alfonsus
de Albuquerque, gouernour of India, sent from the citie of
Ormuz one Fernando Gomes de Lemos as ambassadour
vnto Xec or Shaugh ·Ismael, king of Persia: and it is
declared that they trauailed in it 300 leagues, and that it is
a pleasant countrey like vnto France. This Xec or Shaugh
Ismael went on hunting and fishing for troutes, whereof
there are many. And there be the fairest women in all the
world. And so Alexander the Great affirmed when he
called them the women with golden eies. (And this yeere
this woorthy viceroy Alfonsus de Albuquerque died.)[1]

In the yeere 1516, and one hundred yeeres after the
taking of Ceuta in Barbarie, Lopez Suares being gouernour
of India, there was a dispatch made by the commandement
of the king's highnes vnto one Fernando Perez de Andrada

Marginal notes:
Punta de
Borica.
Cape
Blanco.
Panama
peopled.
Barros,
decad. 2, lib.
10, cap. 5.
Osorius, lib.
10, pag. 277.
An ambas-
sage to
Ismael king
of Persia.

---

dahi à ponta de Borica, & o cabo braço q' esta ē oito graos & meo,
descobrirão dozentas & cincoenta legoas, segundo elles deziam, &
pouvaram a cidade de Penama.

No āno mesmo de 1515 & mes de Mayo mādou Afōso Dalbuq'rq'
gouernador da India, da cidade Dormuz Fernā gomez de lemos
cō embaixada ao Xequismael senhor da Persia, & dize q' atrauessaram por ella trezētas legoas, & q' he hūa bella França, o Xequismael andaua à caça & pescaria de trutas q' hahi muitas, & as mais
fermosas molheres da redondeza, & assi o aproua ho grande
Alexandre quando dezia por ellas que as Persianas eram dor dos
olhos.

No anno de 1516 & cem anos depois da tomada de Cepta, gouernando Lopo soarez a India, despachou por mandado de S. A.
Fernā perez dandrade p'a a grā prouincia da China partio da cidade

---

[1] Not in Portuguese.

to passe to the great countrey and kingdome of China. He went from the citie of Cochin in the moneth of Aprill. They[1] received pepper, being the principal marchandise to be sold in all China of any value. And he was farther commanded by the king, Don Emmanuel, to goe also to Bengala with his letter and dispatch to a knight called John Coelo. This was the first Portugall, as farre as I know, which drunke of the water of the riuer Ganges.

Pepper a principall marchandise in China.

This yeere, 1516, died Don Fernando, king of Spaine.

In the yeere 1517, this Fernando Perez went vnto the citie of Malacha, and in the moneth of July he departed from thence towards China with eight sailes, fower Portugals, and the others Malayans. He arriued in China :[2] and because he could not come on land without an ambassage, there was one Thomas Perez which had order for it: and he went from the citie of Canton, where they came to an anker: they went by land fower hundred leagues, and came vnto the citie of *Pekin, where the king was, for this prouince and countrey is the biggest that is in the worlde. It be-

The death of Fernando, king of Spaine. Osorius, lib. ii, fol, 312. China discouered.

Canton.

---

de Cochim no mes Dabril, & esteue na ylha de Samatra, & cidade de Pacem, tomando a pimenta, por ser a principal mercadoria q' na China tem valia, & mandou daqui a el rey dō Manoel q' tambē fosse a Bengala cō sua carta & recado a hū caualeiro q' se chamaua Ioam coelho. Este foy o primeiro Portugues q' eu saiba q' bebeo agoa do rio Gange. E neste anno de 1516 faleceo el rey dō Fernando de castella.

No anno de 1517, foy Fernā perez ter á cidade de Malaca, & no mes de Iulho partio della p'a a China cō oito vellas, q'tro portuguesas, & as outras malayas. Chegado aa China, como nā pode entrar nella sem embaxada, leuaua ja hū Tome pirez pera isso. E partio da cidade de Cantam, onde elles surgirā, foy por terra quatrocentas legoas, que era a cidade de Pequim, onde el rey estaua,

---

[1] They took in a cargo of pepper at the city of Pacem in Sumatra.
[2] Taken with him for that purpose.   * Or Pakin.

ginneth at Sailana, in [19 or] 20 degrees of latitude towards
the north, and it endeth almost in fifty degrees. Which
must be 500 leagues in length : they say that it containeth
300 leagues in bredth. Fernando Perez was 14 moneths in
the Isle da Veniaga, learning as much as he could of the
[affairs of that country] countrey, according as the king, his
master, had commanded him [they being great and remark-
able]. And although one Raphael Perestrello had beene
there in a junke or barke of certaine marchants of Malaca,
yet vnto Fernando Perez there ought to be giuen the praise
of this discouerie : as well for that he had commandement
from the king, as in discouering so much with [his fleet,
and to] Thomas Perez by land, and George Mascarenhas
by sea, and for coasting vnto the citie of Foquiem, standing in 24 degrees of latitude.

In this same yeere, 1517, Charles, which afterward was
Emperour, came into Spaine, and tooke possession thereof.
And in the same yeere Francis Fernandes de Cordoua,
Christopher Morantes, and Lopez Ochoa, armed three ships,
at their owne proper charges, from the Island of Cuba.

Illha da Veniaga or Tama according to Osorius.

Foquiem.

The comming of Charles the fift into Spaine. Gomar., hist. gen., lib. 3, cap. 2.

porque esta prouincia he a mayor que se agora sabe no mūdo.
Começa dezanoue & xx. graos daltura da parte do norte, & diz q'
acaba perto de cincõeta graos ē q' auera 500 legoas de cōprido, &
q'rē q' tenhā de largo 300. & estue Fernāo pēz. xiiij. meses ē hūa
ylha q' se chama Daueniaga, enformandose das cousas daquella
terra como lhe el Rey mandaua, por serem muy grādes & notaueis,
& ainda que ja la fora Raphael perestrelo, em hum junco de mercadores de Malaca, a Fernam Perez se deue dar a palma deste
descobrimento, assi por ser por el Rey mandado, como por descobrir tanto cō armada e Thome pirez por terra & Iorge mascarenhas por mar & costa atè a cidade de Foquiem, que esta em 24
graos daltura.

Neste mesmo anno de 1517, veyo o emperador dom Carlos a
Espanha tomar posse della. No anno mesmo armou Francisco
fernādez de Cordoua, Christouam morāte, & Lopo ochea tres nauios

They had also with them a barke of Diego Velasques, who
then was gouernor. They came on land in Jucatan, stand- Jucatau.
ing in 20 degrees of latitude, at a point which they called
Punta de las Duennas ; that is to say, The point of Ladies,
which was the first place wherein they had seen temples and
buildings of lime and stone. The people here goe better
apparelled then in any other place. They haue crosses
which they worship, setting them vpon their tombes when
they be buried. Wherby it seemeth that in times past they
had in that place the faith of Christ among them. And
some say that thereabouts were the seven Cities. They The Seuen
went round about it towards the north, which is on the cities.
right hand : from whence they turned backe vnto the Island
of Cuba with some examples of gold, and men which they
had taken. And this was the first beginning of the discouerie of New Spaine.

In the yeere 1518, Lopez Suares commanded Don John Castigneda,
de Silueira to goe to the Islands of Maldiua [and kingdom 36, and 3, 7.
of Bengal] : and he made peace with them [of the islands] : ii, fol. 315,
and from thence he went to the citie of Chatigam, situated Chatigam in
Bengala.

à sua custa da ylha da Cuba, leuará mais hūa barca de Diogo
velhasquez que ja gouernaua, q' meteo nesta armada, forão tomar
terra em Hiucatas, em vinte graos daltura, em hūa ponta que
poseram nome das molheres, q' foy a primcira em que se viram
templos & edeficios de cal & pedra. He gēte milhor atauiada que
ha em neuhūa outra terra, & cruzes em q' os Indios adorauam, &
os punham sobre seus defuntos quando faleciam, donde parecia que
em algum tēpo se sentio aly a fe de Christo, por onde algūs quiseram dizer q' fossē ali as sete cidades, andará derredor della da
parte do norte, que he da mão dereita, dōde se tornaram a ylha
Cuba cō algūas mostras douro & hōmes que tomaram, & este foy o
comēço do descobrimento da noua Espanha.

No anno de 1518, mandou Lopo soarez dō Ioam da silueira ás
ylhas de Maldiua & reyno de Bengala, nas ilhas assentou pazes
com os moradores dellas, & dahi foy a cidade de Chatigam, que

on the mouth of the riuer Ganges, vnder the tropicke of Cancer. For this riuer, and the riuer Indus, which standeth an hundred leagues beyond the citie of Diu, and that of Canton in China, doe all fall into the sea vnder one parallele or latitude. And although before that time Fernan Perez had [been]¹ commanded [Coelho] to goe to Bengala [as has been said], yet notwithstanding John de Silueira ought to beare away the commendation of this discouerie; because he went as captaine generall, and remained there longest, learning the commodities of the countrey, and manners of the people.

Pet. Martyr,
decad. 4,
cap. 3.
Gomar.,
hist. gen.,
lib. 2, cap.
14, and cap.
17.
In the said yeere 1518, the first day of May, Diego Velasques, gouernour of the Island of Cuba, sent his nephew, John de Grisalua, with fower ships and two hundred soldiers, to discouer the land of Jucatan. And they founde in their way the Island *Cosumel standing towards the north in 19 degrees, and named it Santa Cruz, because they came to it the third of May. They coasted the land lying vpon the left hand of the gulfe, and came to an Island called

---

esta situada na boca do rio Gāje no tropico de Cācro porque assi este Rio como o Indo que he çem legoas alē da cidade de Dio, & o de Cantam, na China todos desembarcam num paralelo, mar & terra, & ainda que ja neste tempo tiuesse Fernam perez mandado a Bēgala o Coelho (como he dito) com tudo dom Ioão da silueira deue de leuar a palma deste descobrimento, por hir por capitam mōr, & estar la mais tempo enformādose da terra & dos costumes dos principaes della.

No anno de 1518, o primeiro dia do mes de Mayo mandou o gouernador Diogo velhasq'z que na ilha Cuba estaua, seu sobrinho Ioam de gūjaluarez com quatro nauios & dozentos soldados ao descobrimēto da terra de Hiucatam, & tomaram de caminho a ilha de Cuximel, q' está da parte do norte en dezanoue graos, & poseram lhe nome santa Cruz, por estarem nella aquelle dia, costearam esta costa à mão esquerda per hūa enseada que poseram nome Dasce-

---

¹ Dele.   * Or Acuzamil.

Ascension, because they came vnto it vpon Ascension Day. The Isle of Ascension. They went vnto the end of it, standing in 16 degrees of latitude; from whence they came backe because they could finde no place to goe out at; and from hence they went The Bay of Hunduras. round about it to another riuer, which they called the riuer of Grisalua, standing in 17 degrees of latitude; the people Rio de Grisalua. thereabout troubled them sore, yet notwithstanding they brought from thence some gold, siluer, and feathers, being there in great estimation, and so they turned backe againe to the Island of Cuba.

In the same yeere, 1518, one Francis Garay armed three Gomar., hist., gen., ships in the Isle of Jamaica at his owne charges, and went lib. 2, cap. 12, and 61. towards the point of Florida standing in 25 degrees towards the north, seeming to them to be an island most pleasant, thinking it better to people islands then the firme land, because they could best conquere them and keepe them. They went there on land, but the people of Florida killed many of them, so that they durst not inhabite it. So they sailed along the coast and came vnto the riuer of Panuco, standing Panuco. 500 leagues from the point of Florida in sailing along the

çam por la entrarem em festata manha. Foram ate a fim dela, que esta em dezaseis graos daltura, donde se tornaram por nam acharem saida: & daquy forão derredor della a outro rio que poseram nome de Gūjaluarez, q' está em dezasete graos daltura, & os della os feriram & maltratarā, com tudo trouxeram algum ouro, prata, penachos, que sam la muy estimados, & com isto se tornaram aa ylha da Cuba.

E no mesmo anno de 1518, armou Francisco garai tres nauios na ilha Jamaica á sua depesa: foy atentar a ponta da Florida q' está em vinte cinco graos da parte do norte, parecendolhes que seria ilha q' naquelle tempo mais folgauão de as descobrirem q' terra firme, porq' a podiā milhor conquistar, senhorear, & conservar: sairam em terra, os della lhe feriram & mataram muita gēte polo q' nam ousaram pouoala, & foram se ao lōgo da costa, chegarā ao Rio de Panuco, q' sam 500 legoas da pōta da Florida, nā nos deixarā

coast; but the people resisted them in euery place. Many of them also were killed in Chila, whom the saueges flaied and eate, hanging vp their skinnes in their temples in memoriall of their valiantnes. Notwithstanding all this, Francis de Garay went[1] thither, [and] the next yeere [sent], and begged the gouerment of that countrey of the emperour, because he sawe in it some shew of gold and siluer.[2]

Pet. Martyr, decad. 4, cap. 6.

In the yeere 1519, in the moneth of Februarie, Fernando Cortes went from the Island of Cuba to the land which is called Noua Spania, with eleuen ships and 550 Spanyards in them. The first place where he went on land was the Island of Cosumel [or Santa Cruz], where they immediately destroied all the idols, and set crosses on the altars and the

Gomar., hist. gen., lib. 2, cap. 18, &c.

images of the Virgine Marie [which all worshipped]. From this island they went and arriued on the firme land of Jucatan, at the point De las Duennas, or the point of Ladies,

Tauasco.

and went thence to the riuer of Tanasco, and set vpon a

Potoncian now called Victoria.

citie fast by, called Potoncian, enuironed with wood, and the houses were built with lime and stone, and couered with

---

resgatar, nē conservar em nenhũa parte: mas autes em Chily lhe ferirā & matarā gēte, & os esfolarā & comerā, & poserā as pelles no templo & sacrificio por memoria de sua valētia. Cō tudo tornou lá Francisco de Garai, & o āno seguīte mādou ao emp'ador pedir a gouernança daquella terra, por lhe parecer rica de ouro & prata.

No āno de 1519 em Feuereiro partio Fernā cortez da ylha da Cuba, por a terra a q' elle pos nome noua Espanha cō xj vellas & 550 Espanhoes nellas, & a primcira terra q' tomarā foy a terra de Coxomil, ou S. cruz, onde logo destruyrā todo los ydolos, poserā cruzes nos altares, & imagēs de nossa sñora, a q' todos adorauā. Desta ylha tomarā a terra firme de Jiucatā na ponta das molheres, ao rio de Tauasco, & derā nūa cidade q' está nelle, q' se chama Potochā cercada de madeira, & as casas de cal & pedra, cubertas de ladrilho: pelejaram cō grāde aperto, aparaceolhes o señor Santiago

---

[1] Returned.   [2] Because it appeared to him rich in gold and silver.

tile : they fought there egarly ; and there appeered vnto
them S. James on horsebacke, which increased their courage.
They called that citie Victoria ; and they were the first
people which were subdued to the Spanyards' obedience in
all Newe Spaine. From hence they went discouering the
coast till they came vnto a place named S. John d'Vllhua, dis- _{St. John de Vllhua.}
tant, as they said, from Mexico, where the king of Mute-
çuma was, sixty or seventy leagues : and there was a seruant
of his that gouerned that prouince, named Tendilli, which
gaue them good entertainment, although they vnderstood
not one another. But Cortes had twenty women,[1] whereof one
was called Marine, borne in that countrey : they were the
first that were baptized in New Spaine. And from that
time forward Marine and Aguilar served as interpreters.
Tendilli presently gaue knowledge of this vnto Muteçuma,
that a kinde of bearded people were arriued in his countrey;
for so they called the Castillians. But he was troubled vpon
that newes : for his gods (which are to be thought to be
diuels), had told him, that such people as the Spanyards

---

encima dū caualo, q' lhes dobrou o esforço, & poseram nome a
esta cidade a Vitoria, foram os primeiros vassallos q' o Emperador
teue na noua Espanha.

Daqui forā pela costa descobrindo ate onde se chama S. Ioā
dalua, dōde dizē q' auera de Mexico, 60 ou 70 legoas onde estaua
el rey Matacumací, & gouernaua por elle hū seu criado q' se chamaua Teudali, q' lhe fez bō gasalhado, inda q' senā entenderā senā
leuara Fernā cortez xx molheres, & hūa dellas q' se chamaua
Marina, era de dētro da q'la terra. Fora as primeiras q' receberā
agoa de batismo na noua Espana, & dali por diante Marina, &
Aguilar seruiram de lingoa : & logo Thedelim fez a saber a Matecuma como a gente Barbada, q' assi chamauam aos Castelhanos,
era ali aportada, de que lhe pesou muito, por lhe terem dito os
seus deoses que os tais homēs como aquelles auiam de destruir

---

[1] Although they would not have understood each other, but that
Cortez had with him twenty women, etc.

were should destroy his law and countrey, and be Lords thereof. And therefore he sent gifts vnto Cortes, in value twenty thousand ducats, but would not come to him.

Because S. John de Vllhua was then no place for a nauie to ride in, Cortes sent Francis de Monteio, and the pilot Antonie Alaminos, in two brigadines to discouer that coast, who came to a[1] place where they might ride without danger.

Gomara, historiæ gener., lib. 2, cap. 21, 22, 23, 24. They came to Panuco, standing in 23^2 degrees northward: from whence they came backe vpon an agreement to goe vnto Culuacan, being an hauen of more safetie. They set saile [and went westward], but Cortes went by land westward with the most part of his men on horsebacke, and they

Zempoallan. came vnto a citie called Zempoallan, where they were well receiued. And from thence he went to another towne called

Chianitzlan. Chianitzlan, with the lord of which towne, as with all the countrey besides, he made league to be against Muteçuma. And when he knew that his ships were come, he went vnto

Villa rica de la vera Cruz. them, and there builded a towne, and called it Villa rica de la vera cruz. From whence he sent vnto Charles the empe-

---

sua ley, & terra, & seuhoreala, & por ysso mandou peças a Fernam cortez q' valiam vinte mil cruzados, escusando se de se ver com elle.

Como sam Iohão dalua nam era porto pera estar a armada, mandou Fernam cortez a Francisco de Montejo, & ao piloto Antam de Laminos em dous bargantīs, q' descobrissem aquela costa ate topar sitio onde podesem estar sem perigo. Foram ate Panuco q' está da parte do norte em xxij graos daltura, dōde se tornaram cō acordo se passarse a Culuacā, q' he porto de milhar abrigo. E dada á vella se partiram contra o Ponente, & Cortez por terra com a mais da gente & caualos, & chegaram a hūa cidade q' se chama Leopolão, foy bem recebido. E dahi a outra q' se chama Chesuilam, & com estes & toda a comarca assentou liga contra Matecuma, & sabendo que as naos eram chegadas, foyse a ellas, & fundon ali

---

[1] And find a place.   [2] 22 ?

rour a present [and his fifths], and made report of all that
he had done, and how he determined to goe to Mexico, and
to visite Muteçuma: and besought the emperour to giue
him the gouernment of that countrey. And because his
people should not rise in mutinie, as they began, he destroied all his ships.

Cortez presently went from Villa rica de la vera Cruz,
leauing there 150 Spanish horsemen,[1] and many Indians to
serue them; and the villages round about (became)[2] his friends
[and allies]. He went vnto the citie of [Heopolam, now called
Zeopolam] Zempoallan: there he heard news that Francis
Garay was on the coast with fower ships to come on land:[3] and
by subtiltie he got nine of his men; of whom he vnderstood, Gomara,
that Garay had beene in Florida, and came vnto the riuer historiæ
Panuco, where he got some golde, determining to stay general. lib.
there in a towne which is now called Almeria. 2, cap. 61.

Cortez ouerthrew the idols in Zempoallan, and the tombes Gomar.,
of their kings, whome they worshipped as gods, and tolde hist. gen.,
lib. 2, cap.
25.

hūa villa, a q' pos nome Rica de vera cruz, donde maudou ao Emperador presente & seus quintos, & darem lhe conta do que passaua, & como determinaua dhir a Mexico a ver se com Mantacu-
macim, q' lhe fizesse merce da gouernaça, & por se nã amotinar
agēte, como ja começaua, deu cos nauios á costa.

Partio logo Fernam cortez da villa Rica da vera Cruz, deixando nella cento & cincoenta castelhanos, dous caualos, &
muitos Indios de seruiço, & pouos derredor, seus amigos & aliados.
E elle se foy à cidade de Heopolam, que se agora chama Zeopolam,
onde lhe deram noua q' audaua pella costa Francisco de Garai,
com quatro nauios pera tomar terra, & per manhas & cilladas ouue
delles noue homēs, de q̄ soube como Garai fora aa Florida, &
tocara o rio Pamuco, onde resgatara ouro, cõ tudo leuaua determi-
nado de se assentar, onde se agora chama Almeria.

Cortez em Zeopolam fez derribar os ydolos & os sepulchros dos

---

[1] 150 Spaniards, two horses, and etc.   [2] Not in Portuguese.
[3] Seeking to land.

them that they were to worship the true God. From thence
he went toward Mexico the 16 day of August 1519, and
trauailed three daies iourney [without guides] and came to
the citie of Zalapan, and to another beyond it named Sicuchimatl, where they were well receiued, and offered to be
conducted to Mexico, because Muteçuma had giuen such
commandement. Beyond this place he passed with his companie a certaine hill of three leagues high,[1] wherein there
were vines. (In another place they found aboue a thousand
loades of wood ready cut) ;[2] and beyond they met with a
plaine countrey, and in going through the same, he named
it Nombre de Dios. At the bottome of the mountaine he
rested in a towne called Teubixuacan, and from thence they
went through a desolate countrey, and so came to another
mountaine that was very colde and full of snow, and they
lay in a towne named Zaclotan. And so from towne to
towne they were well receiued and feasted until they came
into another realme named Tlaxcallan, which waged warre
against Muteçuma, and being valiant they skirmished with

Marginal notes:
Zalapan.
Sicuchimatl.

Zaclotan.

Tlaxcallan.

senhores, q' tambem reuerenciauam como a deoses, & adorar ao
Senhor de tudo, partio pera Mexico a xvj Dagosto, caminharam
tres jornados sem guias, chegaram a cidade de Colopam, & outra
mais adiante que se chama Sepochimaco, donde foram bem recebidos, & se offereceram de os leuarem a Mexico, por o Matacuma ter
assi mandado.

Passado hũas serras de tres legoas, em q' auia aruores cõ mil
parreiras duuas, & da outra banda era a terra chãa, & ao passo
desta terra por ser a primeira poseram lhe nome Nõbre de
Dios, & no fundo de serra se aposeutarão em hũa villa que se
chama Tenixuacam, & daly andaram tres dias por terra despouada,
& forã ter a outro serra muy fria & neuada, & pousarão em hũa vila
que se diz Zacotam, & dũ lugar em outro foram bẽ recebidos & agasa-
lhados, ate entrarem em o reyno de Trascalam, que tinha guerra com

---

[1] Three leagues of hills were passed, where there were trees and thou-
sands of grape vines.
[2] Dele.

Cortes ; but in the end they agreed and entred into league
with him against the Mexicans ; and so they went from
countrey to countrey till they came within sight of Mexico.
The king Muteçuma fearing them, gaue them good entertainment, with lodging and all things necessarie : and they
were with this for a time contented : but mistrusting that
he and his should be slaine, he tooke Muteçuma pri- Muteçuma prisoner.
soner, and brought him to his lodging with good garde.
Cortes (demanded how farre his realme did extend, and
sought to know the mines of gold and siluer that were in it,
and how many kings, neighbours to Muteçuma, dwelled
therein, requiring certaine Indians to be informed thereof,
whereof he had eight prouided) :[1] and he [Cortes] ioined to
them eight Spanyards, and sent them two and two into fower
countreyes, namely, into Zuçolla, Malinaltepec, Tenich, and Zuçolla. Malinal-
Tututepec. They which went vnto Zuçolla went 80 leagues : tepec. Zenich. Tututepec.

Matacuma. E como presumiam de valentes, pelejaram cō Fernam
Cortez & suas gentes : & por fim de tudo ficaram amigos & aliados
contra os Mexicanos. E assi forā de terra em terra, & pouco em pouco
descobrindo ate a cidade de Mexico. El rey de Matacuma como os
temia fez lhe bō gasalhado, mādandoos aposentar & darlhe todo o
necessario : estiuerā assi algūs dias cōtentes. Mas como Fernam
cortez se arreceasse de os matarem, prendeo a Matacuma & leuouo
a sua casa & o pos a bom recado.

Desejou Fernam cortez saber camanho este reyno era contra o
ocidente, & o mar gue chamam do sul, & as minas d'ouro & prata
q' nella auia, & os Reys vezinhos que contra aquella parte Matacuma tinha, pera que pedio que lhe dessem algūs Indios q' sou-
bessem dar disso boa conta, elle mandou logo fazer prestes oyto,
& Cortez outros tātos Espanhoes, & de dous em dous se foram a
quatro prouincias que sam, Zocalam, Malinaltepec, Tenih, Tutipec.
Os que foram a Zocalam andarā oytēta legoas que ha de Mexico a

[1] Dele. Desired to learn the extent of this kingdom towards the west,
and how far it was to the South Sea, he therefore begged Montezuma to
provide some Indians who might be able to give this information, and
he immediately ordered eight to be got ready.

for so much it was from Mexico thither. They which went to Malinaltepec went 70[1] leagues, seeing goodly countries, and brought examples of gold, which the naturals of the countrey tooke out of great riuers :[2] and all this prouince belonged vnto Muteçuma.

The countrey of Tenich and vp the river were not subiect to Muteçuma, but had warre with him, and would not suffer the Mexicans to enter into their territorie [but gave them samples of gold taken from the river]. They sent ambassadors vnto Cortes with presents, offering him their estates, and amitie, whereof Muteçuma was nothing glad. They which went to Tututepec, standing neere the South sea, did also bring with them examples of gold, and praised the pleasantnes of the countrey [as a dwelling place], (and the multitude of good harbours vpon that coast, shewing)[3] [Montezuma ordered that houses should be built for the Spaniards. Cortez inquired of him whether on the sea coast there were any harbours in which ships could lie securely. He replied that he did not know, but would ask : and he shewed] to Cortes a cloth of cotton wooll all wouen with goodly workes,

---

elle, & os q' foram a Malinaltepec, andaram setecentas, viram boa terra, & trouxerão mostras d'ouro, que os naturaes tiram dũ gram rio q' passa por ella, tudo isto he da Matacuma.

Tenis & Epolo rio acima, nam obedecião a Matacuma, mas antes tinham com elle guerra, & nam deixarã entrar os Mexicanos, & deranlhes mostras douro que no rio tiraram, & mandaram embaixadores a Fernam Cortez cõ presentes, offerecendolhe seu estado & amizade, de que Matacuma nam folgou nada. Os que foram a Tutipec, que está jūto do mar, tambē trouxeram mostras douro, dizendo que a terra era boa pera fazer nella assento. Matacuma mandou logo fazer casas & aposentos pera os Castelhanos estarem nellas. Pergūtoulhe Fernam Cortez se naquella costa do mar auia portos em que podessem as naos estar seguras, disse que nam sabia, mas que logo pergūtaria, & amostroulhe hum pano dalgodão

---

[1] 700 ?   [2] A great river which flowed through it.   [3] Dele.

wherein all the coast with the hauens and creekes were set
foorth.   But this thing then (could not be prosecuted)[1] by _{Gomara,}
reason of the comming of Pamphilus de Naruaez into the _{lib. 2,cap.48.}
countrey, who set all the kingdome of Mexico in an vp- _{de Naruaez.}
rore.

In this yeere 1519, the tenth day of August, one Fernande
de Magallanes departed from Siuill with fiue ships toward _{Gomara,}
the Islands of Maluco : he went along the coast of Brasill _{lib. 4, cap. 2.}
till he came vnto the riuer of Plate, which the Castillians
had before discouered.   From thence therefore he began his _{The discoue-}
discouerie, and came vnto an hauen which he called The _{lanes from}
Porte of Saint Julian, standing in 49 degrees, and there he _{ward.}
entred and wintred : they endured much cold by reason of
snow and ice : the people of that countrey they found to be
of great stature, and of great strength, taking men by the
legs and renting them in the middest as easily as one of vs
will rend an hen : they live by fruits and hunting.   They
called them Patagones, but the Brasilians doe call them _{Palagones.}
Morcas.

---

todo texido de debuxo, em questaua toda a costa, portos & enseadas, esta obra polla vinda de Pamphilo de Narbais & reuoltas de
Mexico.

Neste mesmo anno de 1519 a dez de Agosto partio Fernam de
magalhães de Seuilla com cinco vellas pera as ilhas de Maluco, foy
costeando a costa do Brazil ate ho Rio da Prata, que era ja descuberto por parte de Castella, da qui por diãte fez o Magalhães seu
descobrimento, & chegado a hum rio que pos nome de sam Juliam
que està em corenta & noue graos, meteose dentro, onde enuerna-
ram, passaram grande frio pollas neues & geadas que avia muitas :
os homẽs daquella terra dizem q' sam de grande estatura & força,
& que tomão outro qualquer pellas pernas & quebram pello meio
como se fosse bũa galinha, mantẽse de caça & fruta, poseran lhe
nome os Patagones, & os Brazis, lhe chamão Morcas.

---

[1] Not in Portuguese, but necessary to make sense.

In the yeere 1520, in the beginning of the moneth of September, growing then somewhat temperate, they went out of the port and riuer of St. Julian, having lost in it one of their ships, and with the other fower he came vnto the streights named after the name of Magallanes standing in 52 degrees and a halfe. From thence one of the ships returned backe vnto Castile, whereof was captaine and pilot one Stephen de Porto, a Portugall, and the other three went forward, entring into a mightie sea called Pacificum, without seeing any inhabited land till they came in 13 degrees towards the north of the Equinoctiall : in which latitude they came vnto islands

Los Jardines.

which they called Los Jardines, and from thence they sailed to the Archipelagus of S. Lazarus, and in one of the islands

Gomara, hist. gen., lib. 4, cap. 3.

called-[Sebu, the principal island] Matan[1] Magallanes was slaine, and his ship was burnt, and the other two went vnto Borneo, and so from place to place they went backe vntill

Pet. Martyr, decad. 5, cap. 7.

they came to the Islands of Malucos, leauing many others discouered, which I rehearse not,[2] because I finde not this voiage exactly written.

No anno de 1520 & entrada do mes de Setembro, que começa o veram naquella terra, sairam do rio tendo ja hum nauio perdido, com os quatro chegaram ao estreito que chamão do Magalhães, que està em cincõeta & dous graos & meio, donde se tornou hũa nao pera Castella, de que era capitam & piloto Esteuão gomez do porto Portugues, com as tres forão seu caminho por hũ grande mar ermo, a q' chamaram pacifico, sem verẽ terra nẽ ilha pouoada ate treze graos daltura da parte do norte, que fora ter ás ilhas pouoadas, a que poseram nome dos prazeres, & dahi ao Archipeligo de são Lazaro, & em hũa ylha que se diz Sebu, & nata, foy ho Magalhães morto & sua nao queymada as outras duas forã a Borneo, & dahy a Midanao & de pedra ẽ pedra ás ilhas do crauo, deixãdo outras muitas descubertas q' nã aponto, por auer muytos escritores deste caminho.

---

[1] Not in Portuguese. [2] As many have written about them.

About this time [it is said] Pope Leo the tenth sent one Gomar., lib. 4, cap. 17. Paulus Centurio as ambassadour to the great Duke of Mos- Ramusius, 1 vol., fol. couie to wish him to send into India an armie along the 374. coast of Tartarie. And by the reasons of this ambassadour the said duke was almost persuaded vnto that action, if other inconueniences had not letted him.

In this same yeere 1520, in Februarie, Diego Lopes de Sequeira, a gouernour of India, went towards the Streight of Mecha, and carried with him the ambassadour of Presbyter John, and Roderigo de Lima, who also went as ambassadour to him. They came vnto the Island of Maçua, standing in Maçua. the Red sea on the side of Africa, in 17 degrees toward the north; where he set the ambassadours on land, with the Portugals that should goe with them. Peter de Couillan had beene there before, being sent thither by king John the Ramusius, 1 vol., fol. second of Portugall: but yet Francis Aluarez gaue princi- 190. pall light and knowledge of that countrey.

In the yeere 1520, the licenciate Lucas Vasques de Gomara, hist. gen., Aillon and other inhabitants of S. Domingo furnished two lib. 2, cap. 7.

Neste mesmo tempo dizem que o Papa Liam decimo mandou miser Paulo Sinturiam cõ embaixada ao gram duq' Moscouia ho prouocara q' enuiasse á India armada ao longo da costa da Tartaria, tais rezões lhes daua q' o mouia a isso se o não estoruara algũs incõuenientes q' auia.

Neste mesmo anno de 1520 em o mes de Feuereiro, partio Diogo lopez de Sequeira gouernador da India pera o estreito de Meca, leuã do consigo o embaixador do Preste: & de Rodrigo de lima que hya tambē com embaixada, chegaram á ilha de Masua, que está da bãda Dafrica da parte do norte em dezasete graos, poseram os embaixadores em terra com os Portugueses que auiam de hir com elles, ainda q' ja la fora Pero de couilhãa, que el Rey dom Joham ho segundo mandara, mas com tudo Francisco Aluarez nos deu enformaçam daquella terra, pollo que escreueo della.

Neste anno de 1520 ho lecenceado vasco de Seilam, & outros vesinhos de sam Domingos, armaram dous nauios q' mandaram ás

ships, and sent them to the Isles of Lucayos to get slaves,
and finding none they passed along by the firme land beyond Florida vnto certaine countreyes called Chicora[1] and
Gualdapé, vnto the riuer Jordan and the Cape of Saint
Helena standing in 32 degrees toward the north. They of
the countrey camé downe to the sea side to see the ships, as
hauing neuer before seene the like : the Spanyards went on
land, where they received good entertainment, and had given
vnto them such things as they lacked. But they brought[2]
many of them into ther ships and then set saile and brought
them away for slaves: but in the way one of their ships
sunke, and the other was also in great hazard. By this
newes the Licentiate Aillon, knowing the wealth of the
countrey,[3] begged the gouernment thereof of the emperour,
and it was giuen him: whither he went to get money to pay
his debt.

About this time Diego Velasquez, gouernour of Cuba,
hearing the good successe of Cortes, and that he had begged

Marginal notes: Chicora. Gualdepé. Gomara, hist. gen., lib. 2, cap. 4, 8.

---

ilhas dos Lucayos tomar escrauos, & como os nam acharam, passaram à terra firme acima da Florida, onde se chama Chiapa, &
Gualdapè, ou rio Jordão, & cabo de S. Elena, q' està da parte do
Norte ē 32 graos, os da terra acodiram à praya ver os nauios, como
quē nunca os vira, os Castelhanos saltaram em terra, onde lhes
fizeram bõ gasalhado, & lhes deram de graça o necessario. Foram
muitos aas naos conuidados, derã às vellas trouxeram nos por
escrauos, & no caminho se foy hũa nao ao fundo, os q' na outra
escaparam passarã cõ trabalho. O Licēceado como la visse ouro,
prata, & aljofre, pedio ao Emperador aq' la gouernança, onde
tornou p'a pagar o q' deuia.

Neste tempo sabendo Diogo Vasquez, q' gouernaua a Cuba, q'
Cortez andaua prospero, & pedia a capitania da noua Espanha, q'
elle tinha por sua, mandou la hũa armada de dezoito velas, & mil

---

[1] Chiapa.   [2] Invited.
[3] The Licentiate; as he had seen there, gold, silver, and seed pearls.

the gouernment of New Spaine, which he held to be his, he furnished out thither against Cortes 18 ships, with 1000 men and 80 horses, whereof he sent as Generall one Pamphilus de Naruaez. He came vnto the towne called Villa rica de la vera Cruz, where he tooke land, and commanded those of the countrey to receiue him as gouernour thereof. But they tooke his messenger prisoner, and sent him to Mexico, where Cortes was. Which thing being knowne of Cortes, he wrote letters vnto Naruaez not to raise any vprore in the countrey which he had discouered, offering him obedience if he had any commission from the Emperour; but he corrupted the people of the countrey with money.[1] Whereupon Cortes went from Mexico and tooke Naruaez prisoner in the towne of Zampoallan, and put out one of his eies.

Naruaez being thus taken prisoner, his armie submitted themselues to Cortes, and obeied him. Whereupon presently he dispatched 200 soldiers vnto the riuer of Garay, and he sent John Vasquez de Leon with other two hundred vnto Cosaalco, and withall sent a Spanyard with the newes of his victorie vnto Mexico. But the Indians being in the meane time risen, hurt the messenger; which being knowne to

The revolt of the Mexicans in absence of Cortes.

homēs, & oitenta cauallos nellas, & por capitam mòr Pamphilo de Narbais, foy se aa villa Rica da vera Cruz, onde tomou terra, & mandou dizer q' o recebessem por gouernador della: prenderam os messageiros, & mandaram nos a Cortez a Mexico. Sabendo isto escreueo a Narbais q' nam amotinasse a terra que le tinha descuberta, que se elle tinha prouisam do Emperador, que lhe obe-deceria, com isto dizem que lhe mandou sobornar a gente com dinheiro : sahio do Mexico, & o prendeo na villa de Sempucol, quebrando lhe hum olho.

Como Narbais foy preso, os de seu exercito se entregaram a Cortez & lhe obedeceram, despachou logo dezētos Espanhoes ao rio Garai, Joam vasquez de Liam cō outros tantos a Cofoalco, & hum Castelhano com noua de sua victoria a Mexico : mas os Indios

---

[1] It may be read that Cortes sent to corrupt the troops of Narvaez.

Cortes, he mustered his men, and found a thousand footemen and two hundred horsemen, with the which he went
towards Mexico, where he found Peter de Aluarado and the
rest which he had left there aliue and in safetie, wherewith
he was greatly pleased, and Muteçuma made much of him.
But yet the Mexicans ceased not, but made warre against
him; and the warre grew so hot that they killed their king,

Muteçuma
slaine.

Muteçuma, with a stone; and then there rose vp another
king, such an one as pleased them, till such time as they
might put the Spanyards out of the citie, being no more than

Gomara,
hist. gen.,
lib. 2, cap.
50.

504 footemen and fortie horsemen.   The Spanyards with
great losse being driuen out of Mexico, retired themselues
with much adoe to Tlaxcallan, where they were well receiued; and so they gathered together 900 Spanyards, 80
horsemen, and two hundred thousand Indians, their friends
and allies: and so they went backe againe to take Mexico in
the moneth of August in the yeere 1521.

Gomar.,
hist. gen.,
lib. 2, cap.
60.

Cortes obtaining still more and more victories, determined
to see further within the countrey; and for this purpose, in
the yeere 1521, and in October, he sent out one Gonzalo de
Sandoual, with 200 footemen and 35 horsemen, and certaine

---

como ja estauā aleuantados o feriram.   Sabēdo Cortez isto, fez
alardo, achou mil de pè, & dozentos de caualo, com que foy a
Mexico, & achou Pero Daluarado, & os que la deixara viuos &
sāos, de q' teue gram contentamento.   Matecuma lhe fez bom
gasalhado, cō tudo os Mexicanos nam deixarā de lhes fazer a
guerra, & tam crua q' lhes mataram seu Rey Matacuma de hūa
pedrada, & aleuantaram outro a elles mais aceito, ate deytarem os
Castelhanos da cidade, que nam eram mais jaa de quinhentos &
quatro de pe, & quarenta de cauallo, & assi desbaratados foram a
Tascalam, dōde os receberão, & se fizerā noue centos Espanhoes,
oitenta de cauallo, & dozentos mil Indios, amigos & aliados, tornaram a tomar Mexico no mes Dagosto, anno de 1521.
    Vēdose Fernam cortez vitorioso & pacifico determinou de desco-
brir pola terra dentro, & pera isso neste anno de 1521 em o mes

Indians his friends vnto Tochtepec and Coazacoalco, which Tochtepec Coaza-
had rebelled, but at length yeelded. And they discouered coalco.
the countrey, and built a towne 120 leagues from Mexico,
and named it Medelin, and another towne they made, naming
it Santo Spirito, fower leagues from the sea vpon a riuer ; and
these two townes kept the whole countrey in obedience.

This yeere 1521, in December, Emmanuell king of Portu- Emmanuels death.
gall died, and after him his sonne, king John the 3, reigned. Osorius, lib. 12, fol. 366.
In the yeere 1521 there went from Maluco one of Gomara, historiæ
Magellans ships laden with cloues [Captain and pilot John general. lib. 4, cap. 8.
Sebastian del Cano]: they victualled themselves in the
Island of Burro [which is in 24 degrees south latitude, and Burro.
passed between Vitara and Malua, which are in 8 degrees],
and from thence went to Timor, which standeth in 11 degrees Timor.
of southerly latitude. Beyond this Island one hundred
leagues they discouered certaine Islands under the Tro-
pic of Capricorn [and further on others. All are peopled
thenceforward : nor did they see land (without inhabitants),[1]

---

d'outubro, mandou Gonçalo de sandoual com dozentos piães &
trinta & cinco de caualo & muytos Indios amigos ate Antepec,
Cosoalco q' se reuelaram, os quaes renderam aquella terra, & a
descobriram & fizeram hũa villa de cento & vinte legoas de Mexico
q' se chama Medelim, & assi outra do Spiritu Sancto, quatro legoas
do mar ao longo de hũa ribeira, com as quaes pacificaram por ali tudo.

Neste mesmo anno no mes. de Dezembro faleceo el rey dom
Manoel, & socedeo dom João o terceiro seu filho.

No anno de 1521 partio de Maluco hũa das naos pera Castella,
em q' o Magalhães fora carregada de crauo, capitã & piloto della
Joam Sebastiam del cano. Foram tomar mantimento aa ilhã de
Burro q' estaa em vinte quatro graos daltura da parte do Sul, passaram por antre Vitara & Malua, que estam em oyto graos : & dahi
foram a Thimor q' estaa em onze, alē delle cem legoas, descobriram hũas ylhas diante outras debaxo do Tropico de Capricornio.
Todas sam pouoadas daqui por diate : nam sey terra que vissem

---

[1] Dele.

except it might be some islet, up to the Cape of Good Hope, where it is said they took in wood and water] (one named Ende, finding the places from thenceforward peopled. Afterward passing without Samatra they met with no land till they fell with the Cape of Bona Sperança, where they tooke in fresh water and wood).[1] So they came by the Islands of Cape Verde, and from thence to Siuill, where they were notably receiued, as well for the cloues that they brought, as that they had compassed about the world.

Gomara,
hist. gen.,
lib. 6, cap. 4. In the yeere 1522, in Januarie, one Gilgonzales armed fower ships in the Island of Tararequi, standing in the South sea, with intent to discouer the coast of Nicaragua, and especially a streight or passage from the South sea into the North sea. And sailing along the coast he came vnto an hauen called S. Vincent, and there landed with 100 Spanyards and certaine horsemen, and went within the land 200 leagues; and he brought with him 200 [thousand] pesoes of gold [although not of fine quality], and so came backe againe to S. Vincent, where he found his pilot, Andrew Nigno, who Tecoante-
pec. was as far as Tecoantepec,[2] in 16 degrees to the north, and had

---

ate o Cabo de boa esperança senam algũa ylheta sem gente : onde diz que tomaram agoa & lenha. E ao lõgo daquella costa vieram aas ylhas do Cabo verde, & dahi aa cidade de Seuilha, onde foram com grande aluoroço recebidos, assi pello crauo que traziam, como por darem hũa volta ao mundo.

No ãno de 1522 & mes de Janeiro, foram ao descobrimento de Nocaraga, & buscar o estreito que diz que passaua da outra banda, Gil gonçaluez Dauila em quatro nauios que diz q' armara na ylha de Tararequi. Yndo assi ao longo da terra, sayo em hum Porto que se chama Sam Vicente, com cem Espanhoes & certos cauallos, entrou pella terra dentro dozentas legoas, & trouxe dozentos mil pesos douro, ainda que baxo. Tornado a sam Vicente, achou ahi ho seu piloto Andre Minho, que dezia que chegara ate Teantepé,

---

[1] Dele   [2] Who said he had reached Teantepé.

sailed three hundred leagues, from whence they returned to Gomara, historiæ general. lib. 6, cap. 12 Panama, and so (ouer land)[1] to Hispaniola.

In the same yeere 1522, in the moneth of Aprill, the Castagneda Historia delle Indie Orientali, lib. 6, cap. 41. other ship of Magallanes (called The Trinitie)[2] went from the Island of Tidoré, wherein was captaine Gonzalo Gomez de Espinosa, shaping their course toward Noua Spania : and Gomar. hist. gen., lib. 4, cap. 8 & 12. because winde was scant they stirred toward the northeast into 16[3] degrees, where they found two islands, and named Two Islands in 16 degrees of northerly latitude. them the Isles of Saint John, and in that course they came to another island in 20 degrees, which they named La Griega, where the simple people came into their ships, of whom they kept some to shew them in Noua Spania. They were in this course fower monthes, vntill they came into 42 degrees of northerly latitude, where they did see sea 42 degrees of northerly latitude. fishes called seales and tunies. And the climate (seemed vnto them, comming newly out of the heat to be)[4] [was] so cold and vntemperate, that they could not well abide it, and therefore they turned backe againe to Tidoré[5] being there-unto enforced also by contrarie windes.[6] [Notwithstanding] these were the first Spanyards which had beene in so high a

---

que estaa em dezaseys graos da parte do Norte, & nauegara tre-zentas legoas : dali se tornaram a Penama, onde foram aa ylha Espanhola.

Neste mesmo anno de 1522 & mes Dabril, partio a outra nao que com o Magalhães fora da ylha de Tidore, capitam della Gon-çalo gomez despinosa na volta da noua Espanha, por escassear o vento, gouernaram ao Nordeste em trinta & seis graos da parte do norte, duas ilhas a que poseram nome de sam Joam, & polo mesmo rumo foram ter a outra em vinte graos, q' se chama a Grega, a gente della como innocente. se veyo meter na nao, & tomaram algūs pera leuar damostra aa noua Espanha. Forão quatro meses nesta volta, ate se poerem em quarenta & dous graos, onde viram

---

[1] Not in Portuguese.
[3] Thirty-six degrees north latitude.
[5] Maluco.

[2] Not in Portuguese.
[4] Not in Portuguese.
[6] By the wind failing.

latitude toward the north [on that side]. And there they found one Antonie de Britto building a fortresse (which tooke from them their goods, and sent forty-eight of them prisoners to Malaca).[1]

Gomar.,
hist. gen.,
lib. 6, cap. 12. In this yeere 1522, Cortes desirous to haue some hauens on the South Sea, and to discouer the coast of Noua Spania on that side, whereof he had knowledge in Muteçuma his time, bicause he thought by that way to bring the drugs from Maluco and Banda, and the spicerie from Jaua, with lesse trauaile and danger, he sent fower Spaniards with their guides to Tecoantepec, Quahutemallan, and other hauens, where they were wel received, and brought some of the people with them to Mexico. And Cortes made much of them [and made them presents which contented them] ; and

The South
Sea first
searched
by Cortes
his pilots. afterwards sent ten pilots[2] thither to search the seas thereabout. They went seventy leagues in the sea,[3] but found

---

lobos marinhos, & toninhas, & era o clima tam frio & destemperado, que se nam podia sostentar nella, pello que tornaram arribar a Maluco, com tudo forã os primeiros Espanhoes que se poseram daquela banda em tam grande altura : & quando tornaram a Maluco, acharam ja neste anno Antonio de Brito fazendo fortaleza.

Neste anno de 1522 desejoso ho Cortez ter terras & portos no mar do Sul, pera descobrir por aly a costa da noua Espanha, de que tinha noticia em vida de Matecuma : & tam bē lhe parecia que trazia por ali as drogas de Maluco, Banda, & especearias da Jaoa com menos trabalho & perigo, mandou la quatro Castelhanos com suas guias a Thoantepè, & a Cotomolam, & a outros portos de que foram bem recebidos, trouxeram homēs que os guiaram a Mexico. Fernam Cortez lhes fez bom gasalhado, & deulhes peças que os contentaram. Depois disso mandou la dez pilotos & guias da terra que os leuaram aa prouincia de Teantepee, & Chicoalco, que se

---

[1] Not in Portuguese.

[2] And guides, that they might examine the province of Zeantepec and Chicoolto, which is now called Joam d'alua.

[3] By sea and land.

no hauen. One Cassique or Lord, called Cuchataquir, vsed them well, and sent with them to Cortes two hundred of his men with a present of gold and siluer, and other things of the country; and they of Tecoantepec did the like [whom Cortez received with honour]; and not long after, this Casique sent for aide to Cortes against his neighbours which did warre against him.

In the yeere 1523 [in the month of March] Cortes sent vnto him for his aide Peter de Aluarado, with two hundred soldiers, footemen, and fortie horsemen, and the Caciques of Tecoantepec and Quahutemallan asked them [for Cortez and] for the monsters of the sea which came thither the yeere past, meaning the ships of Gil Gonsales de Auila, being greatly amazed at the sight of them, and woondring much more when they heard that Cortes had bigger then those; and they painted vnto them a mightie carake with (sixe)[1] masts, and sailes and shroudes, and men armed on

Marginal notes: Tecoantepec. Gomara, hist. gen., lib. 6, cap. 12. A wittie stratagem.

agora diz Joam dalua. Andaram setenta legoas por mar do Sul & costa, sem acharem porto nem fundo, senam hum Cacique que se chamaua Chuchelaquir, que lhes fez bom gasalhado: & mandou com elles dozētos caualeiros com hum presente douro & prata, & doutras cousas que auia na terra, & assi o fezeram os de Toantepe, a que Fernam cortez fez assaz honra: & nam tardou muito que lhe nam mandaram pedir socorro pera contra seus vezinhos que os guerreauam.

No anno de mil & quinhentos & vinte & tres, & mes de Março, mandou la ho Cortez em sua ajuda a Pero Daluarado com dozentos soldados, quarenta de cauallo, ao senhor de Toantepee, & Catamalum, & lhes perguntaram por Cortez, & por os monstruos marinhos que ho anno passado aly chegaram, que eram os Nauios de Gil Gonçaluez Dauila, de que estauam muy espantados, & muito mais foram de lhe dizerē que Fernam Cortez os tinha mayores, & lhes debuxaram hūa Carraca com mastos, & vellas, & enxarcias,

---

[1] Not in Portuguese.

horsebacke.   This Aluarado [was well received and] went
Saut Iago
built. through the countrey and builded there the city of Sant Jago
or Saint James, and a towne which he called Segura, leauing
certaine of his people in it [to hold possession of the
country].

Castagneda
hist. delle
Indie Orien-
tali, lib. 6,
cap. 42. In the same yeere, 1523, in the moneth of May, Antonie
de Britto being captain of the Isles of Maluco, sent his
cosen, Simon de Bren, to learn the way by the Isle of
Borneo to Malaca.   They came in sight of the Islands of
Manada.
Panguen-
sara.
The Islands
of S.Michael. Manada and Panguensara; they went through the straight
of[1] Treminao and Taquy, and to the Islands of Saint Michael
standing in seven degrees, and from thence discouered[2] the
Borneo.
Pedra
Branca. Islands of Borneo, and had sight of Pedra Branca, or the
white stone, and passed through the straight of Cincapura,
and so to the citie of Malaca [acquiring knowledge of many
islands, sea and land.]

Gomera,
hist. gen.,
lib. 2, cap. 61. In this same yeere, 1523, Cortes went with three hundred
footemen, and one hundred and fifty horsemen, and forty

& caualos, com hum homē armado encima, foy Aluarado bem recebido, começou logo a correr aquellas prouincias & senhorealas : &
fez nellas a cidade de Sanctiago, & hūa villa q' pos nome Segura,
& deixou nella gēte cō fe q' segurou a terra.

No anno mesmo de 1523 & mes de Mayo mãdou Antonio de
Brito, que estaua por capitam de Maluco a Simão Dabreu seu
primo a saber ho caminho de Borneo, pera Malaca, ouueram vista
das ylhas de Manada Panguensara.   Foram pollo estreito Dantre-
minao & Taguina ás ilhas de sam Miguel, q' estam em sete graos
daltura da parte do norte & da hi descorreram a ilha de Borneo,
& toda sua costa, ouueram vista da Pedra branca, passaram polo
estreito de Sincapura, foram ter a cidade de Maluca deixando
muytas ilhas, mar, & terra por aly sabidas.

Neste mesmo anno de 1523 foy Cortez com trezentos soldados,
& cento & cincoenta de caualo, quatrocentos Mexicanos a Panuco

---

[1] Between Minao.   [2] They coasted along.

thousand[1] Mexicans to Panuco [as he had settled] both to
discouer it better, and also to inhabite it, and withall to
be reuenged upon them which had killed and eaten the
soldiers of Francis Garay. They of Panuco resisted him
[courageously] ; but Cortes in the end ouerthrew them [kill-
ing many], and conquered the countrey. And hard by
Chila, vpon the riuer he built a towne and named it Santo   Santo Ste-
Stephano del puerto, leauing in it one hundred footemen,   phano del
puerto.
and thirtie horsemen and one Peter de Valleio for lieutenant.
This iourney cost him seventy-six thousand Castilians,[2] besides the Spanyards, horses, and Maxicans which died there.

In this yeere, 1523, Francis de Garay made[3] nine ships   Gomara,
and two brigandines to goe to Panuco and to Rio de las   hist. gen.,
lib. 2, cap.
Palmas to be there as gouernour ; for that the emperour had   61 ; & en la
conquista
granted vnto him from the coast of Florida vnto Panuco, in   de Mexico.
regard of the charges, which he had been at in that discouerie.   He carried with him eight hundred and fifty
soldiers and one hundred and fovty horses, and some men
out of the Island of Jamaica, where he furnished his fleet

---

como tinha assentado, assi por descobrir milhor aq'lla terra, como
por pouoalla, & tomar vingança dos de Guara, que aly mataram &
comerā, os de Panuco os nam receberam, mas antes se defenderam
varonilmente, cō tudo foram desbaratados & muitos mortos, & con-
quistaram a terra : & junto de Chili ao longo do Rio, fundou Cortez hūa villa, a que pos nome santo Esteuam del puerto, deyxou
nella cem infantes, & trinta de cauallo, & por Tenente a Pero de
Valleijo, custoulhe esta hida setenta & seis mil Castelhanos, afora
os Espanhoes, & cauallos & Mexicanos que la ficaram.

Neste anno de 1523 armou Francisco de Garai none nauios, &
dous bargantins, pera hir a Panuco & Rio das palmas por gouernador & adiantado, que lhe o Emperador tinha dado da Florida
ate Panuco, pello gasto que tinha feyto neste descobrimento, leuou
desta vez oito cētos & cincoenta soldados, & cento & quorēta

---

[1] Four hundred.   [2] Dollars or reals ?   [3] Armed.

with munition for the warre ; and he went vnto Xagua, an
hauen in the Island of Cuba, where he vnderstood that
Cortes had peopled the coast of Panuco ; and that it might
not happen vnto him as it did to Pamphilus de Naruaez, he
determined to take another companion with him,[1] and [for
this purpose] he desired the Doctor Zuazo to goe to Mexico
(and procure some agreement betweene Cortes and him).[2]
And they departed from Xagua each one about his busines.
Zuazo came in great ieoperdie, and Garay went not cleere

Rio de las
l'almas. without.   Garay arriued in Rio de las Palmas on S. James
his day, and then he sent vp the riuer one Gonsaluo de
Ocampo, who, at his returne, declared that it was an euill
and desert countrey ; but, notwithstanding, Garay went
there on land with 400 footemen and some horsemen, and he
commanded one John de Grijalua to search[3] the coast, and
he himselfe marched by land towards Panuco, and passed a

Rio Mon-
talto. riuer, which he named Rio montalto : he entred into a great
towne,[4] where they found many hennes,[5] wherewith they

---

cauallos, & algūs Islenos de Jaimaca, onde forneceo a frota de
munições de guerra, & foy se a Xaca porto da ylha da Cuba, onde
soube q' Cortez tinha pouoado a costa de Panuco, & por lhe nam
acontecer como a Pamphilo de Narbais, determinou yr fazer com
elle algum concerto.   Pera isso rogou ao Lecenceado Suaso q'
fosse a Mexico, & partiram de Xaca cada hum a seu negocio :
Suaso correo assaz fortuna, & Garay nam esteue sem algūa.

Chegado ao Rio das Palmas, surgio ahy dia de Santiago : & mandou por elle acima a Gonçalo de o Campo que tornou, dizēdo que
a terra era má & despouoada, com tudo Gara desembarcou nella
cõ quatro centos Espanhoes & cauallos, & mandou a Joam de
gujaluarez costear a costa, & elle caminhou por terra pera Panuco
& passou hum rio a que pos nome Mōte alto, entrou em hū lugar
despouoado, onde achou muitos Galipauos com que refrescarão, &

---

[1] To make an agreement with him.   [2] Dele.
[3] Sail along.   [4] Depopulated village.   [5] Pea fowl ?

refreshed themselues : and he tooke some of the people of
Chila [with a good deal of trouble] (which he vsed for Chila.
messengers to certaine places).[1]   And (after great trauaile)[1]
comming to Panuco they found no victuailes there, by
reason of the warres of Cortes (and the spoile of the soldiers).[1]
Garray then sent one Gonçalo de Ocampo to Sant Isteuan
del puerto to know whether they would receiue him or no.
They had a good answere.   But Cortes his men priuily by
an ambushment tooke forty of Garayes horsemen, alleaging
that they came to vsurpe the gouernment of another; and
besides this misfortune he lost fower of his ships, whereupon he left off to proceede any farther.[2]

While Cortes was preparing to set forward to Panuco,[3] Gomar. en la Conquista
Francis de las Casas and Roderigo de la Paz arriued at de Mexico, fol. 226.

---

tomou algũs de Chily com assaz trabalho, & chegaram ao Panuco,
mas nam acharam mantimento pollas guerras que ho Cortez ay
tiueram.

Mandou Garai a Gonçalo de o campo a sancto Esteuam del
Puerto a saber se ho receberiam, deram boa reposta, & deitaram
lhe cilada, em que prenderam corenta, por dizerem que hiam a
vsurpar aquella terra, em que Garay recebeo muita perda, alem de
quatro nauios que tinha perdidos, & a gente que lhe fogio em ho
Rio de Panuco, & cõ isto temerão a fortuna de Cortez, que sabendo
esta noua, deixou as armadas pera descobrir as figueiras,[4] & Chiapa
& Tomulam, & volueo o rostro a Panuco.

---

[1] Dele.

[2] Garay sent from the camp one Gonçalez to St. Estevan del Puerto
to learn whether they would receive him.   A favourable answer was returned, and an ambush prepared whereby forty prisoners were taken, it
being alleged that they (Garay) came to usurp that land ; by which
Garay suffered much damage, besides four ships that he had lost, and
the people who fled from him in the river of Panuco ; in conse-
quence he dreaded the fortune of Cortez, who learning this news, left
the ships to discover Cape Higueras and Chiapa and Tomulam, and
turned his face to Panuco.

[3] Affairs being in this state.   [4] Higueras ?

Mexico with letters patents, wherein the Emperour gaue the gouernment of Nueua Spagna and all the countrey which Cortes had conquered to Cortes, and namely Panuco. Whereupon he staied his iourney. But he sent Diego de Ocampo with the said letters patents,[2] and Pedro de Aluarado with store of footemen and horsemen. Garay, knowing this, thought it best to yeeld himselfe vnto Cortes his hands, and to go to Mexico, which thing he did, hauing discouered a great tract of land.

Gomara, en la Conquista de Mexico, fol. 242.
San Gil de buena Vista in the Bay of Honduras.
In this yeere, 1523,[3] Gil Gonçales de Auila made a discouerie, and peopled a towne called San Gil de buena vista, standing in 14 degrees toward the north, and almost in the bottome of the bay called the Ascension or the Honduras. He began to conquere it because he best knew the secrets thereof[4] (and that it was a very rich countrey).[5]

Gomara, en la conquista de Mexico, fol. 229, & in sequentibus.
In this yeere, 1523, the sixt day of December, Peter de Aluarado went from the citie of Mexico, by Cortes his commandement, to discouer and conquere Quahutemallan,

---

Estando nisto Francisco de las casas & Rodrigo dela paz, chegaram a Mexico cō prouisões, ẹm q' o Emperador mandaua a Fernã Cortez a gouernança da noua Espanha, & todo o mais q' tiuesse conquistado ate Panuco, polo q' mādoula dinheiro a Diego de ho campo, & Pero daluarado cō gēte de pè & caualo, q' o Garia sabēdo tomou por partido meterse nas mãos de Cortez, & hirse a Mexico deixando muito descuberto. Tābé foy ao descobrimēto neste mesmo anno Gil gonçaluez dauilla, & pouoaçam Gil de Boa vista, que estara em catorze graos daltura da parte do norte, na fim ou quàsi da Baya da Ascensam começou a conquistar aquela terra pera saber milhor os segredos della.

Neste anno de 1523 aos seis dias do mes de Dezēbro partio Pero daluarado da cidade de Mexico por mādado d' Cortez, a cōquista & descobrimēto de Cataimalā & Autalā & Chiapa, &

---

[1] As far as.   [2] Upon this he sent money to Diego from the camp.
[3] Also in this same year.   [4] That he might learn its secrets better.
[5] Not in Portuguese.

Vtlatlan, Chiapa, Xochnuxco, and other townes toward the South Sea.[1] He had with him three hundred soldiers, 170[2] horsemen (foure field peeces),[3] and some noble men of Mexico, with people of the countrey to aide him as well in the warre, as by the way being long. He went by Tecoantepec to Xochmuxco, and other places aboue said, with great trauaile and losse of his men; but he discouered and subdued all the countrey. There are in those parts certaine hils that haue alume in them, and out of which distilleth a certaine liquor like vnto oile, and sulphur or brimstone,[4] whereof the Spanyards made excellent gunpowder. He trauailed 400 leagues in this voiage (and passed certaine riuers which were so hot that they could not well endure to wade through them).[5] He builded a citie, calling it Sant Iago de Quahutemallan. [The country appeared so desirable that] Peter de Aluarado begged the gouernment of this countrey, and the report is that it was giuen him.

Oile distilling out of hils.

Ibidem, fol. 230.

Sant Jago de Quahutemallan.

In the yeere 1523, the 8 day of December, Cortes sent Diego de Godoy, with 100 footemen and 30 horsemen (two

Gomara, en la conquista de Mexico, fol. 233.

Chanuco, & outros pouos q' por ali estauam, leuou. 300. soldados. 140 caualos, & algūs senhores Mexicanos cō gēte da terra q' os ajudaram, assi na guerra como polo caminho q' era cōprido, forā ter a Toātepè & a Chanuco & o mais acima nomeado, & com assaz trabalho & mortos, descobrio & cōquistou tudo, ōde á serras de pedra hume & licor q' pareçe azeite muito bō, & muito bō ēxofre q' sē ser refinado fazē poluora dele, ali andaram quatro cētas legoas, & fizerā hūa cidade, q' poseram nome Sātiago de Cautumalam, pareceo tambem a Pero daluarado aquella terra, que pedio della ha gouernança, & diz qoe lhe foy dada.

Nesta era de 1524[6] a oito de Dezembro mandou Cortez a Diogo de Godoy com cem soldados & trinta cavallos, & muitos amigos & aliados dos Indios contra a prouincia de Chamola, aa villa do

---

[1] And other people in that direction.   [2] 140.   [3] Not in Portuguese.
[4] Which, without being refined, was used to make gunpowder.
[5] Not in Portuguese.   [6] 1523?

field peeces),[1] and many of his friends, Indians [against

Villa del
Espiritu
Santo.

Chamolla.

the province of Chamola], vnto the towne Del Espiritu santo
[and to other countries that lie between Chiapa and Cotu-
molam, where Pedro d'Alvarado had arrived]. He ioined
himselfe with the captaine of that towne, and they went to
Chamolla, the head citie of that prouince; and that being
taken all the countrey grew quiet [and he left it well known].

Gomara,
en la Con-
quista de
Mexico,fol.
234.

In the yeere 1524, in Februarie, Cortes sent one Roderigo[2]
Rangel, with 150 Spaniards and many of the Tlaxcallans
and Mexicans, against the Zapotecas and Nixticas, and vnto
other prouinces and countreyes not so well discouered: they
were resisted at the first, but quickly put the people to the
woorst, and kept them for euer after in subiection.[3]

Gomar. hist.
gen., lib. 3,
cap. 21.

In this same yeere, 1524, one Roderigo de Bastidas was
sent[4] to discouer, people, and gouerne the countrey of Santa
Martha, where he lost his life because he would not suffer the
soldiers to take the spoile of a certaine towne.[5] They

Spirito Sancto, & a outras terras q' estam entre Chiapa & Catumalam, onde Pero Daluarado era chegado Foy, Diogo de Godoi aa
villa do Spiritu Sancto, & ajuntouse com o capitam della, & entraram
ate chamolla que he cidade & cabeça daquella prouincia, & tomada
pacificouse toda a terra & ficou bem descuberta & sabida.

Neste mesmo anno de 1524 & mes de Feuereiro, mandou o
Cortez a Diogo rangel cõ cento & cincoẽta Espanhoes & muitos
Trascaloes & Mexicanos, aos Zapotecas, Nistecas, & a outras prouincias q' nã eram bẽ sabidas & descubertas, tiueram la guerras,
mas por fim de tudo desbarataram, & castigaram nos de maneira,
que nunca mais ajuntaram nẽ boliram consigo.

Neste mesmo anno de 1524 foy Rodrigo de bastidas descobrir,
gouernar, & pouoar sancta Marta, o que lhe custou a vida per nam
deixar aos soldados saquear a terra & destroir a gente della, se

---

[1] Not in Portuguese.   [2] Diego.
[3] They fought long, but in the end they were overcome and punished
in such a way that they never more united against nor troubled him.
[4] Went.   [5] To pillage the country and destroy the people.

ioined with Peter Villa-forte, and he, being sometimes his entire friend,[1] did helpe to kill him with daggers, lying in his bed. Afterward, Don Pedro de Lugo and Don Alfonso, his sonne, were gouernours of that place, which vsed them-selues like·couetous tyrants, whereof grew much trouble [in those parts].

In this same yeere also, 1524, after that the Licentiate Lucas Vasques de Aillon had obtained of the emperour the gouernment of Chicora, he armed for that purpose certaine ships from the citie of Santo Domingo and went to discouer the countrey, and to inhabite it [or to repay the injustice and injury that had been committed in those parts with body, life and goods]; but he was lost, with all his companie, leauing nothing done woorthy of memorie. And I cannot tell how it commeth to passe, except it be by the iust iudge-ment of God, that of so much gold and precious stones as

Gomar., hist., gen., lib. 2, cap. 7.

---

ajuntaram com Pero de villa forte, em q' elle confiaua & fazia muyta conta, & ajudou a matalo aas punhaladas jazendo na cama, & depois forā por gouernadores dō Pedro de lugo & seu filho dō Luis de Lugo, q' se ouueram como tiranos cobiçosos, de que soce-derão muitos males em aquellas partes.

E no mesmo anno de 1524 despois do lecenceado Lucas de Seilam ter do Emperador a gouernança de Chicora, armou pera ella certos nauios da cidade de sam Domingos, q' foy descobrir a terra, & pouoala, ou pagar as injustiças & injurias q' em aquellas partes tinham feitas, com o corpo, vida, & fazenda, porque la se perdeo cō toda armada, sem la fazer cousa dina de memoria, sòmēte verse nela a justiça diuina : & em outras muitas se viram em aquella partes das Antilhas, Indias Portuguesas, pelos roubos, tiranias, & males que se faziam nellas, por onde parece que nunca faltaram Nabuquo do nosores que castiguem nossos males, que sam tantos como vemos. Que foram de tantos Castelhanos, Portu-gueses, como tem hido as Antilhas & Indias, ouro, prata, especea-

---

[1] Whom he trusted and made much of, but who, etc.

haue beene gotten in the Antiles by so many Spaniards, little or none remaineth, but the most part is spent and consumed, and no good thing done.[1]

Gomar., hist. gen., lib. 2, cap. 65, & en la Conquista de Mexico, fol. 243.In this yeere, 1524, Cortes sent one Christopher de Olid, with a fleete, to the Island of Cuba, to receiue the vitailes and munitions which Alonso de Contreras had prepared, and to discouer and people the country about Cape de Higueras and the Honduras [and those parts that were not yet well known]; and to send Diego Hurtado de Mendoça by sea, to search the coast (from thence euen to Darien)[2] to finde out the streight which was thought to run into the South sea, as the emperour had commanded. He sent also two ships from Panuco to search along the coast vnto Florida.

---

rias, drogoas, aljofre, pedraria, & mercadarias que de la trouxeram? Tudo he gastado, consumido sem nenhũ fruito, & algum que quis ter alma, ficou sem vida, & ainda me pareçe que quem se quiser ocupar nesta materia, não na acabaria na de Matusalem dobrado.

Neste mesmo anno de quinhẽtos & vinte & quatro, mandou Fernão cortez Christouam de Olim cõ hũa armada á ilha da Cuba tomar mãtimentos, moniçoes, que Contreiras tinha feitas, & descobrir & pouoar as funduras, & aquellas terras que nam eram ainda bẽ sabidas, q' mãdasse Diogo furtado de Mendoça por mar â costa a buscar o estreito q' deziam passar da outra banda, como o Emperador mandaua, & assi enuiou dous nauios de Panuco ate Florida ao mesmo cabo de Catumalam a Penamoa, por nam ficar cousa q'

---

[1] Only in this is seen the Divine justice: and otherwise it is abundantly visible in those parts of the Antilles or Portuguese India, on account of the robberies, oppression and ills that have been committed, whence it appears that there is always a Nabuchodonosor who punishes our evil deeds, which are so great as we see. What has become of the many Spaniards, Portuguese, who gambled in the Antilles and India ; of so much gold, silver, spice, drugs, pearls, jewels, and merchandise, that was brought thence ? All is wasted and consumed leaving no fruit; and any one who appeared to have any soul lost his life ; and besides it seems to me that whoever would embark in these matters, would never finish, not even if he lived to twice the age of Methusaleh.

[2] Not in Portuguese.

He commanded also certaine brigandines to search the coast
from Zacatullan vnto Panama.[1] This Christopher de Olid
came to the Island of Cuba, and made a league with Diego
Velasquez against Cortes, and so set saile and went on land
hard by Puerto de Cauallos, standing in 10 degrees to the
north, and built a towne, which he called Triumpho de la
Cruz. He tooke Gil Gonzales de Auila prisoner, and killed
his nephew and the Spaniards that were with him, all sauing
one childe, and shewed himselfe an enimie to Cortes, who
had spent in that expedition thirty thousand castellans of
gold to doe him pleasure withall.

Cortes vnderstanding hereof the same yeere 1524, and in
the moneth of October,[2] he went out of the citie of Mexico
to seeke Christopher de Olid to be revenged of him, and
also to discouer [countries as yet unknown to the Span-
iards], carrying with him three hundred Spanish footemen
and horsemen, and Quahutimoc king of Mexico, and other
great lords of the same city [for greater peace.] And comming to the towne called La villa del Espirito santo, he

Gomar.,
hist. gen.,
lib. 2, cap.
66, & en la
Conquista
de Mexico,
fol. 246 &
251.

---

nam fosse sabida. Christouam de olid chegado à ilha da Cuba,
assentou liga com Diogo velhasquez cõtra Cortez, dada á vella, foy
desembarcar jũto do porto de caualos em dez graos de parte do
norte, & fez a villa do Triunfo da Cruz, prẽdeo Gil gonçaluez
Auila, matoulhe hum sobrinho com os espanhoes q' o seguiram
ficou soo no ninho, & decrarou se por imigo de Cortez, que gastou
nesta armada trinta mil Castelhanos, por lhe fazer boa obra.

Sabẽdo Fernam cortez isto, na mesma era de vinte & quatro no
mes de Abril, partio da cidade de Mexico em busca de Christouam
de olid, pera tomar delle vingança, & descobrir a terra & prouincias,
que ainda por Espanhoes nam eram vistas, leuando trezẽtos delles
de pé & caualo, & el rey Catinococim & principes de Mexico pera
mais pacifico, chegado a villa do Spiritu sancto fez asaber aos

---

[1] To the same cape from Catumclam to Panama, so as to leave
nothing unknown.

[2] April ?

[made known his determination and] required guides of the lords of Tauasco and Xicalanco, which they prouided immediately (and they sent him ten of their principall men for guides) :[1] who gaue him also a map of cotton wooll,[2] wherein was painted the situation of the whole country from Xicalanco vnto Naco, and Nito, and euen as farre as Nicaragua, with their mountaines, hils, fields, meadowes, vallies, riuers, cities and townes. And Cortes in the meane time sent for three ships which were at the hauen of Medellin to follow him along the coast.

In this yeere 1524 they came to the citie of Izancanac, where he vnderstood that the king Quahutimoc and the Mexicans that were in his companie were conspired against him and the Spanyards: for the which he hanged the king and two others of the chiefe: and so came to the citie of Mazatlan, and after that to Tiaca, the head citie of a prouince so called standing in the middest of a lake: and here about they began to finde the traine of the Spanyards, which they went to seeke, and so they went to Toscola and Zuzullin [and other places of Nico, and finding a good port, he built a city called Ascensa'm de Nosse Senhora], (and at

Side notes:
An excellent large map of cotton wooll.

Gomara, hist. gen., lib. 2, cap. 67 & 68, & en la Conquista de Mexico, fol. 257

Mazatlan. Tiaca.

Zuzullin.

---

senhores de Tauasco & Picalam sua determinaçam, & pedir que lhe mandassem guias, elles o fizeram logo & em hũ debuxo deram hũ pano dalgodã tecido cm q' estaua toda a terra q' a de Xicalã Anico & Neco, & Nicaragas com mõtanhas, serras, campinas vallas, & ribeiras, cidades, & villas, & mandou a Medelim aparelhar tres nauios cõ mantimẽtos, moniçães & que fossem ao longo da costa.

No anno de 1528,[3] chegaram á cidade de Zacanaca, onde souberam como el Rey Catimococim & Mexicanos se conjurauam contra Cortez & Castelhanos, polo q' el Rey & algũs foram enforcados, donde partiram & chegarão á cidade de Matalam : & despois a Tiaca cabeça da prouincia, está no meyo de hũa alagoa: & ja por aqui achauam rastro dos Espanhoes q' buscauam, & forã a

---

[1] Not in Portuguese.   [2] Woven.   [3] 1524 ?

length came to the towne of Nito : from Nito Cortes with Gomar. in the Con-quest of Mexico, fol. 268.
his owne companie, and all the Spanyards that he found
there, departed to the shore or strand called La Baia de
Sant Andres, and finding there a good hauen he builded a Natiuadad de Nuestra Sennora.
towne in that place and called it Natividad de Nuestra
Señora.)[1]

From hence Cortes went to the towne of Truxillo, standing Truxillo.
in the hauen of the Honduras, where the Spanyards dwell- Honduras.
ing there did entertaine him well : and while he was there,
there arriued a ship which brought newes of the stirre in
Mexico (in Cortes his absence) :[2] whereupon he sent word to
Gonsalo de Sandoual to march with his companie from Gomara in the Con-quest of Mexico, fol. 270 & 273.
Naco to Mexico by land toward the South sea vnto Qua-
hutemallan, because that is the vsuall plaine and safest way,[3]
and he left as captaine in Truxillo Fernando de Saavedra
his cozen : and he himselfe went by sea along the coast of
Jucatan (to Chalchicoeca, now called Sant Juan de Vllhua,
and so to)[4] Medellin, and from thence to Mexico, where he

Toscola & Sucelim & outros logares de Nico, & por ser bom porto
fez aly hũa villa, a que pos nome Ascençam de nossa senhora.

Daqui foy Cortez à villa de Truzilho, q' esta em o porto de
Funduras, & bē recebido polos Espanhoes que ahi estauam, no qual
tempo chegou hum nauio que deu noua dos males de Mexico, pelo
qual mandou logo Cortez, Gonçalo de Sandoual com gēte de pee
& caualo descobrir terra contra o mar do sul a Cotumalam, por
ser mais breue caminho, & deixou em Trugilho por capitã à Fernã
sayauedra seu primo, elle foise por mar & costa de Siucatam a
Medelim & dai a Mexico, onde foy bē recebido auēdo mais de anno
& meo que da ly era partido, repousou dos muitos trabalhos &
perigos que auia passado de quinhentas legoas por terras mui

---

[1] Not in Portuguese.   [2] Not in Portuguese.
[3] Whereupon Cortez sent Goncalo de Sandoval with horse and foot
to Cotumalam to discover the country towards the South Sea, that being
the shortest road.
[4] Not in Portuguese.

was well receiued, hauing beene from thencc 18 monethes,[1] (and had gone fiue hundred leagues, trauelling often out of his way, and enduring much hardness).

Gomara, hist. gen., lib 5, cap. 1 & 2. Peru.

In the yeere 1525 Francis Pizarro and Diego Almagro went from Panama to discouer Peru, standing beyond the line towarde the south, which they called Nueua Castillia. The gouernour Pedro Arias would not entermeddle with this expedition, because of the euill newes which his captaine, Francis Vezerra, had brought [who never reached further than the port of Pinas towards the north].

Francis Pizarro went first in a ship, having with him 140 soldiers, and Almagro went after him in another ship with 70 men. He came to Rio de San Juan, standing in three degrees, where he got two thousand pesoes of gold; and not finding Pizarro, he went[2] to seeke him, repenting his doings by reason of a mishap that he had.[3] But [attracted

---

fragosas, & dellas desponadas, andaram em montanhas muy asperas, & grandes ribeyras comendo eruas de que muitos faleçeram.

No anno de 1525 partio Francisco piçarro & Diogo dalmagro de penama ao descobrimento daquellas terras & prouincias, a que chamam Peru, que estam áquem & alem da linha da parte do sul, a que poseram nome a noua Castela, o gouernador Pedraires nam se quis meter na armada, polla roim noua que lhe trouxera seu capitam Francisco bezerra, que nam chegou mais q' ao porto de Pinas, que está da parte do norte.

Francisco Piçarro diz que foy diante em hũ nauio com cento & quarenta soldados, Almagro tras elle em outro com setenta, deu no Rio de sam Joam, que está em tres graos daq'lla banda, onde tomou vinte mil pesos douro.   E como nam achassem Francisco

---

[1] Here he reposed after the great labours and dangers he had passed through in journeying fifteen hundred leagues through rough and desert countries, over rugged mountains and great marshes, eating herbs, by which many perished.

[2] Returned.

[3] Who had changed his mind, owing to a disaster that had happened.

by the gold of Almagro] he went first to an island called Isla del Gorgona, and afterwards to another called Isla del Gallo, and to the riuer called Rio del Peru, standing in two degrees northwards, whereof so many famous countreyes take their name. From thence they went to Rio de San Francisco, and to Cabo de Passaos, where they passed the equinoctiall line, and came to Puerto Vejo, standing in one degree to the south of the line : from whence they sailed to the riuers of Chinapanpa, Tumbez, and Payta, standing in 4 or 5 degrees, where they had knowledge of king Atabalipa and of the exceeding wealth and riches of his palace. Which newes mooued Pizarro speedily to returne home againe to (Panama, and so into)[1] Spaine, and to request the gouernment of that countrey of the emperour : which he also obtained. He had spent aboue three yeeres before in this discouerie, not without enduring great trauaile and perils.[2]

In the same yeere 1525 there was sent out of Spaine a fleet of seuen ships, whereof was captaine generall Don Garcia de Loaisa to the Islands of Maluco. They went

Marginal notes: Isla del Gorgona. Isla del Gallo. Rio del Peru. Cabo de Passaos. Puerto vijo. Tumbez. Payta. Pet. Martyr., decad. 8, cap. 9. Gomar., hist. gen., lib. iv, cap. 12.

piçarro, tornaram em sua busca, que estaua arrependido por hum desastre que lhe acontecera : mas com effôrço do ouro Dalmagro : foy á ylha de Gorgora, & do Galo, & ao rio do Peru, que está em dous graos donde tantas & tam grandes prouincias tomaram apelido. Dahi foram ao Rio de sam Francisco, & ao cabo de Passao, onde passaram a linha. Chegado ao porto que está hum grao da parte do Sul, dõde foram pellos Rios de Chinapápa, Paita, Trubez, q' esta em quatro ou cinco graos, donde souberam que auia aly muita riqueza del rey Atabalipa & boa terra, q' moueo Frãçisco piçarro tornar a Castella a pedir ao Emperador aquella gouernança : & andou mais de tres annos nesta demanda.

No mesmo anno de 1525 foy enuiado de castella hũa armada de

---

[1] Not in Portuguese.
[2] And he spent more than three years in following up this request.

from the citie of the Groine and passed by the Islands of the Canaries, and went to Brasill, where they found an island in two degrees, and named it S. Matthew: and it seemed to be inhabited, because they found in it orenge trees [and other fruit trees, traces of] hogs, and hennes in caues,[1] and vpon the rindes of most of the trees there were grauen Portugall letters, shewing that the Portugals had beene there 17[2] yeeres before that time. A patache or pinnesse of theirs passed the streight of Magellane,[3] hauing in her one Iohn de Resaga, and ran all along the coast of Peru and Noua Spagna. They declared all their successe vnto Cortes,[4] and told him that frier Garsia de Loaisa was passed to the islands of cloues. But of this fleete the admirall onely came thither, wherein was captaine one Martine Mingues de Carchona: for Loaisa and the other captaines [who

The Isle of S. Mathew.

Gomara in the Conquest of Mexico, page 281.

---

sete vellas, Capitam dellas frey Garcia de Loaes: pera as ilhas de Maluco, partiram da cidade de Crunha, atrauessando das ylhas Canareas ao Brasil, dous graos alem da linha, acharam hũa ylha que poseram nome sam Matheus, parecia ser ja pouoada por ter larangeyras, & outras aruores de fruyto, acharam rastro de porcos: & galinhas no mato, & nos troncos de todas aruores letras Portuguesas: que denunciauam auer oytenta & sete annos que aly esteueram: alem do estreyto do Magalhaes se apartou delles hum nauio de remo que leuauam que chamauam Patax, em que hia dom Joam de recaga, foy ter aa costa do Peru, & aa noua Espanha correndo a toda: deu conta a Fernam Cortez do que vira, & como frey Garcia de Loaes era passado aas ylhas do Crauo. Mas de toda esta frota nam chegou a ellas, se nam a nao Capitaina, hindo por Capitam della, Martim Minguez de carquicena, por Loaes, & outros Capitães que lhe soccederam, todos faleceram. Mas esta

---

[1] The bush.   [2] 87.

[3] Beyond the Strait of Magellan, a row boat, called a patache, which they had, separated from them.

[4] They recounted to Cortez what they had seen.

succeeded him] died by the way. [But this alone sufficed to put the whole country in revolt, so well-affectioned are the Moors of Maluco to the Spaniards.] (All the Moores of Maluco were found well affectioned to the Spaniards.)[1]

In the same yeere 1525 the pilot Stephen Gomes went from the port of the Groine toward the north to discouer[2] the streight (vnto the)[3] Malucos, but to keep Magellan from the route, (to whom)[4] they would giue [him] no charge in the fleete of frier Garsia de Loaisa. But yet the Earle Don Fernando de Andrada, and the Doctor Beltram, and the marchant Christopher de Sarro [did not fail him, but] furnished a gallion for him [to make this discouery so much desired], and he went from (the Groine in)[5] Galicia to the Island of Cuba, and to the point of Florida, sailing by day because he knew not the land [and (not seeing?) in the bay, harbour, river, or inlet, he passed (the bay Angra, and the riuer Enseada, and so went)[6] ouer to the other side. It is also reported that he came to Cape Razo in 46[7] degrees to the north : from whence he came backe againe to the Groine laden with slaues. The

Pet. Martyr., decad. 8, pag. 601. Gomara, historia general, lib. i, cap. 5.

soo abastou pera meter toda ha terra em grande reuolta : tam affeyçoados sam os Mouros de Maluco a Castelhanos.

No mesmo anno da era de mil & quinhentos & vinte & cinco, partio ho piloto Esteuam Gomez do porto [de Crunha?] contra a parte do Norte, descobrindo ho estreito de Maluco, com quanto por fogir ao Magalhães do caminho nam lhe quiseram dar nesta armada de Lois nenhum carrego, mas com tudo nam lhe faltou ho Conde dom Fernando Dandrade, & ho doctor Beltrão, & ho mercador Christouam de Sarro, que lhe armarão hum galeam pera este descobrimento tam desejado. Partio de Galiza, foy tomar ha ylha da Cuba, & a ponta da Florida, nauegando de dia por nam saber a terra, & ver em toda Baya angra, rio, enscada se passaua a outra banda, diz que chegaram ao cabo raso, que estaa da parte do Norte, em quarenta & quatro graos daltura, donde tornaram á cidade de

---

[1] Dele.	[2] Discovering.	[3] Of.
[4] Dele.	[5] Not in Portuguse.	[6] Dele.
		[7] 44.

newes hereof ran by and by through Spaine, that he was
come home laden with cloues as mistaking the word : and it
was carried to the court of Spaine [post haste to ask a re-
ward, which caused great joy and entertainment principally
to those who fitted out the vessel]: but when the truth was
knowne[1] it turned to a pleasant iest. In this voiage Gomes
was ten monethes.

In this yeere 1525 Don George de Meneses, captaine of
Maluco, and with him Don Garcia Henriquez, sent a foyst
to discouer land towards the north, wherein went as captaine one Diego de Rocha, and Gomes de Sequeira for
pilot [who afterwards went as pilot on an Indian voyage].
In 9 or 10 degrees they found certaine islands standing
close together [they passed among them], and they called
them the Islands of Gomes de Sequeira, he being the first
pilot that discouered them. And they came backe againe
[to the fort] by[2] the Island of Batochina [do moro].

The Isle of Batochina by Gilolo.

Crunha carregar descrauos, os que isto ouuiram, cuydando que
deziam crauos, mandaram polla posta aa Corte de Castella, pedir
aluiçara, que pos grande aluoroço & contentamento principalmente
aos que armaram, chegado o Roxo com a noua carta, foy tal
azombaria q' andauam corridos : disso porque gastaram muyto
sem nenhum proueyto: & Esteuão gomez pos dez meses no
caminho.

Neste anno de 1525 estando dom Jorge de Meneses capitam de
Maluco, elle dom Garcia anriquez mandara hũa fusta descobrir
contra ho norte, hya por capitã della Diogo da rocha, & piloto
Gomez de sequeira, que depois andou por piloto na carreira da
India, em noue ou dez graos daltura, acharam hũas ilhas juntas,
andaram por entrellas; poseram lhe nome as Ylhas de Gomez de
Sequeira por ser o primeiro piloto que as descobrio, donde se
tornaram aa fortaleza, por derredor da ilha da Batachina do

[1] There was such joking that they were ashamed ; and this because
there had been much expence and no profit.
[2] Passing round.

In the yeere 1526 there went out of Siuill one Sebastian Cabota, a Venetian (by his father, but borne at Bristol in England),[1] being chiefe pilote to the emperour, with fower ships toward Maluco [islands]. They came to Pernambuco, and staied there three monethes [waiting] for a winde to double the Cape of Saint Augustine. In the Bay of Patos or of ducks [which lies to the south] the admirall ship perished ; and being without hope to get to the Isles of Maluco[2] they there made a pinnesse to enter vp the riuer of Plate, and to search it. They ran 60 leagues vp before they came to the barre :[3] where they left their great ships, and with their small pinesses passed vp the riuer Parana, which the inhabitants count to be the principall riuer. Having rowed vp 120 leagues, they made a fortresse and staied there aboue a yeere : and then rowed further till they came to the mouth of another riuer called Paragioa, and perceiuing that the countrey yeelded gold and siluer they kept on their

Gomara, historiæ general. lib. 3, cap. 39.

Rio Parana.

Rio Paragioa.

---

moro. No anno de 1526 partio de Sevilha Sebastiã gaboto Venezeano, & piloto mòr do Emperador, leuaua quatro vellas p'a as ilhas de Maluco, foram ter a Fernam buco, onde esteueram tres meses aguardando por tempo pera dobrar ho cabo de são Agostinho. Na baya dos patos que estaa em á parte do Sul, perderam a nao capitaina. Desesperados de hirē aas ilhas do Crauo, fizerā hūa galeota aly pera entrarē o rio da prata, & saber o que dentro auia, chegado ao rio que se mete nelle sessenta legoas da Barra, deyxaram os nauios da carrega, & com os menores sobiram pella principal ribeira que os da terra chamam- Parana, por ser grande agoa.

Tendo andado por este rio acima, cēto & vinte legoas, fizeram hūa fortaleza em que gastarā mais de hum anno : despois foram pella mesma ribeira ate a boca doutra, que se diz Paragay, & por verem sinais douro & prata, foram tras sua cobiça, & mandando

---

[1] Not in Portuguese.   [2] Cloves.

[3] Arrived at the river that flows into it sixty leagues from the bar, they left, etc.

course,[1] and sent[2] a brigandine before; (but)[3] those of the
countrey tooke it: and Cabote vnderstanding of it thought
it best to turne backe vnto their forte, and there tooke in
his men which he had left there, and so went downe the
riuer where his ships did ride, and from thence he sailed
home to Siuill in the yeere 1530, leauing discouered about[4]
two hundred leagues within this riuer, reporting it to be

The foun-
taine of the
riuer of
Plata. very nauigable, and that it springeth out of a lake named
Bombo. It standeth in (the firme land of)[5] the kingdome of
Peru [in a cold country], running[6] through the vallies of
Xauxa, and meeteth with the riuers Parso, Bulcasban, Cay,
Parima, Hiucax, with others, which make it very broad
and great. It is said also, that out of this lake runneth the
riuer called Rio de San Francesco; and by this meane the

The biggest
riuers pro-
ceed from
lakes. riuers come to be so great. For the riuers that come out of
lakes are bigger then those which proceede from a spring.

Ramusius,
3 vol., fol.
310. In the yeere 1517[7] one Pamphilus de Naruaez went out
of S. Lucar de Barameda to be generall of the coast and land

hum bargantim diante, os da terra lho tomaram, o que sabendo
Gaboto se tornou aa fortaleza, recolhida a gēte q' nella deixara, se
tornou pello rio abaixo onde as naos ficaram. E dahi a Seuilha no
anno de 1530 deixando descuberto mais de dozentas legoas por
este rio, que dizem ser nauegauel, & nacer de hum lago que se
chama Bombo, estaa no reyno de Peru em terra fria, & diz que
passa polos vales de Xauxa. E adiāte se ajuntam a elle os rios de
Parço, Bulcasbā, Cay, Poryma, Hiucax, & outros que o fazem muy
grande, & tambem dizem que deste lago sae ho rio de sam
Francisco. E por isso estes rios sam tamanhos, q' as mais das
ribeiras q' saem de lagos sam mayores que as que nacem de
fontes.

No anno de 1527 partio Pamphilo de Narbaes de sam Lucas de
Baramedo, por adiantado da costa, da terra da florida, ate o rio

---

[1] Their covetousness followed?   [2] Sending.   [3] Dele.
[4] More than.   [5] Dele.   [6] And is said to run.   [7] 1527.

of Florida as farre as Rio de las Palmas, and had with him
fiue ships, 600 soldiers, 100 horses, besides a great summe
and quantitie of victuailes, armour, clothing, and other
things. He could not goe on land where his desire was,
but went on land somewhat neere to Florida with three
hundred of his companie, some horses, and some victuailes,
commanding the ships to goe to Rio de las Palmas; in which
voiage they were almost all lost: and those which escaped
passed great dangers, hunger and thirst, in an island called
Xamo, and by the Spaniards Malhada, being very drie and   The Isle of
barren, where the Spaniards killed one another, and the   Xamo or
                                                            Malhada.
people also of the countrey did the like. Naruaez and those
which went with him sawe some golde with certaine Indians,
and he demanded of them where they gathered it: and they
answered that they had it at Apalachen. They therefore   Apaluchen.
searched[1] this gold, and in searching came to the said towne,[2]
where they found no gold nor siluer: they saw many bay
trees, and almost all other kinde of trees, with beasts, birds
[of Spain], (and such like).[3] The men and women of this

---

das palmas, leuaua cinco nauios, seis centos soldados, cem caualos,
grande soma de bastimentos, armas vestidos, nam pode tomar
porto onde desejaua, sahio em terra acerca da Florida, com
trezentos companheyros, cauallos poucos, mantimentos, mandou os
nauios aos rios das palmas : em cuja demanda se perderam quasy
todos, os que escaparam passaram tam grande trabalho, fome,
sede, que em hūa ylha que se chama Machado Seco, onde hos
Espanhoes se mataram hūs aos outros, & dizem que aos da terra
asi fizeram. Narbais & os que com elle hiam viram hūs Indios
com ouro, preguntaram lhe donde o tirauam, disseram que em
Palacham, foram em sua busca, acharam hum lugar pequeno &
terra pobre sem ouro nē prata, auia nella loureiros, & quasi todas
aruores, alimarias aues de Espanha, os homēs & molheres, altos,

---

[1] They went in search of.   [2] A small village and a poor country.
[3] Not in Portuguese.

place are high and strong, very light, and so swift runners,
that they will take deere at their pleasure, and will not
grow wearie though they run a whole day.   From Apalachen they went to a towne called Aute ; and from thence
to Xamo, a poore countrey with small sustinance.   These
people bring vp their children very tenderly, and make
great lamentation when any of them dieth ; they neither
weepe nor lament at the death of any olde bodie [they did
not kill the Spainiards nor eat them, as they were then weak
with work and the life they had led].   Here the people
desired the Spanyards to cure their sicke folks, for they
had many diseased (and certaine of the Spanyards being in
extreme pouertie assaied it, and vsed praier, and it pleased
God that they did indeede recouer),[1] as well those that were
hurt[2] as those which were otherwise diseased ;[3] in so much,
that one which was thought verily to be dead, was by them
restored to life, [and this was not much if their faith was as
great as the occasion required] (as they themselues reporte).[4]

---

forçosos, muy ligeiros, tam grandes corredores que tomauam os
veados, & corças, & nam cansauam de correr hum dia todo.

De Palacham foram á villa de Haute, & dahi a Xama, terra
pobre, de pouco mantimēto, criam os filhos com regalo, quando
morrem fazem por elles gram pranto, pellos velhos nam choram,
nam mataram os Castelhanos nem os comeram por estarem magros,
fracos do trabalho : & da vida que passaram.   Mandauam lhes
que curassem os enfermos : que auia aly muitos, & como se vissem
na ora da morte pediram a Deos & a sua māy socorro, foram
ouuidos de maneira que quantos aas suas mãos vinham todos
sarauam, assi aleyjados, como hos de doenças muy incurauees,
atee ressuscitarem hum morto : & nam era muito se tinham a fee
tam ynteyra como ho tempo queria.

---

[1] And as they saw themselves at the point of death, they prayed to
God and to his Mother for help ; their prayers were answered in such a
manner that all at their hands were healed.

[2] Maimed.   [3] As those affected with severe disease.

[4] Not in Portuguese.

They affirme that they passed through many countreies and many strange people, differing in language, apparell, and customes. And because they plaied the physitions, they were as they passed greatly esteemed and held for gods, and the people did no hurt vnto them, but would giue them part of such things as they had. (Therefore they passed quietly, and trauelled so farre till)[1] they came to a people, that vse continually to liue in heards with their cattel as the Arabians doe. They be poore, and eate snakes, lisards, spiders, ants, and al kinde of vermiñe, and herewith they liue so well contented that commonly they sing and dance [and divert themselues.] They buie the women of their enimies, and kill their daughters, because they would not haue them marrie with them (whereby they might increase).[2]   They trauailed through certaine places, where the women gaue sucke vnto their children til they were ten or twelue yeeres of age ; and where certaine men (being hermaphrodites)[3] doe marrie one another [and here are such people which neither weep nor make water, and it is said that if they do it they die]. These

---

Dizem que passaram por muitas terras de gentes diferētes em lingoagēs, trajos, costumes : mas por hos fisicos serem la muy estimados, & mais estes que auiam por deoses nam lhe faziam nenhum dano : antes lhe dauam dessa pobreza que tinham, foram ter aos lagazes que andam em cabildos com seus gados : como Alarues, & sam tam pobres que comem cobras, lagartos, aranhas, formigas, & todos os bichos, com isto viuem tam contentes que sempre cantam, bailam, & se desenfadam : compram as molheres aos imigos, matam as filhas, pellas nam casarem com elles, passauam por terras que os filhos mamauam dez, doze annos : em outras que casam os homēs hūs com outros, & ahi tays pouos que nam choram nem rim : & diz que se o fazem, morrem por isso, andaram os Castelhanos nestes trabalhos mais de oyto centos legoas : & nam ficaram mais de sete, ou oyto que escaparam, foram ter ao mar do

---

[1] Not in Portuguese.   [2] Not in Portuguese.
[3] Not in Portuguese.

Spaniards trauailed aboue 800 leagues; and there escaped aliue in this journey not aboue seuen or eight of them. They came vpon the coast of the South sea, vnto a citie called Saint Michael of Culuacan, standing in 23 degrees and vpward (toward the north).[1]

Gomar., hist. gen., lib. 2, cap. 72, and in the Conquest of Mexico, fol. 281.
This yeere 1527, when Cortes vnderstood by the pinnesse aforesaide that Don Garcia de Loaisa was passed by the Streight of Magelan toward the Islands of cloues, he prouided three ships[2] to goe seeke him, and to discouer by that way of New Spaine as farre as the Isles of Maluco. There went as gouernour in those ships one Aluaro de Saavedra Ceron, cosen vnto Cortes, a man fit for that purpose. He made saile from Ciuatlanejo, now named S. Christopher, standing in 20 degrees toward the north, on All Saints day. They arrived at the islands which Magelan named The Pleasures: and from thence sailed to the islands which Gomes de Sequeira had discouered, and not knowing
Islas de los Reyes.
thereof, they named thē Islas de los Reyes, that is to say, The Isles of the kings, because they came vnto them on

sul, a sam Miguel de Culuacam, que dizem estar de trinta graos pera cima.

Neste anno de 1527 sabēdo Fernam cortez polo petaxo, como frei Garcia de loais era passado ás ilhas do crauo, mandou fazer tres nauios prestes pera jrem em sua busca: & descobrir aquele caminho da noua Espanha ate Maluco, & hia por capitā mor delles Aluaro saiauedra Cerom seu primo, pessoa muyto pera isso, partio dia de todos os sanctos de Siuantaneio q' se agora chama sam Christouam que está em vinte graos da parte do norte: chegaram as ilhas q' o Magalhães pos nome dos prazeres: & dahi foram às que Gomez de sequeira descobrira, por nam saberem isto lhe poseram nome dos Reys pellas verem aquelle dia, aqui ficaram a Sayauedra dous nauios, de que nunca mais ouue noua nem recado, & de ilha em ilha foram ter a de Sarangam, onde resgataram dous

---

[1] Not in Portuguese.   [2] He ordered three ships to be got ready.

Twelfe day. In the way Saavedra lost two ships of his company, of which they neuer after heard newes. But from island to island he still sailed and came to the Island of Candiga, where he bought two [or three] Spanyards for Candiga. 70 ducats, which had beene of the companie of Frier Loaisa, who was lost thereabout.

In the yeere 1528, in March, Saavedra arriued at the Islands of Maluco, and came to an anker before the Isle[1] of Gilolo : he found the sea calme and winde at will, without any tempests : and he tooke the distance from thence to Noua Spagna to be 2050[2] leagues. At this time Martin Yñiquez de Carquiçano died, and Fernando de la Torre was chosen their generall, who then was in the citie of Tidore, who had there erected a gallows and had fierce warre with Don George de Meneses, captaine of the Portugals : and in a fight which they had the fourth day of May, Saavedra tooke from him a galiotte and slew the captaine thereof, called Fernando de Baldaya, and in June[3] he returned [in his ship] towards New Spaine, hauing with him one Simon de Brito Patalin and other Portugals, and hauing[4] beene

---

ou tres Castelhanos por setenta cruzados, da companhia de Loais que se por aly perderam.

No anno de 1528 & mes de Março chegou Sayauedra as ylhas de Maluco, & surgio na ciũade de Grilolo, contaua como achara o mar limpo & vento a popa & sem tormenta, & que lhe parecia auer dali a noua Espanha mil & quinhentas legoas, & neste tempo era ja falecido o capitã Martim minquez de Carquiçano, & aleuantado por capitam Fernãdo dela torre, que estaua na cidade de Tidore com hũa forca feyta, & de crua guerra com dom Jorge de meneses capitam dos Portugueses : & na peleja que teueram a quatro de Mayo, lhe tomou Sayauedra hũa galeota, & matouo capitam della Fernam baldaya. E no mes de Julho tornou no seu nauio pera a noua Espanha, & com elle Simão de Brito Patalim,

---

[1] City.   [2] 1500.   [3] July.   [4] Struggled.

certaine monethes at sea, he was forced backe vnto Tidore, where Patalin was beheaded (and quartered),[1] and his companions hanged [and quartered].

Gomara, hist. gen., lib. 2, cap. 73.
In this yeere 1528 Cortez sent two hundred footemen and 60 horsemen, and many Mexicans, to discouer and plant the countrey of the Chichimecas, for that it was reported to be rich of gold.[2] This being done he shipped himselfe, and came into Castile with great pompe, & brought with him 250,000[3] marks of gold and siluer: and being come to Toledo, where the emperour then lay, he was entertained according to his deserts, and the emperour made him Marques Del Valle, and married him to the Lady Jane de Zuniga, daughter vnto the Earle de Aguilar, and then the emperour sent him backe againe to be generall of New Spaine.

Gomara, hist. gen., lib. 2, cap. 72.
In the yeere 1529, in May, Saavedra returned back againe towards New Spaine, and he had sight of a land toward the south in two degrees, and he ran east along by Noua Guinea. it aboue fiue hundred leagues till the end of August [ac-

---

& outros Portugueses, & depois de espancarem o mar algūs meses, se tornaram a Tidore, onde o Patalim foy degolado, & esquartejados, & enforcados, os que com elle hiam.

Nesta era de 1528 mandou Fernam Cortez dozentos soldados, sesenta caualos, & muitos Mexicanos, a descobrir, & pouoar as terras dos Chichimecas, por dizerem que eram ricas & boas: & partiose pera Castella com grande fausto & dozentos cincoenta marcos douro & prata. Chegado a Toledo ōde o Emperador estaua, como pessoa grata fez lhe bō gasalhado & o Marques del Valle o casou cō dona Joana Destuniga, filha do cōde de Aguilar: & tornou oa mandar por capitam a noua Espanha.

No anno de 1529 & mes de Mayo tornou Sayauedra outravez pera a noua Espanha, & ouue vista de hūa costa da parte do Sul em dous graos daltura, foy em leste ao longo della mais de quin-

---

[1] Dele.   [2] And good.   [3] 250 ?

cording to their account]. The coast was cleane and of ^{Noua} ^{Guinea.}
good ankerage, but the people blacke and of curled haire ;
from the girdle downward they did weare[1] a certaine thing
plaited to couer their lower parts. The people of Maluco ^{Os Papuas} ^{are blacke}
call them Papuas, because they be blacke and friseled in ^{people with} ^{frisled}
their hair : and so also do the Portugals call them [   ]. ^{haire.}

[Alvaro] Saavedra hauing sailed 4 or 5 degrees to the
south of the line, returned vnto it, and passed the equinoctiall towards the north, and discouered an island which he
called Isla de los Pintados, that is to say, The Isle of painted ^{Isla de los} ^{Pintados.}
people : for the people thereof be white, and all of them
marked with an iron : and [according to all appearance] by
the signes which they gaue he conceaued that they were of
China. There came vnto them from the shore a kinde of
boate[2] full of these men, making tokens of threatnings to
the Spanyards ; who seeing that the Spanyards would not

---

hētas legoas, te o fim D'Agosto : & segundo o q' della contauam
era limpa & de bōs Surgidouros, & a gēte da terra preta, & cabello
reuolto : traziā da cinta pera baixo huas faldas de penas, bem
feytas, muyto coradas, com que cobriam suas vergonhas, & os
Maluqueses chamā a estes homēs os Papuas por serem pretos de
cabello frizado, & assi lhe chamam os Portugueses, pello tomarem
delles.

Aluaro Sayauedra, como hia ao Sul quatro ou cinco graos affa-
stado da linha, tornou a buscala, & passado aa outra banda do
norte, descobrio hūa ylha, a q' pos nome das Pintadas, por serem
homēs brancos, todos ferrados, & segundo o q' parecia, & sinais
que dauam, deuiam alli de vir da China, donde sahio hum Parao a
elles com grande oufania, ascenando que amainassem. Vendo que
nam obedeciā, tiroulhes com hūa funda, & logo sahio hum golpe
de Paraos da ylha a elles, todos fundeyros : & começaram hūa
peleja com ho nauio, mais soberba & menos perigosa, que a de

---

[1] Skirts of feathers, well made of various colours.
[2] With great bravado, making signs that they should strike sail.

obey them, they began to skirmish with slinging of stones,[1]
but Saavedra would suffer no shot to be shot at them, because their stones were of no strength, and did no harme.

A little beyond this island, in 10 or 12 degrees, they
found many small low islands full of palme trees and grasse,
Los Jar- which they called Los Jardines, and they came to an anker
dines. in the middest of them, where they taried certaine daies.
The people seemed [from their carriage and complexion] to
descend from them of China, but by reason of their long
continuance there they become so brutish, that they haue
neither law [nor religion], nor[2] yet giue themselues to any
honest labour. They weare white clothing, which they
make of grasse. They stand in maruailous feare of fire,
because they neuer saw any. They eate cocos in steede of
bread, breaking them before they be ripe, and putting them
vnder the sand, and then after certaine daies they take them

Xeuena : pello que Sayauedra mandou mesurar a vella, & foy
esperando sem lhe tirar nem fazer dano, ate que gastaram toda a
meniçam que traziam.

Acima desta ylha em dez ou doze graos daltura, acharam muytas
juntas, pequenas & rasas, cheas de palmeiras & verduras : pello
q' lhe poseram nome bom Jardim, surgiram no meo dellas, onde
esteueram algūs dias, os habitadores pareciam na feiçam & aluura
descenderē da China, & pellos largos tempos que aueria que aly
estauam, eram tam Barbaros que nam tinham ley, nem ceyta, nem
criauam cousa viua. Vestiam panos brancos que faziā dēruas,
espantaram se do fogo, porque nunca o viram : comiā por pāo
cocos, que antes que fossem maduros os cascauā, metiā nos de-

---

[1] And presently came out a number of canoes from the island towards
them, all slingers ; and they commenced a fight with the vessel, more
furious, but less dangerous, than that of Xevena, at which Saavedra
ordered the sail to be shortened, and went on slowly, without firing on
them or doing them any mischief, until they had used all the ammuni-
tion they had brought.

[2] Do they bring up any living thing.

out and lay them in the sunne, and then they will open.
They eate [raw] fish, which they take in a kinde of boate
called a parao, which they make of pine wood, which is ^{Flote} wood.
driuen thither at certaine times of the yeere, they know not
how, nor from whence, and the tooles wherewith they make
their boates are of shels of cockles, —— ? or oysters.

Saavedra perceiuing that the time and weather was then
somewhat better for his purpose, made saile towards the
firme lande and [isthmus of the] citie of Panama [it being
not more than seventeen or eighteen leagues across], where
he might vnlade the cloues and marchandise which he had,
that so in cartes it might be carried [across the plains] fower
leagues, to the riuer of Chagre, which they say is nauigable, running out into the North sea not far from Nombre
de Dios, where the ships ride which come out of Spaine:
by which way all kinde of goods might be brought vnto
them in shorter time, and with lesse danger, then to saile
about the Cape of Bona Sperança.   For from Maluco vnto
Panama they saile continually betweene the Tropickes and
the line : but they neuer found winde to serue that course :

---

baixo darea, & em certos dias os descobriam : & tanto q' lhe o sol
daua se abriam.   També se mantinhā em peyxe cru, q' pescauā
em Paraos, q' faziam de madeira de pinho, q' ali vinha ter em
certo tempo, sem saber donde, & pera fazer a tal obra, era a ferra-
menta de cascas damejias, briguigōes, ou hostras.

Vendo Sayauedra q' ho tempo era mais a seu proposito, se fez
á vela na volta da terra & jsmo da cidade de Penama, por nā ser
mais q' dezasete dezoyto legoas em largo, ōde podiā descarregar o
crauo & mercadoria q' leuaua, & em carretas hiria per cāpinas iiij
legoas, ate o rio Lagre, que dizē ser nauegauel & desemboca no
mar do Norte, jūto de nōbre Dios, onde estā naos de Castella, q'
os podiā leuar a elle em mais breue tēpo, & caminho menos perigoso que do cabo de boa esperança : porque de Maluco a Penama
sempre vam por antre o Tropico em a linha, mas nunca poderam
achar vento nem tempo pera comprir este desejo : pello que se

and therefore they came backe againe to Maluco very sad, because Saavedra died by the way :[1] who, if he had liued, meant to haue opened the land of Castillia de Oro and New Spaine from sea to sea.   Which might have beene done

in fower places : namely from the Gulfe of S. Michael to Vraba, which is 25 leagues, or from Panama to Nombre de Dios, being 17 leagues distance : or through Xaquator, a riuer of Nicaragua, which springeth out of a lake three or fower leagues from the South sea, and falleth into the North sea ; whereupon doe saile great barks and crayers.   The other place is from Tecoantepec through[2] a riuer to Verdadera Cruz in the Bay of the Honduras, which also might be opened in a streight.   Which if it were done, then they might saile from the Canaries vnto the Malucos vnder the[3] climate of the zodiake, in lesse time and with much lesse danger, then to saile about the Cape de Bona Sperança, or

by the streight of Magelan, or by the Northwest.   And yet if there might be found a streight there to saile into the

---

tornarão a Maluco assaz tristes, por Sayauedra ser falecido, do qual diziam que leuaua em proposito de fazer com o emperador, que mandasse abrir esta terra de Castella do ouro & noua Espanha de mar, a mar, porque se podia fazer por quatro lugares, que he do Golfam desam Miguel a Vraba, em que ha vinte & cinco legoas de trauesa, ou de Penama ao nombre de Dios, que ha dezasete, ou pello Sangra douro de Nicaraga, que começa em hũa alagoa tres ou quatro legoas da parte do sul, & vay sair a agoa della ao norte, por onde nauegam barcas, & nauios pequenos. Há outro passo de Tagante pera o rio da Vera Cruz, que tambem se podia abrir estreito, & se se fizese, nauegar se hia das Canarias a Maluco por baixo do zodiaco clima temperada, & em menos tempo & com menos perigo, que pello cabo de Boa esperança nem estreito do

---

[1] Of whom it is said that he intended to arrange with the emperor that he should give orders to open, etc.

[2] The river of Vera Cruz.   [3] Zodiack in a temperate climate.

sea of China, as it hath beene sought (it would doe much good.)[1]

In this yeere 1529 one Damian de Goes, a Portugal, being in Flanders, after that he had trauailed ouer all Spaine, was yet desirous to see more countreyes, and fashions, and diuersities of people ; and therefore went ouer into England and Scotland, and was in the courts of the kings [and of the principal persons] of those parts : and after that came againe into Flanders, and then trauailed through Zealand, Holland, Brabant [Guildres], Luxenburge, [to] Suitzerland, and so [along the riuer] through the cities of Colen, Spyres, Argentine, Basill, and other parts of Alemaine, and then came backe againe into Flanders : and from thence he went [a second time] into France through Picardie, Normandie, Champaine, Burgundie, the dukedome of Borbon, Gascoigne, Languedoc, Daulphinie, the dukedome of Sauoy, and [having visited the whole of beautiful France] passed into Italy into the dukedome of Millaine, Ferrara, Lombardie, and so to Venice, and turned backe againe to the territorie of

---

Magalhães, nem terra dos corte Reays, ainda que se nella achara estreito ao mar da China, como se ja buscara.

Neste anno de 1529 achando se Damiam de goes, Portugues em Frandes, depois de correr toda Espanha, desejoso de ver mais terra, costumes, trajos, diuersidades de gentes della, passou a Inglaterra, Escorcia, & esteue nas cortes dos Reys principaes, & senhores daquellas partes : & bem vistas se tornou ao condado de Frādes, & correo todo em ho ducado de Salandia, Olanda, Barbante, Geldija, Lusamburg, Lotoringia, a Suycia, & ao longo do Rio âs cidades de Costancia, Basilea, Argentina, Espiram, Voimatia, Maguueya, Colonia, & outras de baixa alemanha : donde tornou outra vez a Frandes, & entrou em França polla Picardia, Normandia, Gasconha, & foy ao ducado de Borbō Lingado, o Dalfinado, & ducado de Saboya, & de Borgonha, Campania. Correo toda a bella França, passou a Italia, esteue no ducado de Milam, Fer-

---

[1] Not in Portuguese.

Genoa, and the dukedome of Florence, through all Tus-
cane : and he was in the citie of Rome, and in the kingdome
of Naples, from the one side to the other.

From thence he went into Germanie to Vlmes, and other
places of the empire, to the dukedome of Sueuia and of
Bauier, and the archdukedome of Austrich, the kingdome
of Bœme, the dukedome of Morauia, and the kingdome of
Hungarie, and so to the confines of Græcia. From thence
he went to the kingdome of Poland [Sarmatia], Prussia, and
the dukedome of Liuonia, and so came into the great dukedome of Moscouia. From whence he came backe into High
Alemayne, and through the countreyes of the Lantzgraue,
the dukedome of Saxonie, the countreyes of [Dacier or] Den-
marke, Gotland, and Norway, trauailing [through the greater
parte of it] so farre, that he found himselfe in 70[1] degrees of
latitude towards the north. He did see, speake, and was
conuersant with all the kings, princes, nobles, and chiefe
cities of all Christendome in the space of 22 yeeres [occu-
pied in this work]:[2] so that by reason of the greatnes of his

---

rara, & por toda a Lombardia, foy a Veneza, tornou a ribeira de
Genoua, & ducado de Florença com toda Toscana, & a cidade de
Roma, Romania, & o Reyno de Napoles, dhũa parte & outra da
Marinha.

Dahi se passou Alemanha, esteue na cidade de Vlma, & outras
imperiaes, & no ducado de Sueuia, & de Bauaria, & Archeducado
Daustria, Reyno de Boemia, ducado de Morauia, & no Reyno de
Vngria : ate os Confinis da Grecia. Passou ao Reyno de Polonia,
Sarmatia, Brusia, & ducado de Liuoni, chegou ao gram ducado de
Moscouia, donde se tornou pella alta Alemanha, & terras de Lant-
graue, ducado de Xaxonia, & Reino de Dacia, ou Dinamarcha,
donde passou Agotia, Noruega, andou a mòr parte della, ate se
poer em oytenta graos daltura, da parte do norte, vio, falou, con-
uersou com todos os Reis, principes, nobres, pouos de toda a
Christandade, em vinte & dous annos q' gastou nestes trabalhos,

[1] 80 ?

[2] He traversed the greater part of Europe by his own free will, a

trauell, I thought him a man woorthie to be here remembred.

In the [same] yeere 1529 or 1530 one Melchior de Sosa Tauarez went from the citie of Ormuz vnto Balsera and the Islands of Gissara with certaine ships of warre, and passed vp [the Gulf of Persia] as farre as the place where the riuers Tygris and Euphrates meete one with the other. And although other Portugals had discouered and sailed through that streight, yet neuer any of them sailed so farre vpon the fresh water till that time, when he discouered [the shore of] that river from the one side to the other, wherein he saw many things which the Portugals[1] knew not.

Not long after this one Ferdinando Coutinho, a Portugall, came vnto Ormuz, and being desirous to see the world,[2] he determined to goe into Portugalls, from thence ouer land to see Asia and Europe. And to doe this the better he went

---

vio, & correo a môr parte de Europa, por suas liure vontade, cousa digna de louuor & memoria, pois deu luz a seu patria, de muitas cousas occultas a ella.

No anno mesmo de vinto & noue ou trinta, partio Belchior de sousa Tauares da cidade Dormuz pera Baçora, & ylhas de Gozara com certos nauios, em que ādaua darmada, pello estreito da Persia, & Rio Tygre, & Eufrates acima, ate onde se ajuntam hum cõ ho outro : & ainda que outros Portugueses tiuessem descuberto & nauegado este estreito, nenhum foy tanto pella agoa doce acima, ate aquelle tempo, descobrindo aquella ribeira dūa parte & outra, em q' vio cousas que aos Espanhões não eram sabidas.

Despois disto nam muyto tempo, veio ter a Ormuz Fernam coutinho, desejoso de ver mundo, como ja auia tocado Africa, & a India, determinou de hir a Portugal por terra, & ver a mór parte

---

thing worthy of praise and remembrance, since he enlightened his country with many things unknown to her.

[1] Spaniards.

[2] As he had already visited Africa and India, determined to go to Portugal by land, and to see the greater part of Asia and Europe, and for this purpose he went to Arabia, Persia, etc.

into Arabia, Persia, and vpwards the riuer Euphrates the
space of a moneth; and saw many kingdomes and countreies, which in our time had not beene seene (by the Portugals).[1] He was taken prisoner in Damasco, and afterward
crost ouer the prouince of Syria, and came vnto the citie of
Aleppo.[2] [It is said] He had beene at the holy Sepulchre
in Jerusalem, and in the citie of Cayro, and at Constantinople with the Great Turke; and hauing seene his court
[and the greater part of his country] he passed ouer vnto
Venice, and from thence into Italie, France, Spaine, and so
came againe to Lisbon. So that he and Damian de Goes
were in our time the most noble Portugals, that had (discouered and)[3] seene most countreyes and realmes of their owne
affections[4] [which, as a signal of a noble mind, I wanted here to
relate with the names of the other discoverers and navigators.]

Gomara,
hist. gen.,
lib. 5, cap. 3.   In the same yeere 1530, little more or lesse, one Francis
Pizarro, which had been in Spaine to obtaine the gouern-
ment of Peru, turned backe againe to the citie of Panama

Dasia, Europa, & pera isso diz q' foy Arabia Persia, & pollo rio
Eufrates acima hum mes de caminho, & vio muitos reynos : &
senhorios que em nossos tempos nam eram vistos, foy aa cidade
de Lepe, atrauessou a prouincia da Suria : em Damasco ho prenderam, & diz que esteue na casa Santa de Hierusalem, & na cidade
do Cairo, na de Constantinopla, com ho grande Turco, & depois
de visto sua corte, & a mór parte de sua terra, foy ter aa cidade de
Veneza : & visto Italia, França, Espanha, veo ter aa cidade de
Lisboa, aszi q' elle & Damiam de goes foram em nossos tempos os
mais nobres Portugueses & os que mais prouincias & terras viram
por suas liures vontades : que he sinal de nobre pensamento, quis
aqui com os mais descobridores & nauegadores que tenho aponta-
dos declarar.

No mesmo āno de 1530 pouco mais ou menos tornou Francisco
Piçarro que em Espanha andaua, sobre a gouernança de Peru, aa

---

[1] Not in Portuguese.   [2] Transposed from Portuguese.
[3] Not in Portuguese.   [4] By their own free will.

with all things[1] that he desired : he brought with him fower brethren [bastards], Ferdinand, John, Gonzaluo, and Francis Martines de Alcantara. They were not well receiued by Diego de Almagro and his friends, for that Pizarro had not so much commended him to the emperour as he looked for, but omitted the discouerie, wherein he had lost one of his eies, and spent much : yet in the end they agreed, and Diegro de Almagro gaue vnto Pizarro 700 pezoes of golde, victuailes and munition, wherewith he prepared himselfe the better for his iourney.

Not long after this agreement Francis Pizarro and his brethren went in two ships with the most[2] of their soldiers and horses [as possible]; but he could not arriue at Tumbez as he was minded [on account of contrary winds], and so they went on land in the riuer of Peru ; and went along the coast with great paines, because there were many bogs and riuers in their way, wherein some of his men were drowned [they being swollen]. They came to the towne of Coaché [which is well prouided], where they rested, where they

cidade de Perama, com ella como desejaua. Trazia con sigo quatro irmãos bastardos, Fernando, Johã, Gonçalo Piçarro, Francisco martīz dalcantara. Nam foram bem recebidos de Diogo dalmagro, & seus amigos, por nam fazer delles tanta mençam ao Emperador como deuera, nem ho meteo na gouernança & descobrimento, em q' Diogo dalmagro perdeo hum olho, & fez muyto gasto. Mas por fim de tudo se concertaram, & Diogo dalmagro lhe deu seet cētos pesos douro, vitualhas, armas com que se apercebeo pera ho caminho.

Partio logo Frācisco piçarro & seus hirmãos em dous nauios, cõ os mais soldados & caualos que poderam, teue ventos contrarios pera chegar a Tumbes como era seu proposito, desembarcaram no Rio de Peru, foram ao longo da costa, com muyto trabalho, por ser baixa alagadiça de muytas ribeiras, onde se algūs afogaram por serem crecidos, chegaram à villa de Cos, q' he bem prouida,

---

[1] That which. As many.

Much gold and emeraulds. found much gold and emeraulds, of which they brake some to see if they were perfect. From thence Pizarro sent to Diego de Almagro twenty thousand[1] pezos of gold to send him men, horses, munition, and victuailes ; and so he went on his iourney to the hauen named Porto Viejo : and thither came vnto him one Sebastian de Benalcazar, with all such things as he had sent for, which pleased and pleasured him very much.

Gomara, hist. gen., lib. 5, cap. 4. The Isle of Puna. In the yeere 1531,[2] he hauing this aide, passed ouer into a rich island called Puna, where he was well receiued of the gouernour : yet at last [Pizarro having offended him] he conspired to kill him and all his men : but Pizarro pre-uented him, and tooke many of the Indians, and bound them with chaines of gold and siluer. The gouernour[3] caused those that kept his[4] wiues to haue their noses, armes,

Gomara, hist. gen., lib. 5, cap. 5. and priuie members to be cut off, so jealous was he.[5] Here Pizarro found aboue six hundred men prisoners belonging to the king Attabalipa, who waged warre against his eldest

---

onde descansará, auia ahi muyto ouro, & esmeraldas : quebrará dellas por ver se eram verdadeiras : daqui mandou Francisco piçarro a Diogo dalmagro mil pesos douro, pera que lhe mandasse gente, caualos, armas, vitualhas, elle foy seu caminho ao porto velho, onde chegou Sebastiam de benalcacere com tudo ho que pediam, que os alegrou muyto.

No anno da era de quinhentos & cincoenta & tres, vendo Fran-cisco piçarro tam bom socorro, passouse a hũa ylha rica, que se chama Puna, onde foy bẽ recebido do gouernador della, mas por lhe fazer offensa, determinou matalo, com quantos leuaua, ouue Piçarro victoria, ainda que os Indios com feros douro & prata. Os principaes desta ylha, mandauam cortar narizes, braços, membros a os que guardauam suas molheres, tam ciosos eram : achou aqui

---

[1] One thousand ?
[2] The date in the Portuguese (1553) must be an error.
[3] Chiefs of that island.   [4] Their.   [5] Were they.

brother Guascar. [And] to winne reputation, these he set at libertie, and sent them to the citie of Tombez (who promised to be a meane that he should be well receiued in those partes).[1] But when they saw themselues out of bond-age, they forgat their promise, and incited the people against the Spaniards.[2] Then Pizarro sent three Spaniards to Tombez to treate for peace, whome they tooke and slew and sacrificed, and their priestes wept not for pitie but of custome. Pizarro hearing of this cruell fact, passed ouer to the maine, and set vpon the citie [to take vengeance for the injury wrought upon his people] one night suddenly and[3] killed many of them, so that they presented him with gifts of gold and siluer and other riches, and so became friends. This done, he builded a towne vpon the riuer of Cira, and called it Saint Michael of Tangarara, which was the first S. Michael of Tanga-rara. towne inhabited by Christians in those partes ; whereof Sebastian de Benalcazar was appointed captaine. Then he

---

Piçarro mais de seis centos homẽs presos del rey Atabaliba, de q' soube ter guerra com seu irmão Gascar mais velho, & nã lhe pesou nada, & por cobrar fama, mãdou os aa cidade de Tumbos : mas como se lá viram, disseram quẽ os Barbados erã & como tomauam tudo por força, mandou lá Piçarro tres Castelhanos a pedir pazes, foram mortos, & sacrificados, & os sacerdotes que isto faziam diz que chorauam, nam tãto por piedade, como por ser assi costume.

Sabendo Francisco piçarro isto, passouse á terra firme, pos se sobre a cidade por tomar vingãça da offensa que aos seus fora feyta, estando os immigos de noite descuydados, matou muitos, deram lhe presentes douro, prata, & outras riquezas que auia na terra, ficaram amigos & em Tangara, Ribeira de Choya, edificaram hũa cidade, a que poseram nome sam Miguel de tangara q' foy a pri-meira pouoaçam de Christãos naquella terra capitam & tenente

---

[1] Not in Portuguese.

[2] But when they arrived there, they described the bearded ones or Spaniards as men who took all by force.

[3] And the enemy being careless at night, he.

Payta an excellent harbour in 5 degrees to the south of the line. Gomara, historiæ general. lib. 3, cap. 37.

searched out a good and sure hauen for his ships, and found that of Payta to be an excellent harbour.[1]

In this same yeere 1531, there went one Diego de Ordas[2] to be gouernour in the riuer of Maragnon, with three ships, sixe hundred soldiers, and 36 horses. He died by the way, so that the intention came to none effect. After that (in the yeere 1534)[3] there was sent thither one Hierome Artel[4]

The famous riuer Maragnon.

with 130 soldiers, yet he came not to the riuer, but peopled Saint Michael de Neueri, and other places in Paria. Also there went vnto this riuer Maragnon a Portugall gentleman named Aries Dacugna, and he had with him ten ships, nine hundred Portugals, and 130 horses. He spent much [so that those who fitted out the expedition were great losers], but he

John de Barros, factor of the house of India.

that lost most was one John de Barros [factor of the "casa da India," who being noble and of condition payed largely for Ayres da Cunha and others who died there, out of pity towards their wives and children who were left.] This riuer standeth in three degrees toward the south, hauing at the entrance of it 15 leagues of breadth and many islands inha-

---

della Sebastiam de benalcacere, & mandaram os nauios ao porto de Paeta por ser mais seguro.

Neste mesmo anno de 1531 foy por gouernador ao Rio Maranho Diogo de sordas : cõ tres naos & seis centos soldados, trinta & seis caualos, faleceo no caminho, por onde nã teue seu desejo effecto, depois foy la mandado Hieronimo fortal com cento & trinta companheyros. Nã chegou ao rio, pouvou sam Miguel de neuery & outros lugares. Foy tambē a este rio Maranho hum fidalgo Portugues que se chamaua Aires da cunha, leuou dez nauios, noue centos Portugueses, cēto & trinta caualos : fez grande gasto, em que se perderam os que armaram, & o que mais perdeo nisso foy Joã de Barros feitor da casa da India, que por ser nobre & de condiçam larga pagou por Ayres da cunha, & outros que la falceram com piedade de molheres filhos q' lhe ficaram, & dizem q' este rio

---

[1] The ships were sent to the port of Paita for greater safety.
[2] Sordas ?   [3] Not in Portuguese.   [4] Fortal.

bited, (wherein grow trees that beare)[1] incence of a greater bignes then in Arabia, gold, rich stones, and one emeraud was found there as big as the palme of a mans hand. The people of the countrey [said that higher up the river were rocks, and they] make their drinke of a kinde of dates, which are as big as quinces.

In the yeere 1531 one Nunnez de Gusman went from the citie of Mexico towards the north-west to discouer and conquer the countreies of Xalisco, Ceintiliquipac, Ciametlan, Toualla, Quixco, Ciamolla, Culhuacan, and other places. And to doe this he caried with him 250 horses, and fiue hundred soldiers. He went through the countrey of Mechuacan, where he had much gold, ten thousand marks of siluer, and 6000 Indians to carrie burdens. He [discouered and] conquered many countreyes, called that of Xalisco Nueua Galicia, because it is a ragged countrey, and the people strong. He builded a citie which he called Compostella, and another named Guadalajara, because he was borne in the citie of Guadalajara in Spaine. He likewise builded the townes de Santo Espirito (de la Conception),[1]

Gomara, hist. gen., lib. 6, cap. 16.

Nueua Galicia.
Compostella.
Guadalajara.
Santo Espirito, De la conception.

esta em tres graos da parte do sul, em que terá em boca quinze legoas, & muitas ilhas pouoadas, encenso mais crecido que o de Arabia, ouro, pedraria, & que se achara hūa esmeralda como hūa palma, & diziam os da terra que pella ribeira acima auia rocas, & que faziam aqui vinho de tamaras como marmelos.

Nesta era de 1531 foy Nuno de Guzmão da cidade de Mexico contra o Norte, descobrir & conquistar Xalisco, Suntelipac, Chamelam, Tanola, Quisco, Chimola, Huluacam. E leuou pera ysso dozentos & cinquēta caualos & quinhētos soldados, passou por Mexuacão, onde ouue muito ouro, dez mil marcos de prata, seys mil Indios pera carrega. Descobrio & conquistou muita terra, pos nome a de Xalisco noua Galiza, por ser regiam aspera, & de gente esforçada, pouoou Compustella, Guadalajara por ser natural della, & has villas do Spirito sancto, Sam Miguel de Saluaçam, que

---

[1] Not in Portuguese.

San Miguel. and de San Miguel [de Salvacam], standing in 34 degrees of
northerly latitude.

Gomara,
hist. gen.,
lib. 2, cap.
74.

In the yeere 1532 Ferdinando Cortes sent one Diego
Hurtado de Mendoça vnto Acapulco, 70 leagues from
Mexico, where he had prepared a small fleete to discouer
the coast of the South sea as he had promised the emperour. And finding two ships readie, he went into them, and
sailed [westward] to the hauen of Xalisco, where he would
haue taken in water and wood : but Nunnez de Gusman
caused him to be resisted, and so he went forward : but
some of his men mutinied against him, and he put them all
into one of the ships, and sent them backe into New Spaine.
They wanted water, and going to take some in the bay of
the Vanderas, the Indians killed them. But Diego Hurtado sailed 200 leagues along the coast, yet did nothing
woorth the writing.

Gomara,
hist. gen.,
lib. 5, cap. 6,
7, & 8.

In the yeere 1533 Francis Pizarro went from the citie of
Tumbes to Caxamalca, where he tooke the king Attabalipa,
who promised for his ransome much gold and siluer : and to

---

dizem estar em trinta & quatro graos daltura da mesma banda do
Norte.

No anno de 1532 mandou Fernã cortez Diogo furtado de mendoça a Capulco cento & vinte legoas de Mexico, onde mãdaua
fazer armadas pera descobrir a costa da banda do Sul, como cõ o
Emperador tinha assentado, achou Diogo furtado dous nauios
prestes, meteose nelles. Foy ao ponente ao porto Xalisco, onde
quisera tomar agoa & lenha, Nunho de guzmão mandou defen-
derlha, passou diante, amotinou selhe algũa gête, meteos ē hũ dos
nauios, enviou os á noua Espanha, teuerã falta dagoa, sayrã a
tomala na baia das bãdeiras, os Indios os mataram, Diogo furtado
andou bem dozentos legoas ao longe da costa, sem fazer cousa que
de contar seja.

No anno de 1533 partio Francisco piçarro da cidade de Tumbez
pera Xamalca, onde prendeo el Rey Tabaliba, que prometeo por si
muyto ouro, & prata, & pera isso foram a cidade de Cusco, que diz

accomplish it they went to the citie of Cusco standing in 17 degrees on the south side [principal city of that country], Peter de Varco,[1] and Ferdinand de Sotto (who)[2] discouered that iourney,[3] being 200 leagues, all causies of stone, and bridges well made of it, and from one iourney to another, lodgings made for the Yngas : for so they call their kings. Their armies are very great and monstrous. For they bring aboue an hundred thousand fighting men to the field. They lodge vpon these causies ;[4] and haue their prouision sufficient and necessarie, after the vse and custome of China (as it is[5] said). [This people appear to be all of one descent.] Ferdinando Pizarro with some horsemen went vnto Paciacama, 100 leagues from Caxamalca, and discovered that prouince : and comming backe he vnderstood how Guascar, brother to Attabalipa, was by his commandement killed, and how that his captaine Ruminaguy rose vp in armes with the citie of Quito. After this Attabalipa was by the commandement of Pizarro strangled.[6]

Guacas slaine.
Gomar, hist. gen., lib. 5, cap. 11.
Attabalipa strangled.

---

que estaa em dezasete graos da parte do Sul, cabeça daquelle imperio, Pero daluarado, & Fernam do souto, descobriram aquella terra & caminho, em que auia dozentas legoas, todas calçadas de pedra, & pontes bem feytas dellas ; & de jornada em jornada, aposentos pera os Inguas, que assi chamão la aos Reys, & seus exercitos, cousa monstruosa : por q' leuariam mais de cem mil homẽs de guerra, & tudo se nestes paços aposentauam, & tinham mantimento & o necessario em abastança, ao costume da China (como ja disse). Esta gente parece toda dũa costa. Piçarro co algũs de caualo foy a Pachacoma, cem legoas de Caxamalca, descobrio aquella prouincia, & tornado soube como Guascar, hirmão de Tabaliba, era por seu mandado morto, & seu capitam Reymmegay aleuantado com a cidade de Quito, & Atabaliba depois disto, foy por mandado de Piçarro degolado.

---

[1] D'Alvarado.　　　　　[2] Dele.　　　　　[3] Country and route.
[4] And all are lodged in these buildings.
[5] As has been already.　　　　　　　　　[6] Beheaded ?

In the yeere 1534 Francis Pizarro, seeing that the two kings were gone, began to enlarge himselfe in his signiories, and to build cities, forts, and townes, to haue them more in subiection.   Likewise he sent Sebastian de Benalcazar, the captaine of S. Michael of Tangarara, against Ruminaguy vnto Quito.   He had with him two hundred footemen and 80 horsemen.   He went discouering and conquering 120 leagues from the one citie to the other, east, not farre from the equinoctiall line :[1] where Peter Aluarado found mountaines full of snow, and so cold, that 70[2] of his men were frosen to death.   When he came vnto Quito, he began to inhabite it, and named it S. Francis.   In this countrey there is plentie of wheate, barlie, cattell and plants of Spaine, which is very strange [and not to be expected under the line].   Pizarro went straight to the citie of Cusco, and found by the way the captaine Quisquiz (risen in armes, whome shortly he defeated).[3]   About this time there came vnto him a brother of Attabalipa named Mango, whom he made ynga or king of the country [by that means quieting a great part

Gomara, historiæ general. lib. 5, cap. 18.

Cruell snow vnder the line. Gomara, historiæ general. lib. 5, cap. 19. Gomara, hist. gen., lib. 5, cap. 16.

No anno de 1534 Vendo Francisco piçarro estes dous Reys fora do mundo, começouse a estender por seu senhorio, & a fazer nelle forças, cidades, villas pello ter mais sojecto, & mandou logo Sebastiam de Benalcacer, que por capitam em S. Miguel de Tangara estaua, contra Remuregai a Quito, leuou dozentos de pee & oytenta de cauallo, foy descobrindo & conquistandos aquellas cento & vinte legoas, que ha dũa cidade a outra contra o leuante ao longo da linha, onde acharam serras neuadas : & tam frias que se enregelauam algũas pessoas.   Chegado a Quito : começou a pouoalo, & pos lhe nome sam Franciso, diz que se da nesta terra muito trigo, ceuada, gados, plantas de Castella, cousa espantosa de que se nam esperaua debaixo da linha.   Francisco piçarro partio logo a cidade de cusco, & achou no caminho aleuantando o capitam Quisquis, mas veo a elle hum hirmão de Atabaliba que se

---

[1] Towards the east along the line.   [2] Several.
[3] Not in Portuguese.

of the countrey]. (Thus marching forward on his iourney after certaine skirmishes he tooke that exceeding rich and wealthie citie of Cusco.)[1]

In this same yeere 1534 a Briton,[2] called Jaques Cartier, with three ships, went to the land of Cortorealis, and the Bay of Saint Laurence, otherwise called Golfo Quadrato, and fell in 48 degrees and an halfe towards the north; and so he sailed till he came vnto 51 degrees, hoping to haue passed that way to China, and to bring thence drugs and other marchandise[3] into France. The next yeere after he made another voiage into those partes, and found the countrey abounding with victuailes, houses, and good habitations,[4] with many and great riuers. He sailed in one riuer toward the southwest 300 leagues, and named the countrey thereabout Noua Francia: at length finding the water fresh he perceiued he could not passe through to the South sea (and hauing wintered in those parts, the next yeere following)[5] he returned into France.

In the yeere 1534, or in the beginning of the yeere 1535,

---

chamaua Mango, que elle fez Ingua & Rey da terra, com que pacificou grande parte della.

Neste mesmo anno de 1534 diz que foy hũ Frances chamado Jaques cartiel, cõ tres galeões á terra dos Cortes Reais, & Golfam quadrado tomaua em quarenta [oito?] graos da banda do Norte: foy por ella ate cincoenta & hum por ver se achaua saida á outra banda da China, & trazer della a França as especearias, & drogas das Indias: & segundo contauam a terra era abastada de mantimentos, casas, & bem pouoada, q' auia nellas muitas & grandes ribeiras, & que foram por hũa contra o ponente trezentas legoas, poseram lhe nome a Noua França: & como agoa era doçe bem viram que nam atrauessava a outra parte pello que se tornaram.

Neste anno de 1534 ou na entrada de quinhentos & trinta &

---

[1] Not in Portuguese.   [2] Frenchmen.   [3] Spice.
[4] Well peopled.   [5] Not in Portuguese.

Gomar.,
hist. gen.,
lib. 2, cap.
74, & lib. 2,
cap. 98.
Don Antonie de Mendoça came vnto the citie of Mexico as viceroy of New Spaine. In the meane while Cortes was gone for more men to continue his discouerie, which immediately he set in hand, sending foorth two ships [towards the west]'(from Tecoantepec)[1] which he had made readie. There went as captaines in them Fernando de Grijalua, and Diego Bererra de Mendoça, and for pilots there went a Portugal named Acosta, and the other Fortunio Ximenez, a Biscaine. [Making sail they went forth to discover the secrets of those coasts.] The first night they deuided themselues.[2] Fortunio Ximenez killed his captaine Bezerra and hurt

Plaia de
Santa Cruz.
many of his confederacie : and then he went on land to take water and wood in the Bay of Santa Cruz, but the Indians there slue him, and aboue 20 of his companie. Two mariners (which were in the boate escaped, and)[3] went [in a small boat] vnto Xalisco, and told Nunnes de Gusman that they had found tokens of pearles : he went into the ship, and so went to seeke the pearles, he discouered along the coast aboue 150 leagues. They said that Ferdinando de

cinco chegou dom Antonio de mendoça à cidade de Mexico, por Visorey da noua Espanha & era ja partido Fernã cortez catar gente pera continar seu descobrimento, & mandou logo a ella contra ocidente dous nauios que achou acabados, & capitães dellas Fernam de grijaluarez, & Diogo bezerra de mẽdoca, & pilotos hum Portugues que se dizia da costa, & do outro Furtum Ximenez Biscainho. Dadas as vellas foram descobrindo os secretos daquellas ribeiras, & apartados hum do outro, Furtũ ximenes matou o capitam Bezerra & feriram os de sua valia, & deitados em terra tomou agoa & lenha na Baya de Sancta Cruz, onde os Indios ho mataram com vinte & tantos companheyors : & dous marinheyros foram no batel a Xalisco, & dixeram a Nuno de guzman como acharam mostras de perolas, meteose no nauio, foy buscalas : descobrio por esta costa mays de cento & cincoenta legoas, Fernam de Grijal-

---

[1] Not in Portuguese. [2] And separated one from the other. [3] Dele.

Grijalua sailed three hundred leagues (from Tecoantepec)[1] without seeing any land, but only one island, which he named the Isle of Saint Thomas, because he came vnto it on that saints day : it standeth in 20[2] degrees of latitude.

The Isle of
S. Thomas.

In this yeere 1535 Pisarro builded the citie de los Reyes vpon the riuer of Lima.   The inhabitants of Xauxa went to dwell there, because it was a better country, standing in 12 degrees of southerly latitude.   In this same yeere of 1535 he caused the citie of Truxillo to be builded on a riuers side vpon a fruitfull soile, standing in 8 degrees on that side.   He built also the citie of Saint Jago in Porto Viejo : besides many others along the sea coast and within the land : where there breede many horses [mares], asses, [baggage] mules, kine, hogs, goates, sheepe, and other beasts ; also trees and plants, but principally rosemary,[3] oranges, limons, citrons, and other sower fruits [vineyards], vines, wheate, barlie, and other graines [cabbages], radishes [pot herbs], and other [things] (kinde of herbage and fruits)[4] brought out of Spaine (thither to be sowne and planted).[4]

Lima
builded.
Gomar.,
hist. gen.,
lib. 4, cap.
92.
Lib. 5, cap.
23.
Truxillo.

S. Jago de
Porto viejo.

---

uarez diz que andou trezentas sem ver terra, se nam hūa ylha a que poz nome de sam Thomas, pella descobrir em tal dia, & que estaua em dezanoue graos daltura.

No anno de 1535 fundou Francisco piçarro aa cidade dos Reys, na ribeira de Lima, passou a ella os vezinhos de Xauxa, por ser melhor terra esta da parte do sul em doze graos daltura.   Neste mesmo anno de cincoenta,[5] edificou a cidade de Trogilho, ao longo dūa ribeira, terra fresca, em oyto graos da mesma banda, & assi foy feyta a cidade de Santiago, em porto velho & outros muytos ao longo do mar, polla terra dentro : em que se criam muytos caualos, egoas, asnos ; azemelas, vacas, porcos, cabras, ouelhas, & outras alimarias, & assi aruores & outras prantas, principalmēte romeyras, laranjas, limões, sidras, & outras fruytas agras, vinhas, parreiras, trigo, ceuada, grãos, couues, rabãos, ortaliça, & outras cousas q' leuaram d'Espanha.

---

[1] Not in Portuguese.   [2] 19.   [3] Pomegranates.   [4] Dele.
[5] Trinta e cinco ?

In the same yeere 1535 one Diego de Almagro went
from the citie of Cusco to the prouinces of Arequipa and
Chili, reaching [upwards] (beyond Cusco)[1] towards the
south vnto 30 degrees. This voiage was long, and he discouered much land, suffering great hunger, cold, and other
extremities, by reason of the abundance of [snow and] ice,
which stoppeth the running of the riuers [at least after sun-
set, while at midday they melt]; so that men and horses
die in those parts of the colde.[2] About this time Ferdinando Pisarro came out of Spaine to the citie de los Reyes,
and brought with him the title of marquisate of Atanillos
for his brother Francis Pisarro, and vnto Diego de Almagro
he brought the gouernment of 100 leagues ouer and besides

that which was discouered, and named it The New kingdome of Toledo. Ferdinando Pisarro went straight to the
citie of Cusco: and one John de Rada went to Almagro into
Chili with the emperours patents.

Diego de Almagro hauing receiued the letters patents
which the emperour had sent him, went straight from Chili

No mesmo anno da era de mil & quinhentos & vinte[3] cinco, foy
Diogo Dalmagra da cidade de Cusco pera aas prouincias de Ari-
quipa, Chily que estam daly pera cima da parte do Sul ate trezentos graos daltura, & neste caminho por ser comprido, descobriram muita terra, passaram muyta fome, frio, trabalho, grandes
neues, & geadas, que ha tantas naquellas partes: que dizem que
os Rios nam correm se nam depois do Sol fora, & alto dia que as
derrete, pella qual causa lhe morreram muitos caualos & homes
enregelados. Neste meio tempo chegou Fernam piçarro a cidade
dos Reys de Castella & trazia o marquesado de Tuuilhos a seu
jrmaõ Francisco piçarro, & a Diogo dalmagro a gouernança de
çem legoas, alẽ do descuberto a que poseram nome o Nouo reyno
de Toledo, foy logo Fernam piçarro pera á cidade de Cusquo, &
Joam de Rada a Chily [onde?]. Almagro estaua com as pro-

---

[1] Dele. [2] Frozen. [3] Trinta?

vnto Cusco, to haue it, seeing[1] it did appertaine vnto him.
Which was the cause of a ciuill warre. They were mightily
oppressed with want of victuailes and other things in this
their returne,[2] and were enforced to eate the horses, which
had died fower moneths and a halfe before, when they
passed that way [and it is said they were as fresh as when
they died].

In this same yeere 1535, Nunnez Dacuña being gouernour of India, while he was making a fortresse at the citie
of Diu, he sent a fleete to the riuer of Indus, being frō
thence 90 or 100 leagues towards yᵉ north vnder the Tropicke of Cancer. The captaines name was Vasques Perez
de San Paio : also he sent another armie against Badu the
king of Cambaia, the captaine whereof was Cosesofar, a
renegado. They came to the barre of that mighty riuer in
the moneth of December, of the water whereof they found
such trial[3] as Quintus Curtius writeth of it, when Alexander
[the Great] came thither.

The fortresse of Diu.

Badu, king of Cambaia.

---

uisões que lhe o Emperador mandaua, ho qual se partio logo de
Chily a Cusco pera tomalo, dizendo que lhe pertencia, de que se
começou naquella parte a guerra ciuil, nam lhe faltaram fomes &
frios, como á yda, ate comerem os caualos, que auia quatro meses
q' lhe morreram quãdo por aly passaram, & diz que estauam tã
frescos como se entam os mataram.

No mesmo anno de 1535 fazendo Nuno dacunha gouernador da
India a fortaleza da cidade de Dio, mandou hũa armada ao Rio
Indio, que estaua della nouenta, ou cem legoas contra o Norte
debaxo do Tropico de Cancro, & era capitam della Vasco pirez de
Sampayo, & assi hia outra armada do Badu Rey de Cambaya, que
era capitam Cojeçofar arrenegegado. Chegaram á barra daquelle
gram Rio no mes de Dezembro : & contaua o mesmo daquella
terra & agoa que Quinto Curcio deixou escripto quando o grande
Alexandre ali chegara.

---

[1] Saying.   [2] Journey.
[3] And related the same of that land and river as, etc.

Gomara, historiæ general. lib. 2, cap. 61.

In this yeere 1535 one Simon de Alcazaua went from Siuill with two ships and 240 Spaniards in them. Some say they went to New Spaine, others that they went to Maluco, but others also say to China, where they had beene with Ferdinando Perez de Andrada. Howsoeuer it was, they went first vnto the Canaries, and from thence to the streight of Magelan, without touching at the land of Brasill or any part at all of that coast. They entred into the streight in the moneth of December with contrarie windes and cold weather. The soldiers would haue had him turne backe againe, (but he would not).[1] He went into an hauen on the south side in 53 :[2] there the captaine Simon of Alcazaua commanded Roderigo de Isla with 60 Spanyards to goe and discouer land : but they rose vp against him, and killed him, and appointed such captaines and officers as pleased them, and returned. Comming thwart of Brasil they lost one of their ships vpon the coast, and the Spanyards that escaped drowning were eaten by the sauages. The other ship went

Neste anno de 1535 partio Simço Dalcaçoua cõ duas naos de Seuilha, dozentos q'rēta castelhanos nellas. Hūs dizem q' hiam pera a noua Espanha, outros querem dizer q' pera Maluco, outros à China, onde ja esteueram com Fernam perez Dandrade : como quer q' seja foram às Canarias, dahi atrauessaram ao estreito que Magalhães tinha descuberto, sem tocar na terra do Brasil & toda sua costa. Entraram o estreito no mes de Dezembro com tempo contrario, & frio : diz que lhe requereram os soldados que se tornasse pera fora, meteo se em hū porto da parte do Sul em quarenta & cinco graos daltura, donde mandou Simão Dalcaçoua o capitā Rodrigo de Hisla com sessenta Castelhanos descobrir terra, & elles se amotinaram & o prenderā & tomaram as naos, & mataram Simão Dalcaçoua, & poseram capitães officiaes quem quiseram, no Brasil deram cõ hūa nao á costa, os da terra os comeram. A outra nao

---

[1] Not in Portuguese.

[2] From what follows, and if the latitude 45 written in the Portuguese is correct, it seems that he did return.

to Saint Jago in Hispaniola, and from thence to Ciuill in Spaine.

In this same yeere 1535 Don Pedro de Mendoça went [Gomara, historiæ general, lib. 3, cap. 39.] from Cadiz towards the riuer of Plate with twelue ships [the largest and finest vessels that euer went to those parts], and had with him two thousand men : (which was the greatest number of ships and men that euer any captaine carried into the Indies).[1] He died by the way returning homewards. The most part of his men remained in that riuer, (and builded a great towne containing now about two thousand houses, wherein great store of Indians dwell with the Spanyards).[2] They discouered and conquered[3] the countrey till they came to the mines of Potossi and to the towne La [The riuer of Plata runneth vp to Potossi.] Plata [by which the Spaniards of Peru with those of this river, and it is said that more than 600 leagues were discovered by other fleets that ascended the river] (which is 500 leagues distant from them).[4]

In the yeere 1536 Cortes [being at Tagantepec] vnder-

de que era capitão Rodrigo de Hisla, & vinha hum filho de Simão Dalcaçoua, foy ter á cidade de Santiago da ylha Espanhola, & dahi a Seuilha.

Neste mesmo anno de 1535 partio dō Pedro de Mendoça de Calex pera o Rio da prata com doze naos, as mayores & melhores que nunca foram aquellas partes, leuaua dous mil homẽs, por hir mal desposto tornou se, mas faleceo no caminho, & ficou no Rio a mòr parte da gente, q' foy por elle dentro descobrindo, conquistando, & pouoando ate chegar ás minas de Patoci, & villa da prata: por onde se comunicam os Castelhanos de Peru com os deste Rio, & diz q' tem descuberto mais de seis centas legoas com ajuda doutras armadas que foram a este Rio & por elle dentro.

Dizem que no anno de 1536 estando Fernã Cortez em Tagante-

---

[1] Dele.　　　　　　　　　　　　[2] Not in Portuguese.
[3] They went up the river discovering and conquering, etc.
[4] Not in Portuguese.

Gomara,
hist. gen.,
lib. 2, cap.
74 & 98.]

standing that his ship (wherein Fortunio Ximenez was pilote)[1] was seased on by Nunnez de Guzman, he sent foorth three ships [which he had prepared at Chimalam] to the place where Guzman was, and he himselfe went by land well accompanied, and found the ship which he sought all spoiled and rifled. When his three other ships were come about, he went aboord himselfe with the most part of his men and horses, leauing for captaine of those which remained on land one Andrew de Tapia. So he set saile, and comming to a point the first day of May he called it Saint Philip, and an island that lieth fast by it he called

Sant Jago Isle.

Sant Jago. Within three daies after he came into the bay where the pilot Fortunio Ximenez was killed, which he

La plaia de Santa Cruz.

called La Plaia de Santa Cruz, where he went on land, and commanded Andrew de Tapia to discouer.[2] Cortes [having given him time to ariue] tooke shipping againe and came to

Rio de San Pedro y San Paulo.

the riuer now called Rio de San Pedro y San Paulo, where by a tempest the ships were separated, one was driuen to

---

pee, soube como a sua nao era por Nuno de Guzmão tomada, despachou tres nauios que acabados tinha pera Chimalão a onde Guzmão estaua, & foy se por terra bem acompanhado, & achou a sua nao roubada, & a traues deitada. Chegados os tres nauios que mandara embarcou se nelles com a mais gente & cauallos que pode, deixando por capitão dos que sobejara Andres de Tapia. Dada a vela foy tomar hũa ponta ho primeiro dia de Mayo, & por isso lhe pos nome Felipe, & hũa ylheta que ahi está perto Santiago. Dahi a tres dias entrou na baya, em que mataram o piloto Furtum ximenes, & chamou Sancta Cruz, sahio em terra mandou ali vir Audres de Tapia por ser bõ porto, & descobrir a terra dentro. Cortez embarcado deu lhe hum tempo, foy ter a dous Rios q' se agora chamã sam Pedro & Paulo, carregou tanto vento, que se apartaram hũs nauios dos outros, & foy hum ter à baya de Sãta

---

[1] Not in Portuguese.

[2] To come there, it being a safe harbour, and to discover the country inland.

the bay de Santa Cruz, another to the riuer of Guajaual, _{Guajaual Rio.}
and the third was driuen on shore hard by Xalisco, and the
men thereof went by land to Mexico.

Cortes long expected his two ships that he wanted :[1] but _{Mar Vermejo or the}
they not comming he hoised saile & entred into the gulfe now _{Gulfe of California.}
called Mar de Cortes, Mar Vermejo (or the Gulfe of Califor-
nia),[2] (and shot himselfe)[3] 50 leagues within it [under the tropick of Cancer] : where he espied a ship at anker, & sailing
towards her [he ran his ship ashore] he had beene [well nigh] _{Gomara, in the Conquest of Mexico, fol. 290, 291, 292.}
lost [and deprived of everything], if that ship had not suc-
cored him. But hauing graued his ship, he departed with both
the ships from thence. Hee bought victuals (at a deere rate)[3]
at Saint Michael (of Culhuacan);[4] and from thence he went to
the hauen of Santa Cruz, where hee heard that Don Antonio de
Mendoça was come [to Mexico] out of Spaine to be viceroy.
He therefore left to be captaine of his men one Francis de
Vlloa [and went himselfe to Tagante for the purpose of sending thence,] (to send him certaine)[5] ships to discouer that
coast. While he was at Acapulco messengers came vnto him

Cruz & outro a Gayal, outro encalhou junto de Xalisco, os delle se
tornarã por terra a Mexico.

Fernam Cortez esperou pellos nauios, & vendo que nam apare-
ciam, mandou dar á vella, & entrou o estreyto que se agora chama
de Cortez, & mar vermelho, cinquenta legoas por elle dẽtro, até o
Tropico de Cancro, vio hũa nao surta, arribou a ella, foy dar em
seco, esteue quasi perdido, & fora de todo se lhe a Nao nam socorrera, & pos a sua em terra, & corregela. Ambos se tornaram a
comprar em sam Miguel mãtimento, & dahi ao porto de sancta
Cruz, onde deixara a gente, aq' lhe disseram como dom Antonio
de mendoça era chegado a Mexico, o gouernador da noua Españia,
deixou aq' por capitã da gente Francisco dilhoa, foyse a Tagante
p'a de lá mandar nauios em q' fosse descobrir a costa. Chegado
a Capulco, lhe veo mesageiro do viso rey dõ Antonio, em q' lhe

---

[1] Waited for the ships.   [2] Not in Portuguese.
[3] Dele.   [4] Not in Portuguese.   [5] Dele.

from Don Antonio de Mendoça the viceroy to certifie him of his arriuall: and also he sent him the coppie of a letter, wherein Francis Pisarro wrote that Mango Ynga was risen against him, and was come to the citie of Cusco with an hundred thousand fighting men, and that they had killed his brother, John Pisarro, and aboue 400 Spaniards (and 200 horses),[1] and he himselfe was in danger,[2] so that he demanded succour and aide. Cortes being informed of the state of Pisarro, and of the arriuall of Don Antonio de Mendoça [in order that he might not rob him of the blessing or glory] (because he would not as yet be at obediēce; first he)[3] determined [to be the first] to sende to Maluco to discouer that way a long vnder the equinoctial line, because the Islands of Cloues stand vnder that paralele : and for that purpose he prepared 2 ships with prouision, victual[4] & men, besides all other things necessarie. He gaue the charge of one of these ships to Ferdinando de Grijalua, and of the other vnto one Aluarado, a gentleman. They went first[5] to Saint Michael de Tangarara in Peru to succour Francis Pisarro, and from thence to Maluco all along neere the line as they were com-

---

daua cōta de como era naq'la terra : & tābē lhe derā hū trelado dūa carta q' Francisco piçarro dezia como selhe leuantara Māgro ingou, & viera sobre a cidade de Cusco cō cē mil homēs de peleja, & lhe matara seu irmā Joā piçarro, & mais de 400 soldados & o tinha ē grāde ap'to, pelo q' pedia a todos socorro. Vendo Cortez isto, & a chegada de dō Antonio de mēdoça, por lhe nā furtar a bēçam determinou primeiro mādar a Maluco descobrir aq'le caminho ao lōgo da linha, por estarē as ylhas do crauo naq'le paralelo, & p'a isso mādou aparelhar dous nauios de mātimētos, armas, gētes, & todo necessario, deu a capitania dūa nao a Fernā de grijaluerez, & a outra a hū Aluarado homē fidalgo. Forā direitos a S. Miguel de Tangaraga pera fauorecerē Fracisco picarro, & dahia Maluco ao lōgo da linha como lhe era mandado, & deziam q' andariā mais de mil legoas sē verē terra dhūa parte & outra da linha

---

[1] Not in Portuguese. [2] And kept him on the alert ?
[3] Dele. [4] Arms. [5] Direct.

manded. And it is declared that they sailed aboue a thousand leagues without sight of land, on the one side nor
yet on the other of the equinoctiall. And in two degrees
toward the north they discouered one island named Asea, Asea Island.
which seemeth to be[1] one of the Islands of Cloues : 500
leagues little more or lesse [to the west] as they sailed, they
came to the sight of another, which they named Isla de los Isla de los Pescadores.
Pescadores. Going still in this course they sawe another
Island called Hayme towards the south, and another named Hayme Island.
Apia : and then they came to the sight of Seri : turning Apia Island.
towards the north one degree, they came to anchor at Seri.
another Island named Coroa, and from thence they came to Coroa.
another vnder the line named Meousum, and from thence Meosum.
vnto Bufu standing in the same course.[2] Bufu.

The people of all these islands are blacke, and have their
haire frisled, whom the people of Maluco do call Papuas. Ospapuas.
The most of them eate man's flesh, and are witches, so giuen
to diuilishnes, that the diuels walk among them as cōpa-
nions. If these wicked spirits do finde one alone, they kill
him with cruell blowes or smother him. Therefore they
vse not to goe, but when two or three may be in a com-

& en dous graos do norte, descobrirā hūa ylha q' se chama o
Acea, q' parece estar das ilhas do crauo quinhentas legoas pouco
mais ou menos a loeste : pera onde hiā ouuerā vista doutra q'
poserā nome dos pescadores. Indo assi nesta derrota virā hūa
ylha q' se chama Haime, da parte do sul, outra q' se diz Apia, foy
logo ver Seri : tornados ao norte ē hū grao, surgirā ē outra q' se
chama Coroa. Daqui forā ter a outra debaxo da linha q'se diz
Meōsū, & day a de Bufu no mesmo paralelo.

Todas estas ylhas sam de gētes pretas, cabelo reuolto, a q' os
de Maluco chamā Papuas, os mais comē carne humana, grādes
feiticeiros, tā dados aos diabos q' andā antrelles como cōpanheiros,
se achā hū só matāno as pancadas, ou o afogam, por onde nā sam
ousados de andarē sena o dous ou tres jūtos. Ha aq' hūa aue do

---

[1] Five hundred leagues more or less from the islands of Cloves, to the
west. [2] Parallel.

These
seeme to
be like
ostriches. panie.   There is heere a bird as bigge as a crane : he flieth
not, nor hath any wings wherewith to flee, he runneth on
the ground like a deere : of their small feathers they do
make haire for their idols.   There is also an herbe, which
being washed in warme water, if the leafe thereof be laide
on any member and licked with the toong, it will draw out
all the blood of a mans body : and with this leafe they vse
to let themselues blood.

From these islands they came vnto others named the
Guelles, standing one degree towards the north, east, and
west[1] from the Isle Terenate, wherein the Portugals haue a
fortresse : these men are haired[2] like the people of the
Malucoes.   These islands stande. 124 [or 125] leagues from
the Island named Moro ; and from Terenate betweene 40
and 50.   From whence they went to the Isle of Moro, and
the Islands of Cloues, going from the one vnto the other.
But the people of the countrey would not suffer them to
come on lande, saying vnto them : Go vnto the fortresse
where the captain Antonio Galuano is, and we[3] will receiue
you with a good will : for they would not suffer them to

Guelles
Islands.
Ternate.

Moro.
Molucco.

Antonio
Galuano the
author of
this booke.

---

tamanho dhū grou, nã voa nē tē penas p'a isso, corre a pè como
hū veado, das penas delles fazē cabellos p'a seus ydolos, & assi ha
hūa erua q' lauando cō agoa quēte qualq'r mēbro do corpo, ē
pōdoa encima lābēdo cō alīgoa, tirarã o sangue todo dūa pessoa, &
cō elle se sangrã.   Destas ylhas foram a outras q' se chamā os
Gueles, está ē hū grao da parte do norte leste oeste cō a ylha
de Ternate em q' está a fortaleza portugueza.   Estes homēs sam
bassos de cabelo corredio como os Maluq'ses, estam estas ilhe-
tas 124 ou 125 legoas da ylha de Moro, & esta de Ternate 40
ate 50 donde foram ter ao Moro & ylhas do Crauo, & andaram
hūas & outras, sem os da terra lhe deixarem tomar porto, dizendo
q' se fossem aa fortaleza q' achariam o capitã Antonio galuão q' o
receberia com boa vontade, q' eles o nam fariam sem sua licença,
por ser pay da patria, que assi lhe chamauā : cousa digna de notar,

---

[1] In the same parallel.   [2] Have lank hair.   [3] Who.

come on land without his licence : for he was factor[1] of the countrey, as they named him. A thing woorthie to be noted, that those of the countrey were so affectioned to the Portugals, that they would venture for them their liues, wiues, children and goods.

The case is now much altered.

In the yeere 1537 the licenciate John de Vadillo, gouernour of Cartagena, went out with a good armie from a[2] porte of Vraba called Saint Sebastian de buena Vista (being in the gulfe of Vraba),[3] and from thence to Rio verde, & from thence by land without knowing any way (nor yet hauing any carriages),[4] they went to the end of the countrey of Peru, and to the towne of La plata, by the space of 1200 leagues [from that river] : a thing woorthie of memorie. For from this riuer to the mountaines of Abibe the countrey is full of hils,[5] thicke forests of trees [valleys of jungle], and many riuers [which descended from the mountain over which they travelled], (and)[6] for lacke of a beaten way [and sure guides ?] (they had pierced sides).[7] The mountaines of Abibe as it is recorded haue 20 leagues in bredth. They

Pedro de de Cieça, parte primera de la Chronica del Peru, cap. 9, & 107.

La Plata.

The mountaines of Abibe.

porq' os daq'lla terra sam afeiçoados a castelhanos[8] q' põe por elles vidas, molheres, filhos, & fazendas.

No anno de 1537 gouernando a prouincia de Cartagena o Licēceado João de vadilho sahio della com boa armada, & foram ao porto d'Uraba, & à cidade de Sam Sebastiam de boa vista, & dahi ao Rio verde : & por terra caminharam sem caminho nem carreira, ate fim da prouincia do Peru & villa da prata, mil & dozētas legoas desta ribeira. Feito digno de memoria, porq' deste Rio ate as montanhas de Abibi auerá quinhentas legoas de terra chãa, & campina, bosques, valles espessos, muitos aruoredos, rios q' descendē da serra por onde hiã, por falta d'estrada & carreira, pera q' hã mister guias certas.

---

[1] Father.   [2] And went to the.   [3] Not in Portuguese.   [4] Dele.
[5] There were five hundred leagues of burning land, flat open country.
[6] Dele.   [7] Dele.   [8] Portuguese ?

must be passed ouer in Januarie, Februarie, March and Aprill. And from that time forward it raineth much, and the riuers will be so greatly encreased, that you cannot passe for them. There are in those mountaines many (heards of swine, many dantes),[1] lyons, tygers, beares, ounses, and great cats (and monkeis, and mightie)[2] snakes and other such vermine.[3] Also there be in these mountaines abundance of [swine, deer of two kinds, hares, rabbits, and other game], partridges, quailes, turtle doues, pigeons, and other birds and foules of sundrie sorts. Likewise in the riuers is such plentie of fish, that they did kill of them with their staues : and carrying canes and nets they affirme that a great army might be sustained [pleasantly] (that way without being distressed for want of victuals).[4] Moreouer they declared the diuersities of the people, toongs, and apparell that they obserued in the countries, kingdomes, and prouinces which they went through, and the great trauels[5] and dangers that they were in till they came to the towne called Villa de la Plata, and vnto the sea [on the other side] (thereunto adioyning).[6] This was the greatest discouerie that

Villa de la Plata.

Estas montanhas Dabibi, diz q' teram vinte legoas de largo, ham se de atrauessar no mes de Janeiro, Feuereiro, Março, Abril, porq' dahi por diante choue tanto que vã as ribeiras crecidas, & nam se pode caminhar por ellas. Ha tambem muitos leões, tygres, hussos, onças : & grandes gatos, cobras, & outras feras diuersas. Nestas montanhas assi hà tantos porcos, veados, corços, Guazelas, lebres, coelhos : & outras muitas caças, perdizes, codirnizes, pombos, rolas : & outras aues de diuersas castas. E nos Rios tãtos pescados, q' com os paos os matauan, & leuando cães, redes, diz q' poderam manter hũ exercito com desenfadamento. Assi contauam das muitas prouincias, regnos, senhorios q' atrauessaram, & diuersas gentes, linguages, & trajos q' viram, muitos trabalhos & perigos q' passarão, ate chegarem á villa da prata, & mar da outra

---

[1] Dele.　　　　[2] Dele.　　　　[3] Wild beasts.
[4] Dele.　　　　[5] Troubles.　　　[6] Dele.

hath beene heàrd of by land, and in so short a time.   And
if it had not beene done in our daies, the credite thereof
would haue beene doubtfull.

In the yeere 1538 there went out of Mexico certaine ^{Ramusius,} friers of the order of Saint Francis towards the north to ^{356.} preach to the Indians the catholicke faith.   He that went
farthest was one frier Marke de Nizza, who passed through ^{Frier Marke de} Culuacan, and came to the prouince of Sibola, where he ^{Sibola.} found seuen cities [of which he related marvels] : and the
farther he went, the richer he found the countrie of gold,
siluer, previous stones, and sheepe bearing very fine wool.
Vpon the fame of this welth the viceroy don Antonio de
Mendoça, and Cortes, determined to send a power thither.
But when they could not agree[1] thereupon Cortes went ouer
into Spaine in the yeere 1540, where afterward he died.

In this yeere 1538 began the ciuil warre betweene Pisarro
and Almagro, wherein (at the last)[2] Almagro was [overcome]
taken and beheaded.

---

banda : & foy o mōr descubrimento q' se ainda vio por terra : em
tam breue tempo, que se não fora no nosso tiuera duuidoso
credito.

No anno de 1538 sahiram da cidade de Mexico frades Fran-
ciscos contra o Norte, pregar aos Indios a nossa sancta fee catholica, & o q' mais se meteo pella terra, foy fre Marcos de missa, q'
passou por Culuacão, & chegou â prouincia de Sibola : & dezia
auer nela sete cidades de q' coutauam marauilhas : & quanto mais
hiã adiante, tanto mais achauam a terra rica d'ouro, prata, pedraria,
& gados de lãa muy fina.   Era tãta a fama desta terra, & riqueza,
q' se desauierão o Viso rey dom Antonio de mendoça, & Fernã
Cortez sobre mandar a ella, pello q' se passou Cortez a Castella no
ãno de 1540 & acabou l' sua vida.   E nesta de 1538 foy começada

---

[1] So rich was this country considered, that the viceroy and Cortez
disagreed about sending thither.

[2] Dele.

Gomara,
hist. gen.,
lib. 5, cap.
84.

Antonie
Galuano,
chiefe cap-
taine of
Maluco,
author
of this
worke.

In the same yeere 1538, Antonie Galuano being chiefe captaine in the isles of Maluco, sent a ship towards the north, whereof one Francis de Castro was captaine, hauing commandement to conuert as many as he could to the faith. [having been asked to do so by many of those parts.] He himselfe christened many, (as the lords)[1] of the Celebes, Macasares, Amboynos, Moros, Moratax, and diuers other places. When Francis de Castro arriued at the Island of Mindanao [and other islands near them], six kings receiued the water of baptisme, with their wiues, children and sub-iects: and the most of them Antonie Galuano gaue com-mandement to be called by the name of John, in remem-brance that king John the third raigned then in Portugall [so much had he that name in his memory].

The Portugals and Spaniards which haue beene in these islands affirme, that there be certaine hogs in them, which besides the teeth which they haue in their mouthes, haue other two growing out of their snouts, and as many behinde their eares, of a large span and an halfe in length. Like-

---

a guerra ciuil antre Piçarro & Almagro, por onde elle foy desba-ratado, & preso, & degolado.

No mesmo anno de 1538 mandou Antonio galuano, q' estaua por capitã em Maluco, cõtra o norte hu nauio, & capitã dele Fra-cisco de castro, cõ regimēto q' fizesse quantos christãos podesse, por ser dalgũs daq'las partes req'rido p'a isso, & o mesmo Antonio galuão ter muitos feitos [fieis] dos celebres[2] Mocasares, Amboynos, Moros, Maratax, & outras diuersas partes. Chegado Francisco de Castro à ylha de Midanao, & outras q' descobrio acima dellas, tomarã seis Reys agoa de baptismo cõ molheres, filhos, vassalos, & aos mais deles mandou Antonio galuã por nome Joannes, em memoria do terceiro q' em Portugal reynaua, tanto trazia na sua.

Os Portugueses & Castelhanos q' por estas ylhas andaram, con-tauam q' auia nellas porcos, q' alē dos dētes q' tinha na boca, lhe suyã outros dous pelos focinhos, & outros tãtos por detrás das orelhas, & tinhã de cõprido palmo & meo. E auia hũa aruore q' o

---

[1] Dele.   [2] Celebes ?

wise they say there is a tree, the one halfe whereof, which standeth towards the east, is a good medicine against all poyson, and the other side of the tree, which standeth toward the west, is very poison; and the fruite on that side is like a bigge pease; and there is made of it the strongest poyson that is in all the world. Also they report that there is there another tree, the fruite whereof whosoeuer doth eate, shall be twelue houres besides himselfe [and shall act without judgment], and when he commeth againe vnto himselfe he shall not remember what he did in the time of his madnes. Moreouer there are certaine crabs of the land, whereof whosoeuer doth eate shall be a certaine space out of his wits. Likewise the countrey people declare that there is a stone in these islands whereon whosoeuer sitteth shall be broken in his bodie.[1] It is further to be noted, that the people of these islands do gild their teeth [and fix across their privy parts a bar of gold or silver, and rivet the points in the form of a rose, which causes a woman to bleed].

In the yeere 1539 Cortes sent three ships with Francis Vlloa to discouer the coast of Culuacan northward. They

Gomar., hist. gen., lib. 2, cap. 74, & Ramusius, 3 vol.,fol.329.

meio dela q' estaua cōtra o oriēte, era muy medicinal, & cōtra toda peçonha, o outro meio da aruore q' estaua cōtra o ponēte he muy peçonhēto, & o fruito daq'la bāda he todo como tramasso, & se faz delle a mais forte peçonha q' ha na redōdeza, & assi se dizia q' auia outra aruore q' quē comia seu fruto estaua doze oras fora de si, & fazia cousas de homem sem siso, quando tornaua nam daua nenhum acordo disso, & auia hūs cangrejos da terra que quē os comia, tambē estaua certas oras da mesma maneira. Assi diziam os da terra que auia ahi hūa pedra q' quē se assentaua nela criaua potra, os homēs destas ylhas douram os dentes, & atrauessam sua natura cō hūa barra douro ou prata, & nas pontas rebatem hūas rosas, com que ensanguentam hūa molher toda.

No anno de 1539 mādou Fernā cortez tres nauios a Frācisco guil-

---

[1] Ruptured.

went from Acapulco, and touched at S. Jago de buena sperança, and entred into the gulfe that Cortes had discouered,

The bot-
tome of the
gulfe of
California
discouered. and sailed till they came in 32 degrees, which is almost the
farthest end of that gulfe, which place they named Ancon de
Sant Andrew, because they came thither on that saints daie.
Then they came out a long the coast on the other side, and

California
doubled. doubled the point of California and entred in betweene certaine islands and the point,[1] and so sailed along by it, till
they came to 32 degrees, from whence they returned (to
newe Spaine),[2] enforced thereunto by contrarie windes (and
want of victuals) ;[2] hauing beene out about a yeere.   Cortes,
according to his account, spent 200,000 ducates[3] in these discoueries.

Cabo del
Enganno.
The dis-
tance be-
tween Ame-
rica and
China in 32
degrees is
1000 leagues.
Gomara,
hist. gen.,
lib. 6, cap.17. From Cabo del Enganno to another cape called Cabo de
Liampo in China there are 1000 or 1,200 leagues sayling, [of
which] Cortes and his captaines discouered [and conquered]
(new Spaine),[2] from 12 degrees to 32 from south to the north,
being 700 leagues [of coast from east to west], finding it more
warm then cold, although snow do lie vpon certaine moun-

---

hoa p'a descobrir a costa de Culuacam p'a cima. Partiram de Capuleo
tocaram Santiago de boa esperança, entrarã no estreito q' Cortez
descobrira : chegaram por ele acima até trinta & dous graos daltura, que he o fim dagoa, poseram lhe nome Ancon de sancto
Andre por ser em seu dia.   Tornaram p'a fora ao longo da costa
da outra banda, dobrarã a põta de California, & meterã se por
antre as ylhas & a terra : foraõ ao longo della ate se poerẽ em 32
graos, donde arribaram por vento contrario auendo hũ anno q' la
andauam, dizem q' gastou Fernã cortez nestas armadas & desco-
brimẽtos dozentos mil cruzados, & q' desta ponta do engano auera
à outra de Liampo da China mil ou mil & dozentas legoas de rota
abatida, & q' o q' descobrio & conquistoro Fernão Cortez & seus
capitães he de doze graos ate trinta & dous de Leste oeste, em q'
auera setecentas legoas pella terra dentro, que he mais quente que

---

[1] Main.   [2] Not in Portuguese.   [3] Crusadoes.

taines most part of the yeere. In new Spaine there be many
trees, flowers and fruits of diuers sorts and profitable for many
things. The principall tree is named Metl [or the honey tree]. It groweth not very high nor thicke. They plant and dresse it as we do our vines. They say it hath fortie kinde of leaues like wouen clothes, which serue for many vses.[1] When they be tender they make conserues of them, paper, and a thing like vnto flaxe : they make of it mantles, shooes, mats, girdles, and cordage. These trees haue certaine prickles so strong and sharpe, that they sewe with them [as with an awl]. The roots[2] make fire and ashes, which ashes make excellent good lie. They open the earth from the roote and scrape it, and the iuice which commeth out is like a sirrupe. If you do seeth it, it will become honie ; if you purifie it it will be sugar. Also you may make wine and vinegar thereof.[3] (It beareth the coco).[4] The rinde (rosted and)[5] crushed [and squeezed] vpon sores and hurts healeth and cureth.[6] The iuice of the tops[7] and roots mingled with [the

Metl an ex-cellent tree.

---

fria, ainda que ha serras que dura a neue & geada quasi todo o anno.

Hà na noua Espanha muito aruoredo de flores & fructos, diuersos & proueitosos pera muitas cousas, & a mais principal della se chama aruore metel, ou do mel, não he muy grande nem grossa: prantã na, podã na, concertã na como vinha : diz q' tem quarenta folhas de feiçam de telhas & seruem disso & quando sam tenras fazem conseruas dellas, papel, fiãmes como linho, fazem dellas mãtas, alpargates, esteiras, cintas, xaquemas : tem estas aruores hũas espinhas tã duras & agudas q' cozem cõ ellas como com souellas, & o tronco dá bõ lume & cinza pera de coada, escauam na ao pee, & agoa q' estila he como arrobe se a cozem fica mel, se a purificã, açuquere, se lhe deitam patalim, vinho, se a destemperam, vinagre, as pencas assadas & exprimidas sobre chagas ou

---

[1] Like tiles, and are used as such.   [2] Stem.
[3] If —— be thrown into it, wine, if diluted, vinegar.
[4] Not in Portuguese.   [5] Dele.   [6] Forms a crust.   [7] Ears.

juice of] incense are[1] good against poyson, and the biting of a viper. (For these manifold benefits)[2] [Thus] it is the most profitable tree knowne (to growe in those parts).[2]

Also there be there certaine small birds named Vicmalim. Their bill is small[3] and long. They liue of the dewe [honey] and the iuice of flowers and roses. Their feathers be verie small and of diuers colours. They be greatly esteemed to worke golde with. They die or sleepe euerie yeere in the moneth of October : sitting[4] vpon a little bough in a warme and close place,[5] they reuiue or wake againe in the moneth of Aprill after that the flowers be sprung, and therefore they call them the reuiued birds.

The reuiued birds.

Likewise there be snakes in these parts, which sound as though they had bels when they creepe. There be other which engender at the mouth, euen as they report of the viper. There be hogges which haue a nauell on the ridge of their backs, which assoone as they be killed and[6] cut, will by and by corrupt and stinke.

---

ferida, sara & encoura, o sumo das espigas & rayzes emburilhadas com sumo de encenso, he bõ contra a peçonha & mordedura de bibora, assi que he mais proueitosa aruore que se la sabe.

Há la hūs passarinhos q' se chamã Vicincilim sam pequenos, o bico delgado & comprido, mãtem se do rocio, mel, licor de flores, & rosa, tem as penas meudas & de diuersus cores, prezã nas muito pera laurar ouro, morre ou adormece cada āno : no mes Doutubro posto em hum raminho em lugar abrigado resuscita, ou acorda no mes Dabril depois & que ha flores, pello q' lhe chamam o resuscitado. Ha cobras q' sam como cascaneis quando andã : ha outras q' emprenhã pella boca, como dizē da bibora : ha porcos cõ embigos no espinhaço, que matandoos se lho nam cortam fede logo : ha pexes que guincham como porcos & roncam, per onde lhe chamam roncadores.

---

[1] Is.   [2] Not in Portuguese.   [3] Slender.
[4] Placed.   [5] Sheltered place.   [6] If it be not.

Besides these there be certaine fishes which make a noyse like vnto hogs, and will snort, for which cause they be named snorters. Snorting fishes.

In the yeere 1538 and 1539, after that Diego de Almagro was beheaded, the Marquis Francis Pisarro was not idle. For he sent straight one Peter de Baldiuia with a good companie of men to discouer and conquere the countrey of Chili. He was wel receiued of those of the countrey, but afterwards they rose against him and would haue killed him by treason. Yet for all the warre that he had with them, he discouered much land, and the coast of the sea toward the southeast,[1] till he came into 40 degrees and more in latitude. While he was in these discoueries he heard newes of a king called Leucengolma, which commonly brought to the field two hundred thousand fighting men[2] against another king his neighbour [who brought as many], and that this Leucengolma had an island, and a temple therein with two thousand priestes : and that beyond them were the Amazones, whose queene was called Guanomilla, that is to say, the golden heauen [whence the Spaniards concluded that there Gomara, hist. gen., lib. 5, cap. 15.
Chili.
This might be the temple in the lake of Titicaca. Cieça, cap. 103.

No anno de 1538 & 1539, depoys de Diogo Dalmagro degolado, ho marquez Fernam Piçarro nam esteue ocioso, mandou logo Pero de baldiua com muita gente ao descobrimento & conquista de Chily, foy bem recebido dos da terra, & depois o quiseram matar por enganos, & com toda a guerra que teue descobrio muita terra & costa, do mar da banda de Leste ate quarenta & tantos graos daltura : & ouuiram dizer dos naturaes de Hulcham, que juntaua dous mil homēs de peleja, contra outro rey seu vezinho, q' traria o mesmo : & Hulcham colma tinha hūa ylha & templo cō dous mil sacerdotes. Dētro & mais adiante auia amazonas, & a raynha dellas se chamana Ganomilha, q' quer dizer ceo douro, donde os Castelhanos tomaram auer ali muita riqueza, & assi de hūa ylha

---

[1] The coast runs nearly north and south.

[2] They heard tell by the natives of Hulcham, who collected two thousand fighting men, etc.

were great riches to be found there, and also at an Island
called Solomon]. But as yet there are none of these things
discouered. About this time Gomez de Aluarado went to
conquer the prouince of Guanuco : and Francis de Chauez
went to subdue the Conchincos, which troubled the towne
of Truxillo, and the countreyes adioyning. Peter de Vergara went to the Bracamores, a people dwelling toward the
north from Quito. John Perez de Vagara went against the
Ciaciapoians : Alfonsus de Mercadiglio went vnto Mulu-
bamba. Ferdinando and Gonzaluo Pisarros went to subdue
Collao, a [healthy] countrey very rich in gold [and silver].
Peter de Candia went [above] (to the lower part of)[1] Collao
[a barren country with a warlike population]. Peranzures
also went to conquer the said countrey. And thus the
Spanyards dispersed themselues, and conquered aboue seuen
hundred leagues of countrey in a very short space, though
not without great trauailes and losse of men.[2] [In the year
1540 Captain Fernando Alcarano went, by command of the
Viceroy Don Antonio de Mendoza, with two ships to discover
the coast.]

---

que se chama de Salamam, tambem dizem ser muy rica, mas nada
disto se vio ategora. Gomez Daluarado foy á prouincia de Ganuco,
Francisco de Chaues aos Conchucos q' corriam a Trozilho, por
serem vezinhos, Pero de Vergara ao Bracamoros que estam ao
norte de Quito, Joam perez de veragar contra os Chachapoyos,
Alonso de mercadilho a Malubumbo, Fernando & Gonçalo piçarro,
ao Colao terra sadia & rica douro & prata, Pero de Candia acima
de Colao, terra aspera de gente belicosa. Perancuris tambem foy
descobrir, cōquistar, & pouoar terra, & outros per outra banda se
estenderam mays de setesentas legoas com gram presteza.

No anno de 1540 foy o capitā fernā alcarāo por mādado do viso
rey dō Antonio de mēdoça com dous nauios descobrir a costa.

---

[1] Dele.

[2] Perancuris also went to discover, conquer, and people fresh country; and others on the other side extended themselves more than seventy
leagues very rapidly.

The countreyes of Brasill and Peru stand east and west almost 800 leagues (distant).[1] The neerest[2] is from the Cape of Saint Augustine vnto the hauen of Truxillo : for they stand both almost in one parallele and latitude [of six degrees]. And the farthest is[3] [more than] 950 leagues, reckoning from the riuer of Peru to the streits of Magellan, which places lie directly north and south, through which countrey passe certaine mountaines named the Andes, which diuide Brasill from the empire of the Ingas. After this maner the mountaines of Taurus and Imaus diuide Asia into two parts : which mountaines begin in 36 and 37 degrees of northerly latitude at the end of the Mediterran sea ouer against the Isles of Rhodes and Cyprus, running still towards the east vnto the sea of China. And so likewise the mountaines of Atlas in Africa diuide the tawnie Moores from the blacke Moores which haue frisled haire, beginning [at the Red Sea] (at mount Meies about the desert of Barea),[4] and running along vnder the Tropicke of Cancer vnto the Atlanticke Ocean.

The mountaines of Andes.

Estas terras do Brasil & Peru teram de Leste oeste perto de oitocentas legoas pello mais largo, q' he do cabo de Sancto Agustinho ao porto de Trozilho : porque estam ambos em hum paralelo em seis graos daltura, & de comprido mais de nouecentas & cinquenta, q' se contem do Rio Peru ao estreito q' ho Magalhães descobrio norte sul dereitas, em que ha hũas serras a que chamam os Andes, que apartam o Brasil do imperio dos Inguas, assi & da maneira que os mõtes Taurus & Imãos, o fazem em Asia os Indidios dos Sytas, os quaes montes começam em trinta & seis ou trinta & sete graos daltura, na fim do mar Mediterraneo, defronte das ylhas de Rodes & Chipre, & vam sempre a leste ate o mar da China, como os montes Atalantes : diuidem em Affrica os mouros brancos dos negros de cabello reuolto, começando no mar roxo, vam ao longo de Tropico de Cancro, ate o mar chamado Atalantico.

---

[1] Dele. [2] Widest part. [3] Of length.
[4] Not in Portuguese.

The mountains of the Andes be high, ragged [craggy], and in some places barren without trees or grasse, whereon it raineth and snoweth most commonly. Vpon them are windes and sudden blastes; there is likewise such scarcitie of wood, that they make fire of turffes, as they do in Flanders. In some places of these mountaines and countries the earth is of diuers colours, as blacke, white, red, greene, blew, yellow, and violet, wherewith they die colours without any other mixture. From the bottomes of these mountaines spring[1] many small and great riuers, principally from the east side, as appeereth by the riuers of the Amazones, ·[and Maranhan], of S. Francis, of Plata, [of St. John], and many others which runne through the countrey of Brasil, being larger then those of Peru, or those of Castilia del oro. There grow on these mountaines many turneps, rapes,[2] and other such like rootes and herbes. One there is like vnto Aipo or rue[3] which beareth a yellow flower, and healeth all kinde of rotten sores, and if you apply it vnto whole and cleane flesh it will eate it vnto the bone : for that it is good for the vnsound and naught for the whole.

Earth of diuers colours good to dy withall.

As montanhas dos Andes, sam altas, asperas, fragosas, & ha lugares escaluados, sem aruores, nē heruas, chouendo & neuando de contino nellas, cō vētos & trouoadas, carecē tāto de lenha, q' fazē fogo de terra como em Frandes. Ha partes nestas serras, & terras de cores diuersas, hūa preta, outra branca, vermelha, verde, azul, amarella, & mirada, de que fazem tintas sem mais mesturas. Saem das rayzes destas montanhas muitas ribeiras pequenas & grandes, principalmente da parte de Leste, como se parece no rio das Amazonas & Maranho de sam Francisco, da prata, sam Ioam, & outros muitos q' ha na terra do Brasil, por ser mais largo q' o do Peru & noua Castela. Criam se nesta serra muitos nabos, tramossos, & outras : ha hūa como aypo, dá flor amarela, q' sara toda chaga podrida, & se a pōe em carne saá & limpa come até o osso, assi q' he boa pera o mao & mà pera o bō.

---

[1] Run.   [2] Beans.   [3] ?

They say there be in these mountains tigers, lions, beares, woolues, wilde cats, foxes, [antas],[1] (dantes, dunces),[2] hogs, [goats], and deere : birdes as well rauenous as others, and the most part of them are blacke, as vnder the north both[3] beasts and birdes be white. Also there be great & terrible snakes which destroied a whole armie of the Ingas passing that way, yet they say that an olde woman did inchant them in such sort that they became so gentle, that a man might sit vpon one of them.[4] The countrey of Peru adioining vnto the mountaines of Andes westward toward the sea, [is divided into three parts, the Andes, which are very high, some mountains which skirt them, and in the flat valleys which are along the coast, running inland from 15 to 20 leagues], (and containing 15 or 20 leagues in bredth, is)[5] all of very hot sand, yet fresh, bringing foorth many good trees and fruites because it is well watered : where there growe abundance of.[6] [reeds] flags, rushes, herbes, and trees (so slender and loose),[7] that laying your hands vpon them the leaues

---

Dizem q' ha nestas montanhas, tigres, liões, hussos, lobos, gatos, raposos, antas, porcos, veados, guazelas, aues, assi de rapina como destroutras, & as mais sam pretas como debaxo do norte : as mesmas alimarias & aues sam brancas. Ha também grandes cobras & tam feras, q' passando hum exercito dos Inguas o destruyram, mas dizem q' hũa velha as encantou de maneira, q' ficaram tam mansas q' andão homẽs caualgados sobre ellas. As terras do Peru q' jazẽ das serras dos Andes, a loeste cõtra a marinha, he em tres partes diuidida, os Andes q' sam muy grãdes, & algũs montes q' jazem na fralda delles, & ẽ campos, valles, q' vam ao longo da costa, & alargamse pella terra dentro quinze ou vinte legoas, todas d'areaes muy quentes, frescos de diuersos aruoredos & fruitos, per serem regados : & por debaxo canas, espadanas, juncos, heruas, & aruores, q' pondo a mão nellas, caelhe a folha : & por antre estas

---

[1] Tapir ?   [2] Dele.   [3] The same.
[4] That men rode astride upon them.   [5] Dele.
[6] And in the low grounds.   [7] Not in Portuguese.

28

will fall off.   And among these herbes and fresh flowers the
men and women liue and abide without any houses or bed-
ding, euen as the cattell doe in the fields ; and some of them
haue tailes.   They be grosse, and weare long haire.   They
haue no beards, yet haue they diuers languages.

Those which line on the tops[1] of these mountains of Andes
betweene the cold and the heate for the most part be blinde
of one eie, and some altogether blinde, and scarce you shall
finde two men of them together, but one of them is halfe
blinde.   Also there groweth in these fields, notwithstanding the
great heate of the sand, good maiz, and potatos, and an herbe
which they name coca, which they carrie continually in their
mouthes, as in the East India they vse another herbe named
betele, which also they say satisfieth both hunger and thirst.
Also there are other kindes of graines and rootes whereon
they feede.   Moreouer there is plentie of wheate, barly,
millet, vines, and fruitful trees, (which are brought out)[2] of
Spaine and planted there.   For all these things prooue well
in this countrey, because it is so commodiously watered.

---

verduras, flores, & frescuras, se criaõ os homẽs & molheres sém
casas, & camas, como os gados nos campos : & algũs tem rabos,
sam grosseiros, cabellos, compridos, nam tem barbas, mas diuersas
lingoas.

Os q' viuem nas fraldas destas mõtanhas dos Andes, antre a
frialdade & quentura, sam pela mayor parte tortos, & algũs cegos :
de marauilha se acham dous homẽs juntos, q' hum delles nam
seja torto.   Tambẽ se dá por estes campos, ainda q' d'area cali-
dissimos, muito bõ maiz & batatas, & hũas heruas a q' chamam
coca, q' trazẽ sempre na boca, como na India o betele, q' dizẽ q'
mata a sede & fome.   E assi ha outros graõs & rayzes q' la comem,
muito trigo, ceuada, milho, vinhos, & outras aruores Despanha q'
la prantaram, porq' tudo se dá bem naquella terra, por ser regada.
Tambem se semea muito algodam, q' de seu natural he branco,

---

[1] Skirts.   [2] ?

Also they sow much cotton wooll, which of nature is white, red, blacke, [blue], greene, yellow, orange, tawnie, and of diuers other colours.

Likewise they affirme, that from Tumbez southward it doth neither raine, thunder, nor lighten, for the space of fiue hundred leagues of land : but at some times there falleth some little shower [or dew]. Also it is reported, that from Tumbez to Chili there breede no peacocks, hennes, cocks, nor eagles, falcons, haukes, kites, nor any other kinde of rauening fowles, and yet there are of them in all other regions and countreies : but there are many duckes, geese, herons, pigeons, partriges, quailes, [owls, nightingales], and many other kindes of birdes. There are also a certaine kinde of fowle like vnto a ducke, which hath no wings to flie withall, but it hath fine thinne feathers [or veil] which couer all the body. Likewise there are bitters[1] that make war with the seale or sea wolfe : for finding them out of the water they will labour to picke out their eies, that they may not see to get to the water againe, and then they doe kill them. They say it is a pleasant sight to behold [this sport] (the fight betweene the said bitters and seales).[2] With the

---

vermelho, preto, azul, verde, amarelo, aleonado, & doutras diuersas cores.

Assi dizem q' de Tumbez por diante, não choue, nem trouoeja, ne relampaguea, mais de quinhentas legoas, ás vezes cae algũ orualho, & tãbem querē dizer q' de Tumbez a Chili, nam se criem pauas, galinhas, nem galos, nem aguias, falcões, açores, gauiães, nem outras aues de rapina auendoas em toda a outra terra & co-marca : mas ha muitos patos, adēs, garças, rolas, pōbos, perdizes, codornizes, mouchos, petos, roxinoes, & outras aues, hũas como patos sem penas, tem hum veo delgado q' as cobre todas : ha butres q' tem guerra com os lobos marinhos, como os acham fora dagoa quebram lhe os olhos aas picadas, por se nam acolheram a

---

[1] Vultures.   [2] Not in Portuguese.

Xacos a
kinde of
great
sheepe
that men
ride vpon.

beards of these seales men make cleane their teeth, because they be wholesome for the toothach.   There are certaine beastes which those of the countrey call Xacos, and the Spanyards sheepe, because they beare wooll like vnto a sheepe, but are made much like vnto a deere, hauing a saddle backe like vnto a camell.   They will carrie the burthen of 100 weight.   The Spanyards ride vpon them, and when they be wearie they will turne their heads backward, and void out of their mouthes a woonderful stinking water.

From the riuer of Plata and Lima southward[1] there breede no crocodiles nor lizards, no snakes, nor any kinde of venemous vermine,[2] but great store of good fishes breede in those riuers.   On the coast of Saint Michael in the South sea there are many rocks of salt couered with egges.   On the point of Saint Helena are certaine well-springs which cast foorth a liquor, that serueth in stead of pitch and tarre.   They say that in Chili there is a fountaine, the water whereof will conuert wood[3] into stone [and clay into great stones].   In the hauen of Truxillo there, is a lake of fresh

---

ella, assi os matam : diz q' he pera folgar de ver esta caça : cō as barbas dos lobos alimpam os dentes, por ser bom pera a dōr delles. Ha hūas alimarias que os da terra chamã xacos, os Castelhanos ouelhas por terem lāas como elles, sam da feiçam de ceruos : tem gibas como camellos, leuam peso de quatro arrobas, os Castelhanos caualgã nellas, quando cansam volvem a cabeça, & deitão hūa agoa muy fedorenta.

Dos Rios da prata & Lima pera cima nam se criam lagartos, cobras, nem bichos peçonhētos por onde ha muitos & bōs pescados.   Na costa de sam Miguel, no mar ha grãdes pedras de sal cubertas d'ouas.   Na pōta de sancta Elena ha fontes q' deitam licor q' serue de pez & alcatram.   Dizem q' em Chicha ha hūa fonte q' sua agoa cōuerte a terra em pedra, & o barro penedo.   No porto de Trugilho ha hūa alagoa d'agoa doce, & o fundo de bom

---

[1] Upwards.   [2] For which reason there be great store of good fish.
[3] Earth.

water, and the bottome thereof is of good hard salt. In the Andes beyond Xauxa there is a riuer of fresh water, in the bottome whereof there lieth white salt. Also they affirme by the report of those of the countrey, that there haue dwelt giants in Peru, of whose statures[1] they found in Porto viejo, and in the hauen of Truxillo, bones and iawes with teeth, which were three and fower fingers long. (In the yeere 1540 the captaine Ferdinando Alorchon went by the commandement of the Viceroy Don Antonio de Mendoça with two ships to discouer the bottome of the gulfe of California, and diuers other countries.)[2] Ramusius, 3 vol., fol. 363.

In this yeere 1540 Gonsaluo Pizarro went out of the citie of Quito to discouer the countrey of Canell or Cinamome, a thing of great fame in that countrey. He had with him two hundred Spanyards horsemen and footemen, and three hundred Indians to carrie burthens. He went forward til he came to Guixos, which is the farthest place gouerned by the Ingas : where there happened a great earthquake with raine and lightning, which sunke 60 houses. They passed ouer cold and snowie hils, where they found many Indians frozen to death, maruelling much of the great snowe that Gomara, hist. gen., lib. 5, cap. 36.

---

sal coalhado. E nos Andes detras de Xauxa ha hum Rio dagoa doce, & o fundo de sal branco : assi dizem os da terra que ouue gigãtes nella, cujas estatuas acharam em Porto velho, & no de Trugilho grãdes ossos & cauernas cõ dẽtes de tres ou quatro dedos em largo.

No anno de 1540 partio Gonçalo piçarro da cidade de Quito ao descobrimento da canella, cousa muito nomeada naquella terra, leuaua dozentos Espanhoes de pè & cauallo, trezentos Indios de carrega, caminhou ate Quixos que he a derradeira cousa q' os Inguas senhorearam, onde lhe tremeo a terra, & choueo, & relampagueou, tanto que se fundiram sessenta casas : passaram hũas serras muy frias & neuadas, onde lhe ficaram muitos Indios rege-

---

[1] Statues.   [2] Not in Portuguese.

they found vnder the equinoctiall line. From hence they
went to a prouince called Cumaco, where they tarried two
monethes because it rained continually. And beyond they
sawe the cinamome-trees, which be very great, the leaues
thereof resembling bay leaues, both leaues, branches, rootes,
and all tasting of Cinamome. The rootes haue the whole
taste of Cinamome. But the best are certaine knops like
vnto alcornoques or acornes, which are good marchandise.[1]
It appeereth to be wilde cinamone, and there is much of it
in the East Indies, and in the Islands of Jaoa or Jaua.

[In this year 40 Fernando Cortez returned with his wife
to Castile and died of disease.] From hence they went to
the prouince and citie of Coca, where they rested fifty daies.
From that place forwards they trauailed along by a riuers
side being 60 leagues long, without finding of any bridge,
nor yet any forde, [nor meanes] to passe ouer to the other
side. They found one place of this riuer, where it had a
fall of 200 fathomes deepe, where the water made such a
noise, that it would make a man almost deafe to stand by it.
And not far beneath this fall, they say they found a chanell

Margin notes:
Cumaco.
Cinamomtrees.
Wild cinamom in the Islands of Jaua.
Coca.
El pongo, a mighty fall of a riuer.

---

lados, & elles espantados da gram neue q' auia debaixo da linha.
Daqui foram a hũa prouincia q' se chama Cumaco, onde esteuerã
dous meses por lhes chouer contino : & ao diante viram as aruores
de canella q' sam grandes, & as folhas como de loureiro, & ellas,
& codea, & rayzes tem tudo sabor de canella, mas o melhor della
he hũs capulhos como dalcornoques, de que ha gram trato : &
segundo parece deue ser canella braua que ha muyta na India, &
ilhas de Java. E neste anno de quarenta foy Fernam Cortez com
sua molher pera Castella, & faleceo lá de doença.

Daqui foram à prouincia ou cidade de Coca, onde repousaram
cinquẽta dias. Dahi por diãte caminharam ao longo de hũa ribeira
muy grande sessenta legoas sem acharem ponte, vao, nem por
onde passassem a outra banda, somẽte acharam o rio de dozentos

---

[1] With which there is great trade.

of stone very smooth, of two hundred[1] foote broad, and the riuer runneth by :[2] and there they made a bridge to passe ouer on the other side [it is said to be a better country] ; where they went to a country called Guema, which was so Guema. poore, that they could get nothing to eate but onely fruits and herbes [some like truffles]. From that place forward they found a people of some reason, wearing certaine clothing made of cotton wooll, where they made a brigandine [payed with resin] ; and there they found also certaine canoas, wherein they put their sicke men, and their treasure and best apparell, giuing the charge of them to one Francis de Orellana: and Gonsaluo Pizarro went by land with the rest of the companie along by the riuers side, and at night went into the boates, and they trauailed in this order two hundred leagues as it appeereth. When Pizarro came to the place where he thought to finde the brigandine and canoas, and could haue no sight of them nor yet heare of them, he thought himselfe out of all hope, because he was in a strange countrey without victuales, clothing, or any

---

estadios, onde a agoa fazia tam grande roydo q' parecia q' emmouq'cia a quē junto estaua : & nam muito abaxo diz q' acharam hum canal de pedra, talhada de vinte pès em largo, por onde todo o Rio passa, em q' fezeram ponte pera a outra banda : dizem ser melhor terra. Foram a hūa que se chama Gema, tam pobre que nam comiam se nam frutas & heruas, & hūas como tubaras da terra. Adiante acharam gente de razam, que vestiam algodam, onde fezeram hum bergantim brado com rasina, & acharam algūas canoas em q' meteram os doentes, & o melhor vestido & peças q' leuauā: & deram carrego desta armada a Frācisco dorilhana, & Gōçalo piçarro foy por terra cō a mais gente ao longo da ribeira, & como era noite recolhiam se aos nauios, & caminhariam assi dozentas legoas segundo lhe parecia.

Chegado Piçarro onde esperaua achar o bergantim & canoas, &

---

[1] Twenty.   [2] Through which the whole river passes.

thing else : wherefore they were faine to eate their horses, yea and dogs also, because the countrey was poore and barren, and the iourney long, to goe to Quito. Yet notwithstanding, taking a good hart to themselues, they went on forwards in their iourney, trauailing continually 18 monethes, and it is reported that they went almost five hundred leagues, wherein they did neither see sunne nor any thing else whereby they might be comforted, wherefore of two hundred men which went foorth at the first, there returned not backe past ten vnto Quito, and these so weake, ragged, and disfigured that they knew them not. Orellana went five hundred or sixe hundred leagues downe the riuer, seeing diuers countreyes and people on both sides thereof, among whom he affirmed some to be Amazones. He came into Castile, excusing himselfe, that the water and streames draue him downe perforce. This riuer is named The riuer

Rio de Orellana.

of Orellana, and other name it the riuer of the Amazones, because there be women there which liue like vnto them.

In the yeere 1540 Cortes went with his wife into Spaine, where he died of a disease seuen yeeres after.[1]

---

como as nam vio nē nouas dellas ficou muito agastado por se ver em terra alhea, sem mantimento, vestido, nem cousa algūa q' ate os cauallos & cāes comeram, & a terra pobre, fragosa, caminho comprido pera tornar á cidade de Quito, & com tudo poseram se a isso & no caminho andaram anno & meo : & diz q' andariam quatrocentas ou quinhentas legoas, onde nam acharam sol nem cousa que os podesse confortar, por onde de dozentos que eram nam tornaram a Quito dez, & estes tam fracos, rotos, & trasfigurados, que os nam conheciam. Orilhana andaria quinhentas ou seis centas legoas pello Rio abaxo, vendo diuersas terras & gentes de hūa parte & de outra, & diz q' ha Amazonas. Veyo ter a Castela desculpado se q' a agoa o trouxera por força : a qual se chama o rio Dorilhana, & outros das Amazonas pelas auer nesta terra, ou molheres q' viuē como elas.

---

[1] See back, page 222.

In the yeere 1541 it is recorded that Don Stephan de Gama, gouernour of India, sailed toward the streit of Mecca. He came with all his fleete vnto an anker in the Island of Maçua, and from thence vpwards in small shipping[1] he Maçua. went along the coast of the Abassins and Ethiopia [step by step] till he came to the Island of Suachen, standing in 20 Suachen. degrees towardes the north, and from thence to the hauen of Cossir, standing in 27 degrees, and so he crossed ouer to Cossir. the citie of Toro, standing on the shore of Arabia, and along Toro. by it he went vnto Suez, which is the farthest ende of the Suez. streit, and so he turned backe the same way, leauing that countrey and coast discouered so far as neuer any other Portugall[2] captaine had done, although Lopez Suares, go-uernour of India, went to the hauen of Juda, and the hauen of Mecca, standing on the coast of Arabia, in 23 degrees of latitude, and 150 leagues from the mouth of the streit. Don Stephan (de Gama)[3] crossing ouer from Cossir to the citie of Toro, as it is reported, found an Island of Brimstone, which An Island of was dispeopled by the hand of Mahumet, wherein many brimstone in the Red Sea.

No anno de 1541 diz q' partio dõ Esteuã da gama gouernador da India pera o estreyto de Meca : foy com toda armada surgir á ylha de Masua, & dahi pera cima em nauios de remos, costeãdo a costa do Abexim & Affrica, de pedra ē pedra ate a ilha do Suaquē, q' estará ē xx graos daltura da parte do norte, dahi ao porto Dal-corer q' está ē xxvij atrauessou p'a a cidade de Toro da parte da ribeira, & ao longo della foy a Suez, que he o fim do estreito, por onde se tornaram pello mesmo caminho, deixando aquela terra & costa descuberta, onde capitam Espanhol nunca chegara : ainda q' Lopo Soarez gouernador da India foy à cidade Juda, & porto de Meca, q' está da banda Darabia em vinte & tres graos daltura, & cento & cinquenta legoas da boca do estreito.

Atrauessando dom Esteuam Dalcocer pera o Toro, dizem q' se achou hūa ylha d'enxofre q' foy da mão de Mafamede despouoada,

---

[1] In row boats.   [2] Spanish ?   [3] Not in Portuguese.

crabs doe breede, which increase[1] nature : wherefore they be greatly esteemed of such as are vnchaste. Also they say that there are in this streit many roses which open when women are in their labour.

John Leo writeth in the (very end of his)[2] geographie which he made of Africa, that there is in the mountaines of Atlas a roote[3] called surnag, ouer which if a maid [pass] (chance to make water)[4] shee shall loose her virginitie.

In the same yeere 1541 [on twelfth day] Don Diego de Almagro killed the Marques Francis Pizarro, and his brother Francis Martinez of Alcantara (in the citie de los Reyes, otherwise called Lima),[5] and made himselfe gouernour of that countrey.

Gomara, hist. gen., lib. 6, cap. 17.

Sibola.

In the [same] yeere 1540[6] the Viceroy Don Antony de Mendoza sent one Francis Vasquez de Coronado by land vnto the prouince of Sibola with an armie of Spaniards and Indians. They went out of Mexico, and came to Culuacan, and from thence to Sibola, which standeth in 30 degrees of latitude.

& muytos cangrejos nella q' ajudam a natureza : pelo q' sam muy estimados, principalmente dos pouco castos. Assi dizem q' há neste estreito muitas rosas das q' se abrem quando as molheres parem. Joam Liam escreue na geographia q' fez Dafrica, q' nos montes Atalantes há hũa herua que a molher que passa per cima, perde a virgindade. Neste mesmo anno de 1541 naũdade[7] dos Reis matou dom Diogo Dalmagro ao Marquez Frãcisco piçarro, & a seu yrmão Francisco mẽz dalcãtara, & se aleuãtou por gouernador da terra.

Neste mesmo anno de 1539[6] mandou o Viso rey dõ Antonio de mẽdoça por terra à prouincia de Sibolla Francisco vasquez coronado cõ bõ exercito de Castelhanos & Indios. Partiram de Mexico, foram a Culuacam, dahi a Sibolla, que està em trinta & oito graos daltura, requereram aos da terra pazes & mantimentos,

---

[1] Assist.   [2] Not in Portuguese.   [3] A herb.
[4] Dele.   [5] Not in Portuguese.   [6] 1541 ?   [7] No dia?

They required peace with the people and some victuals, being thereof destitute. But they answered that they vsed not to giue any thing to those that came vnto them in war-like manner. So the Spaniards assalted the towne and tooke it, and called it Nueua Granada, because the generall himselfe was borne in Granada. The soldiers found[1] them-selues deceiued by the words of the friers, which had beene in those parts before; and because they woulde not returne backe to Mexico againe with emptie hands, they went [from Sibolla] to the towne of Acuco, where they had knowledge Acuco. of Axa and Quiuira,[2] where there was a king very rich, that did worship a crosse of golde, and the picture of the queene of heauen.[3] They indured many extremities in this journey [and crossed frozen riuers], and [one night all] the Indians fled away from them, and in one morning[4] they found thirtie of their horses dead. From Cicuic they went to Circuic. Quiuira,[5] which was two hundred leagues off, according to Quiuira. their account, passing all through a plaine countrey [with-out tree or stone], and making by the way certaine hillocks

que leuauam disso falta. Responderam q' nam dauā nada a quem hia de guerra : combateram a vila, foy tomada, poseram lhe nome Granada, por o Viso Rey ser natural della.

Achando se os soldados dos frades enganados, por nam tornarē com as mãos vazias a Mexico, foram de Sibolla á cidade de Suco, donde teueram noua de Xaqueuira onde estaua hum Rey muito rico, q' adoraua hūa Cruz douro, & hūa molher de prata, q' o ceo senhoreaua. Neste caminho passaram muito trabalho, perigo, & Rios neuados, & lhe fogiram hūa noite todos os Indios, & aman-heceram trinta caualos mortos. E de Suco foram a Xaqueuira, que segundo sua conta eram dozentas legoas, tudo campina rasa pelada, sem aruore nem pedra. Faziam por ella montes de bostas

---

[1] Finding.   [2] Xaqueuira.
[3] And a woman of silver who governed heaven.
[4] At dawn.   [5] From Suco they went to Xaqueuira.

of cowe dung, because thereby they might not loose their
way in their returne. [It is said] they had there haile-
stones as bigge as oranges [which caused them fear and
tears]. Now when they were come to Quiuira [said to be
in 42 degrees of latitude], they found the king (called
Tatarrax)[1] which they sought for, with a iewell of copper
hanging about his necke, which was all his riches. They
saw neither any crosse [of gold], nor any image of [siluer]
(the queene of heauen),[2] nor any other token of Christian
religion. It is written of this countrey that it is but
smally inhabited, principally in the plaine and champion
places, because the men and women goe in herds with
their cattell, whereof they haue great plenty euen as the
Arabians do in Barbarie, and they remooue from place to
place, euen as the season serueth, and the pastures to
feede their cattle. In these parts are certaine beasts almost
as bigge as horses, they haue very great hornes, and
they beare wooll like vnto sheepe, and so the Spaniards
call them. They haue abundance of oxen verie monstrous,
being camel backed, and hauing long beards, and on their

*Gomara,
hist. gen.,
lib. 6, cap. 18
& 19.*

*Sheepe as
big as
horses.*

---

de vaca, por se nam perderem á tornada : diz que lhe choueo &
cahio pedra do tamanho de laranjas, pello que ouue temor & lagri-
mas. Chegados a Xaqueuira que dizem estar em quarenta & dous
graos daltura, acharam ho Rey que buscauam com hũa joya de
cobre ao pescoço, q' era toda sua riq'za, nã viram cruz douro, nẽ
molher de prata, nem quem lhe desse razam da nossa sancta fe
catholica.

O q' contauam desta terra era ser pouco pouoada, principalmente
na campina, porq' os homẽs & molheres costumam andar por ella
com seus gados, q' tẽ muitos, como os alarues : & mudã se segundo
o tempo & pasto. Diziam q' auia ahi hũas alimarias do tamanho
da zemelas, tinham grandes cornos, & lãa como carneyros, & assi
lhe chamam os Castelhanos. As vacas sam muitas & muy mon-
struosas, com grandes corcouas sobre as espaduas, & compridas,

---

[1] Not in Portuguese.   [2] Dele.

necke long manes like vnto horses. [In this prouince there
is neither wheat nor barley, millet nor maize, nor do they
make bread.] They liue with eating of these oxen and
drinking of their blood, and apparell themselues with the
skins of the same. The most parte of the flesh that they
do eate is rawe, or euill rosted, for they lacke [wood] (pots
to seeth it in).[1] They cut their meat with certaine kniues
made of flint stone. Their fruite are (damsons, hazel nuts),[2]
walnuts, melons, grapes [plums], pines,[3] and mulberies.
There be dogges [and mastiffs] so bigge, that one of them
alone will hold a bull, though he be neuer so wilde. When
they remooue, these dogs do carrie their children, wiues,
and stuffe vpon their backes (and they are able to carrie
fiftie pound waight.)[4] [Also there are many dogs in the
jungle, wild, in droues like cattle.] I passe ouer many
things, because the order which I follow will not permit me
to be long.

Dogs carying 50 pound waight on their backes.

In the yeere of our Lord 1542 one Diego de Freitas being
in the realme of Siam, and in the citie of Dodra as captaine
of a ship, there fled from him three Portugals in a junco

barbas pelo espinhaço, & pescoço, sedas como de cauallos. Nam
ha nesta prouincia trigo, ceuada, milho, mayz, nem fazem pão de
nenhũa cousa : das vacas comem, bebem seu sangue, vestem,
calçam, a mais da carne crua, ou mal assada aa mingoa de lenha :
cortam na cõ facas de pederneyra. As frutas sam nozes, melãas,
huuas, ameixas, pinhões, & amoras. Ha cães & rafeyros tamanhos, que hum so tem hum touro por brauo que seja. Quando se
mudam leuam o fato, filhos, & molheres encima : tambẽ ha muitos
cães no mato brauos em manadas como gados : por muitas cousas
passo, porque a regra q' sigo me nam da a mais espaço.

No anno de 1542 achandose Diogo de freytas no Reyno de
Syam na cidade Dodra capitam de hũ nauio, lhe fogiram tres Por-

---

[1] Dele.   [2] Dele.   [3] Cones of the pine tree.
[4] Not in Portuguese.

(which is a kind of ship) towards China. Their names were Antony de Mota, Francis Zeimoro, and Antony Pexoto, directing their course to the citie of Liampo, standing in 30 and odde degrees of latitude. There fell vpon their sterne such a storme, that it set them off the land, and in fewe daies they sawe an island towards the east standing in 32

Japan dis-couered by chance.

degrees, which they do name Japan, which seemeth to be the Isle of Zipangri, whereof Paulus Venetus maketh mention,[1] and of the riches thereof. And this Island of Japan hath gold, siluer, and other riches.

In this [same] yeere 1542 Don Antonio de Mendoça, Viceroy of Nueua Spagna, sent his captaines and pilots to discouer the coast of Cape del Enganno, where a fleete of Cortez had been before. They sailed till they came to (a place called Sierras Neuadas, or)[2] The snowie mountaines, standing in 40[3] degrees toward the north, where they saw ships with merchandises, which carried on their stems [for device or crest] (the images of certaine birdes called)[4] alcatrarzi [and other birds of gold and silver], (and had the

---

tugueses em hū junco q' hia pera a China, chamauãse Antonio da mota, Francisco zeimoto, & Antonio pexoto. Hindo se caminho p'a tomar porto na cidade de Liampo, q' está em trinta & tātos graos daltura, lhe deu tal tormenta aa popa, q' os apartou da terra, & em poucos dias ao Leuāte viram hūa ylha em trinta & dous graos, a q' chamam os Japoes, que parecem ser aquelas Sipangas de que tanto falam as escripturas, & suas riquezas : & assi estas tambem tem ouro, & muyta prata, & outras riquezas.

Neste mesmo anno de 1542 mandou dom Antonio de mendoça Viso rey da noua Espanha seus capitães piloto, descobrir a costa do cabo del enganho, onde os de Cortez chegarā pera cima, foram até as serras neuadas, que dizē estar ē quarenta & cinco graos da parte do norte, onde viram naos cō mercadorias, q' traziam nas proas por diuisas alcatrazes, & outros passaros douro & prata, q'

---

[1] Of which writers say so much.   [2] Dele.   [3] 45 ?   [4] Dele.

yards of their sailes gilded, and their prowesse laid ouer
siluer).[1] They seemed to be of the Isles of Japan, or of Gomara,
hist. geu.,
lib. 6, cap. 18.
China ; for they said that it was not aboue thirtie daies sail-
ing vnto their country.

In the (same)[2] yeere 1542, [in the month of October],
Don Antony de Mendoça [the viceroy] sent vnto the Islands
of Mindanao [Cebu and Nota, where Magellan died] a Gomara,
hist. gen.,
lib. 4, cap. 13.
Ramusius, 1
vol., fol. 375,
pag. 2.
fleete of sixe ships, with fower or fiue hundred soldiers,
and as many Indians of the countrey, the generall whereof
was one Rui Lopes de villa Lobos, being his brother in
law and a man in great estimation. They set saile from
the hauen of Natiuidad, standing in 20 degrees towards
the north, vpon All Saints eeue, and shaped their course
towards the west [and in the south-west quarter in 19
degrees]. They had sight of the Island of S. Thomas, Saint
Thomas.
which Hernando de Grijalua had discouered, and beyond
in 17 degrees they had sight of another island, which they
named La Nublada (that is, The cloudie Island). From La Nu-
blada.
thence they went to another island named Roca partida Roca
Partida.
(that is, The clouen Rocke). The 3 of December they

---

pareciam serē dos Japoēs ou Chinas, & diziam q' auia pouco mais
de trinta dias de nauegaçam a sua terra.

No anno de 1542 em mes Doutubro, mādou o viso rey dō Antonio ás ylhas de Mindanao, Cebu, & Nata, ōde Magalhāes fora
morto hūa armada de seis velas, q'trecētos ou quinhētos soldados
nelas, & outros tātos Indios da terra : & por capitam môr Ruy
lopez de Vilhalobos seu cunhado, pessoa de muita estima. Partiram do porto do Natal, q' està em vinte graos ao norte, vespera de
todos os sanctos gouernaram a loeste, & á quarta do Sudoeste em
dezanoue graos, ouueram vista da ylha de sancto Thomas q' Fernam de grijaluerez descobrira. Mais a diante em dezasete graos
viram outra, a q' poseram nome a Nublada. Dahi foram a outra
q' chamam Roca partida. A tres dias de Dezēbro acharam hūs
baxos de seis ou sete braças de fundo. A vinte & cinco deste

---

[1] Not in Portuguese.   [2] Dele.

Baxos.

found certaine baxos or flates of sixe or seuen fathoms deepe. The 15[1] of the same moneth they had sight of the islands, which Diego de Roca, and Gomez de Sequeira, and

Los Reyes.

Aluaro de Saauedra had discouered, and named them Los Reyes, because they came vnto them on Twelfe day. And beyond them they found other islands in 10 degrees all standing round, and in the midst of them they came to an anker, where they tooke fresh water and wood.

In the same yeere 1542 Don Diego de Almagro was slaine in Peru by the hands of one Don Vaca de Castro.

In the yeere 1543, in Januarie, they departed from the foresaid islands with all the fleete, and had sight of certaine islands, out of which there came vnto them men in a certaine kinde of boats, and they brought in their hands crosses, and saluted the Spaniards in the Spanish toong saying, Buenas dias, Matelotes, that is to say, Good morrow, companions ;[2] whereat the Spaniards much marueiled, being then so farre out of Spaine, to see the men of that countrey with crosses, and to be saluted by them in the Spanish toong, and they seemed in their behauiour to incline somewhat to our Catholique faith. The Spaniards not knowing

---

mes viram as ylhas q' Diogo da Rocha, & Gomez de Sequeira, & Aluaro Sayauedra descobrirā, poseram nome dos Reis por a verē em seu dia. E ao diante acharam outras em dez graos, todas em roda : & da mesma maneira surgirā nelles, & tomaram agoa & lenha. Neste mesmo āno de 1542 foy desbaratado em Peru dom Diogo dalmagro por Vaca de castro.

No anno de 1543 em mes de Janeiro se fezeram aqui à vella com toda a armada, & ouueram vista dalgūas ylhas, de q' sahiram paraos & calaluzez com gēte, & traziam nas naos cruzes, & os saluaram com bōs dias matalotes, de q' ficaram marauilhados por se verem de Castella tam alongados, & homēs naquella terra cō cruzes, & saudarē nos em lingoa Espanhol, & traziam diuisa que

---

[1] 25 ?　　　　　　　　　　[2] Sailors.

that many thereabout had beene christened by Francis de
Castro, at the commandement of Antony Galuano, some of
them named these islands, Islas de las cruzes, and others
named them Islas de los Matelotes. The Isles of
Matelutes.

In the same yeere 1543, the first of February, Rui Lopez
had sight of that noble island Mindanao, standing in 9 Mindanao.
degrees : they could not double it nor yet come to an ancre
as they would, because the christened kings and people
resisted them, hauing giuen their obedience to Antonie.
Galuano, whom they had in great estimation, and there
were fiue or sixe kings that had receiued baptisme, who by
no meanes would incurre his displeasure. Rui Lopez perceiuing this, and hauing a contrary winde, sailed along the
coast to finde some aide,[1] and in 4 or 5 degrees he found a
small island, which they of the countrey call Sarangam, Sarangam.
which they tooke perforce, and in memory of the vizeroy
who had sent them thither they named it Antonio, where
they remained a whole yeere, in which time there fell out
things worthie to be written ; but (because there are more

---

parecia sentirem algūa cousa da nossa sancta fe catholica, por
nam saberem que auia muytos della que Francisco de Castro por
mandado de Antonio Galuam baptizara, hūs lhes chamam as ylhas
das Cruzes, & outros dos matalotes.

Neste mesmo anno de 1543, o primeiro de feuereiro ouue Ruy
lopez vista daq'lla nobre ilha de Mindanao, em noue graos daltura,
nam pode dobrala, nem surgir como desejaua, porq' os Reys
Christãos & pouo della lho defenderam, por terem dado a obedi-
ēcia a Antonio galuam, q' elles muito estimauam, & nam queriam
anojalo cinco ou seis Reys q' tinham tomado agoa de baptismo.
Vendo Ruy lopez ysto, & o vēto contrario, foy se ao longo da costa
buscar algū abrigo, & em quatro ou cinco graos daltura acharam
hūa ylha pequena, a q' os da terra chamam Saranguam : & tomada
perforça, em memoria do Viso rey que os la mandaua, poseram
lhe nome Antonio, onde esteueram hum anno, socederam lhe

---

[1] Shelter.

histories that intreat of the same)[1] I leaue them, meaning to meddle with the discoueries onely.[2]

In the same yeere 1543, and in the moneth of August, the generall Rui Lopez sent one Bartholomew[3] de la torre in a (smal)[4] ship into new Spaine, to acquaint the vizeroy don Antonio de Mendoça with all things. They went to the Islands of Siria, Gaonata, Bisaia, and many others, standing in 11 and 12 degrees towards the north, where Magellan had beene, and Francis de Castro also, who [had given eternal life to many who were] there baptized (many),[5] and the Spaniards called thē the Philippinas in memory of the prince of Spaine. Here they tooke victuals and wood, and hoised sailes : they sailed for certaine daies with a farewinde, till it came vpon the skanting,[6] and came right vnder the tropique of Cancer. The 25 of September they had sight of certaine islands, which they named Malabrigos (that is to say, The euil roads). Beyond them they discouered Las dos Hermanas (that is, The two sisters). And beyond them also they saw 4 islands more, which they called los

The relation of John Gaietan in the first vol. of Ramusius, fol. 376.

The Philippiuas.

Malabrigos.

Las dos Hermauas.

---

cousas dignas de serem escritas, nam me meto antre ellas por serem mais historias que descobrimento.

No mesmo anno de 1543 em mes Dagosto, mandou ho Geral Ruy lopez a Bernaldo dela torre em hum nauio á noua Espanha dar conta a dom Antonio de mēdoça o q' la passara. Forā ter aa ylha de Syria, Gaonata, Bisaya, & outras q' ahi muytas em onze & doze graos da parte do Norte, por onde o Magalhães andara, & Francisco de Castro dera saude perpetua a muytos que por aly se baptizaram, & hos Castelhanos lhe poseram nome as Filipinas, em memoria do principe de Castella. Tomaram mantimento, agoa, & lenha, & se fezeram à vella : foram algus dias em Léste vento a popa, ate que lhe foy escasseando, & se poseram porto do Tropico de Cancro : em xxv do mes de Setēbro virā hūas ylhas, a q' pose-

---

[1] Dele.   [2] As they belong more to general history than to discovery.
[3] Bernard ?   [4] Not in Portuguese.   [5] Dele.   [6] Fell light.

Volcanes. The second of October they had sight of Far- Los Volcanes.
fana, beyond which there standeth an high pointed rock, La Farfaua.
which casteth out fire at 5 places. So sayling in 16 degrees
of northerly latitude [700 leagues] from whence they had
come, as it seemeth,[1] wanting winde they arriued againe at
the Islands of the Philippinas. They had sight of 6 or 7 Sixe or seuen
islands more, but they ankered not at them. They found also islands more.
an Archipelagus of Islands well inhabited with people, lying An archipelagus of
in 15 or 16 degrees : the people be white [well disposed], islands.
and the women (well proportioned, and)[2] more beautifull
and better arraied then in any other place of those parts,
hauing many iewels of gold, which was a token that there
was some of that metal in the same countrie. Here were
also barkes of 43 cubits in length, and 2 fathomes and a
halfe in bredth, and the plankes 5 inches thicke, which
barkes were rowed with oares. They told the Spaniards,
that they vsed to saile in them to China, and that if they
would go thither they should haue pilots to conduct them, Pilots for China.
the countrie not being aboue 5 or 6 daies sayling from

---

ram nome Mal abrigo. E alē delas descobrirāo as duas yrmāas :
& mais auante quatro, a q' chamarā os Balcones. A dous d'Outubro ouuerã vista da Forfana : & alem della ha hū penedo alto, q'
deita fogo por cinco partes.

Hindo assi em xvi graos daltura setecētas legoas donde partirā
segūdo o q' lhes pareciã, por nā acharē tēpo arribarā as ylhas
Felipinas, ouueram vista de seis ou sete, mas nam surgirã nellas :
acharam em hū archipelago de ylhas bem pouoadas de gente, q'
estam em quinze ou dezaseis graos daltura, aluas, bē despostas
molheres mais fermosas & atauiadas q' ha naquellas partes, com
muitas joyas douro, q' era sinal auello na terra. Auia tabē nauios
de remo de quarenta & tres couados ē cōprido, duas braças & mea
de largo, & o taboado de v dedos ē grosso, & diziā q' nauegauā
nelles p'a a China, q' se la quisessem hir, q' lhes dariam pilotos
pera ysso, q' nam erāo mais q' cinco ou seis dias de caminho.

---

[1] Seemed to them. [2] Not in Portuguese.

thence. There came vnto them also certaine barkes or boates handsomely decked,[1] wherein the master and principall men sate on high, and vnderneath were very blacke moores with frizled haire [as if for parade or state]: and being demanded where they had these blacke moores, they answered, that they had them from certaine islands standing fast by Sebut, where there were many of them, a thing that the Spaniards much maruailed at, because from thence it was aboue 300 leagues to the places where the black people were. Therefore it seemed, that they were not naturally borne in that climate, but that they be in certaine places scattered ouer the whole circuite of the world [like other races]. For euen so they be in the Islands of Nicobar and Andeman, which stand in the gulfe of Bengala, and from thence by the space of 500 leagues we doe not know of any blacke people. Also (Vasco Nunez de)[2] Valboa declareth, that as he went to discouer the South sea, in a certaine land named Quareca, he found black people with frizled haire, whereas there were neuer any other found either in Noua Spagna, or in Castilia del Oro, or in Peru [called New Castile].

Tambē vierā a elles paraos & calaluzes bē laurados & guarneci-dos : & os señores vinhā assētados ē alto, & por baxo certos negros de cabello reuolto, como por estado : pergūtando dōde os ouuerā. Respōderam q' de hūas ylhas. Junto de Sebue mantam auia muitos, de q' se os Castelhanos marauilhauam, por q' dali a mais de trezentas legoas, nam auia gentes pretas, por onde parece q' nam sam naturaes da Clima, se nam ha os em manchas pella redondeza, como qual q'r outra casta : porque assi os ha nas ylhas de Nicober & Andamam, que estam no golfam de Bengala, & dali a quinhentas legoas nam sabemos gentes pretas. Valboa tambem conta que hindo descobrir ho mar da outra banda do Sul, que em hūa certa terra que se chama Cauça, achou gente preta de cabello frisado, nam os auendo em toda a Noua Espanha, nem em Castella

---

[1] Well built and fitted.   [2] Not in Portuguese.

In the yeere 1544 Don Gutierre de Vargas, bishop of Placenza, sent a fleet from the city of Siuil vnto the streits of Magellan: which is reported to haue beene done by the counsel of the vizeroy Don Antonie de Mendoça his cousin.[1] Some suspected that they went to Maluco, others to China, others that they went onely to discouer the land betwixt the streite and the land of Peru on the other side of Chili, because it was reported to be very rich in gold and siluer [which would enrich them speedily]. But this fleete[2] by reason of contrary windes could not passe the streit, yet one small barke passed the same, and sailed along the coast [following the land on the right hand], and discouered all the land, till he came vnto Chirimai, (and Arequipa),[3] which was aboue 500 leagues, for the rest was alreadie discouered by Diego de Almagro, and Francis Pizarro, and their captaines and people at diuers times. By this it appeereth, that from the streit to the equinoctial line on both sides is wholly discouered.

Gomara, hist. gen., lib. 4, cap. 14.

---

do ouro, nem nas terras do Peru, aque elles chamam Noua Castella.

No anno de 1544 mandou dom Guterre de Vargas, Bispo de Plazencia, hũa armada da cidade de Seuilha ao estreyto do Magalhães, & diziam q' por conselho do Viso rey dom Antonio de mẽdoça seu cunhado: algũs sospeitam se hiriam a Maluco, outros á China, outros q'rem dizer q' fossem a mais q' a descobrirem terra q' há do estreito á terra do Peru, da outra banda do Chily: por dizerem q' auia la muyto ouro & prata, q' cedo os enriqueceria. Mas esta armada dizem q' teue ventura contraria, porque nam passou á outra banda do estreito senam hũ galeão q' seguio a costa ao longo da terra sobre a mão dereita, & descobrio toda ate Chirima q' auera quinhentas legoas, q' a outra era ja descuberta por Diogo Dalmagro, & Francisco piçarro, & seus capitães, &

---

[1] Brother-in-law.
[2] Is said to have been unlucky, for it did not pass, etc.
[3] Not in Portuguese.

In the yeere 1545, and in the moneth of Januarie, Rui Lopez de villa Lobos, and Giraldo, with the Castilians,[1] came to the Island of Moro, and the citie of Carnaf, where they were well receiued of the kings of Gilolo and Tidore, and of the people of the countrey (because Antony Galuano was gone), and put the captaine Don George de Castro to great trouble, as appeered by those things which passed betweene him and the Portugals, and the great expences whereunto he put the fortresse.

The Isle of Moro.

Antonio Galuano gon out of the Malucas.

In the same yeere 1545 Rui Lopez de villa Lobos sent from the Island of Tidore another ship towards New Spaine by the south side of the line, wherein was captaine one Inigo Ortez de Rotha, and for pilot one Jaspar Rico [a native of Almada]. They sailed to the coast of Os Papuas, and ranged all along the same, and because they knew not that Saauedra had beene there before, they chalenged the honor and fame of that discouerie. And because the people there were black and had frisled haire, they named it Nueua

Os Papuas.

---

gentes em diuersas vezes & segūdo isto tudo he descuberto do estreito de Magalhães ate a linha de hūa parte & de outra.

No anno de 1545 em mes de Janeyro, chegou Ruy lopez de Vilhalobos geral dos Castellanos, á ylha do Moro & cidade de Samofo : foy bem recebido dos Reis de Geilolo, & Tidore, & gente da terra : por Antonio galuam ser ja partido, q' deu assaz de tra- balho ao capitam dom Jorge de Castro, segūdo parece que lhe socedeo, & aos Portugueses que cō elle estauam, & muyto gasto à fortaleza.

No mesmo āno de 1545 tornou mandar Ruy lopez de Vilhalabos da ylha de Tidore, onde ja estaua da parte do Sul outro nauio pera a Noua Espanha, capitam delle Ynhigo ortiz de Roda, piloto Gaspar Rico, natural Dalmada : foram ter aa costa dos Papuas, correram na toda, & como nam sabiam q' por ali andara Saya- uedra, adquiriram assi esta honra & descobrimēto, por a gente ser

---

[1] Commander of the Spaniards.

Guinea. For the memorie of Saauedra as then was almost Nueua Guinea.
lost, as all things else do fall into obliuion, which are not
recorded, and illustrated by writing.

In this yeere 1545 and in the moneth of June, there went
a junk from the citie of Borneo, wherein went a Portugall
called Peter Fidalgo, and by contrary windes he was driuen
towards the north; where he founde an island standing in
9 or 10 degrees, that stretched it selfe to 22 degrees of
latitude, which is called The Isle of the Luçones, because The Isle of Luçones.
the inhabitants thereof were so named. It may haue some
other name and harborowes, which as yet we know not: it
runneth from the north vnto the south-west, and standeth
betweene Mindanao and China. They say they sailed along
by it 250 leagues, where the land was fruitfull[1] and well
couered,[2] and they affirme, that there they will giue two
pezos of gold for one of siluer : and yet it standeth not farre Siluer more esteemed than gold.
from the countrey of China.

In the yeere 1553[3] there went out of England certaine
shipping, and as it appeered they sailed northward along

preta & de cabelo reuolto, poseram lhe nome noua Guinea, por ser
ja perdida a memoria de Sayauedra, q' assi faz tudo o que nam
alumea a escriptura.

No anno de 1545 en mes de Junho, partio hum junco da cidade
de Borneo, em que hia hũ Portugues que se chamaua Pero fidalgo,
arribaram com tẽpo contrario, ao norte acharam hũa ylha de noue
ou dez graos, ate vinte & dous daltura, a que chamaram dos
Lucões, por assi auerẽ nome os habitadores della, pode ter outros,
& assi seus portos q' indagora nam sabemos. Corre se de Nordeste a Sudoeste: jaz antre Mindanao & a China, diz q' foram ao
longo della dozentas & cinquẽta legoas, em q' a terra era fresca &
bẽ assombrada, & contam q' dam ali dous pesos douro por hum de
prata, ainda q' he muy vezinha da terra da China.

No anno de 1550 em Inglaterra se fez hũa armada, & segundo

---

[1] Pleasant ?   [2] Well favoured.   [3] 1550 ?

the coast of Norway and Finmark, and from thence east,
[because there is no certainty about the route they followed
nor the latitude they reached, unless from a letter of the
Grand Duke of Moscovy, in which it is declared that there
arrived at his Port an English vessel, of which was captain
Richard Trebuli, and that there was brought to him by an
Englishman called Geneloux, a letter from the king, in
which he asked that his subjects might come and go and
trade in his country.   He gave leave and safe conduct.
This Muscovy, according to his description, extends from
sixty to seventy degrees] (till they came betweene 70 and
80 degrees vnto Moscouia, for so far one of the ships went :
but)[1] I know not what became of the rest : & this was the
last discouery made vntil this time.   From this lande of
Moscouie eastward you saile vnto Tartary, and at the farther
end of it standeth the countrey and prouince of China.   It
is said that betweene China and Tartary there is a wall
aboue 200 leagues in length, standing neere vnto 50 degrees
of latitude.

Moscouie discouered by sea by the English.

---

parece foy ao norte ao longo da costa de Gotea : & dahi ao leuante,
porq' o caminho q' fezeram, & altura em q' se poseram, aindagora
nam ha certeza, somente ver hūa carta do gram Duque de Mascouia, em q' declaraua q' chegara a seu porto hūa Nao Dinglaterra,
de q' era capitam Richarte Trebuli, q' lhe mandara por hum
Ingres q' se dizia Geneloux, hūa carta del Rey em q' lhe pedia q'
seus vasallos podessem hir & vir, & tratar em sua terra, elle dera
saluo conduto & licença.   Esta Mascouia segundo sua descripção
mostra, de sessenta graos pera setenta.   Os outros nauios nam sey
q' fim ouueram, somente ser este derradeiro descobrimento a q'
ate esta era feyto era : & desta terra de Mascouia pera o Leuante
vay a Tartaria, & na fim della aa prouincia da China, q' dizem ter
hū muro de mais de dozentas legoas, antre hūa & a outra porto de
cincoenta graos daltura.

---

[1] Dele.

Now I gather by all the precedent discoueries, that the whole earth is in circuite 360 degrees according to the geometrie thereof: and to every degree the ancient writers allow 17 leagues and a halfe, which amount vnto 6,300 leagues [the moderns make the degree 16⅔, making 6,000 leagues], yet I take it that euerie degree is iust 17 leagues, so that the circuit of the earth is about 6,200. Howsoeuer it be, all is discouered and sailed from the east vnto the west almost euen as the sunne compasseth it: but from the south to the north there is great difference; for towardes the north pole there is found discouered no more then 77 or 78 degrees, which come to 1326[1] leagues: and towards the south pole there is discouered from the equinoctiall to 52 or 53 degrees, that is, to the streit which Magellan passed through (which amounteth to about 900 leagues); and putting both these saide maine sums togither, they amount to 2226[2] leagues. Now take so many out of 6300[3] leagues,

O que disto tenho alcançado he ser a redõdeza de trezentos & sessenta graos, segũdo sua geometria, a q' deram os antiguos dezasete legoas & mea, em q' se montam seis mil & trezentas, os modernos poẽ o grao em xvj & dous terços por virem seis mil legoas. Com tudo eu tenho q' sam dezasete largas, em q' saem o ambito da terra en seis mil & dozentas. Como q'r q' seja toda he descuberta & nauegada de Léste oeste, quasi por onde o sol anda, mas de Sul ao norte ha muita deferença, porq' contra elle nam se acha mais descuberto, q' ate setenta & sete, ou setenta & oito graos daltura, em q' se montam mil & trezẽtas & tantas legoas. E da parte do Sul ate nouecentas, por ser descuberto cincoẽto & dous, ou cincenta & tres graos, que o estreito por onde o Magalhães passara, juntas todas fazẽ em soma duas mil & dozentas,

---

[1] 1,300 and odd. [2] 2,200. [3] 6,200.

31

there remaineth as yet vndiscouered (north and south aboue the space of)[1] 4000 leagues.

FINIS.

To the praise of God, and of the glorious Virgin Mary, this account is finished of the discoueries of the Antilles and of India.   It was printed in the house of John Barreira, printer to the king our lord, on the 15th of December, 1563.

tiradas de seis mil & dozentas, ficam por descobrir quatro mil legoas.

LAUS DEO.

A louuor de Deos, & da gloriosa Virgem Maria, se acabou o liuro dos descobrimentos das Antilhas & India.   Imprimio se em casa de Joham da Barreira, impressor del Rey nosso senhor.   Aos quinze de Dezembro.   De mil & quinhētos & sessenta & tres annos.

---

[1] Not in Portuguese.

For EU product safety concerns, contact us at Calle de José Abascal, 56–1°, 28003 Madrid, Spain or eugpsr@cambridge.org.

www.ingramcontent.com/pod-product-compliance
Ingram Content Group UK Ltd.
Pitfield, Milton Keynes, MK11 3LW, UK
UKHW010341140625
459647UK00010B/740